The Philosophy of Poetry

The Philosophy of Poetry

EDITED BY

John Gibson

OXFORD
UNIVERSITY PRESS

OXFORD
UNIVERSITY PRESS

Great Clarendon Street, Oxford, OX2 6DP,
United Kingdom

Oxford University Press is a department of the University of Oxford.
It furthers the University's objective of excellence in research, scholarship,
and education by publishing worldwide. Oxford is a registered trade mark of
Oxford University Press in the UK and in certain other countries

First Edition published in 2015

Impression: 1

Published in the United States of America by Oxford University Press
198 Madison Avenue, New York, NY 10016, United States of America

British Library Cataloguing in Publication Data
Data available

Library of Congress Control Number: 2014955302

ISBN 978–0–19–960367–1

Printed and bound by
CPI Group (UK) Ltd, Croydon, CR0 4YY

Contents

List of Contributors   vii

Introduction: The Place of Poetry in Contemporary Aesthetics   1
John Gibson

1. Semantic Finegrainedness and Poetic Value   18
   Peter Lamarque

2. The Dense and the Transparent: Reconciling Opposites   37
   Ronald de Sousa

3. Poetic Opacity: How to Paint Things with Words   63
   Jesse Prinz and Eric Mandelbaum

4. Unreadable Poems and How They Mean   88
   Sherri Irvin

5. Can an Analytic Philosopher Read Poetry?   111
   Simon Blackburn

6. The Spoken and the Written: An Ontology of Poems   127
   Anna Christina Soy Ribeiro

7. Poetry and Truth   149
   Roger Scruton

8. Poetry's Knowing: So What Do We Know?   162
   Angela Leighton

9. Ethical Estrangement: Pictures, Poetry, and Epistemic Value   183
   Alison Denham

10. The Inner Paradise   205
    Tzachi Zamir

11. "To Think Exactly and Courageously": Poetry, Ingeborg Bachmann's Poetics, and her Bohemia Poem   232
    Richard Eldridge

Index   251

List of Contributors

SIMON BLACKBURN is Fellow of Trinity College, Cambridge, half-time Research Professor at UNC Chapel Hill, and Professor at the New College of the Humanities. He is the author of many books, including *Spreading the Word* (1984), *Essay in Quasi-Realism* (1993), *Ruling Passions* (1998), *Think* (1999), *Being Good* (2001), *Lust* (2004), *Truth: A Guide for the Perplexed* (2005), *Plato's Republic* (2006), *How to Read Hume* (2008), and, most recently, *Mirror, Mirror: The Uses and Abuses of Self-Love* (2014).

ALISON DENHAM is Senior Research Fellow in Philosophy, St Anne's College, Oxford, and Associate Professor of Philosophy at Tulane University. Her books include *Metaphor and Moral Experience: An Essay in the Psychology of Value* (2000) and, as editor, *Plato on Art and Beauty* (2012). Her essays have appeared in the *British Journal of Aesthetics*, *Proceedings of the British Academy*, and *Modern Fiction Studies* and in volumes such as *Music and Morality* (forthcoming), *Nietzsche on Art* (2013), and *Iris Murdoch, Philosopher* (2011).

RICHARD ELDRIDGE is Charles and Harriett Cox McDowell Professor of Philosophy at Swarthmore College. In addition to many essays, he is the author of *Literature, Life, and Modernity* (2008), *On Moral Personhood: Philosophy, Literature, Criticism, and Self-Understanding* (1989), *An Introduction to the Philosophy of Art* (2003), *The Persistence of Romanticism: Essays in Philosophy and Literature* (2001), *Leading a Human Life: Wittgenstein, Intentionality, and Romanticism* (1997), and, as editor, *Stanley Cavell and Literary Studies: Consequences of Skepticism* (2011), *Oxford Handbook of Philosophy and Literature* (2009), *Stanley Cavell* (2003), and *Beyond Representation: Philosophy and Poetic Imagination* (1996).

JOHN GIBSON is Associate Professor of Philosophy at the University of Louisville. He is the author of *Fiction and the Weave of Life* (2007) and co-editor of *The Routledge Companion to Philosophy of Literature* (forthcoming), *Narrative, Emotion and Insight* (2011), *A Sense of the World: Essays on Fiction, Narrative, and Knowledge* (2007), and *The Literary Wittgenstein* (2004).

SHERRI IRVIN is Presidential Research Professor and Associate Professor of Philosophy at the University of Oklahoma. Her essays have appeared in the *Journal of Aesthetics and Art Criticism*, *British Journal of Aesthetics*, *Canadian Journal of Philosophy*, *Journal of Applied Philosophy*, *Museum Management and Curatorship*, and *Philosophiques*, among others. She is working on a book, tentatively titled *Immaterial: A Philosophy of Contemporary Art*. She is on the editorial boards of the *Journal of Aesthetics and Art Criticism* and the *Standford Encyclopedia of Philosophy* and is past editor of the Aesthetics and Philosophy of Art section of *Philosophy Compass*.

PETER LAMARQUE is Professor of Philosophy at the University of York and past editor of *British Journal of Aesthetics*. He is the author of many articles, and his books include *The Opacity of Narrative* (2014), *Work and Object: Explorations in the Metaphysics of Art* (2012), *The Philosophy of Literature* (2008), *Fictional Points of View* (1996), co-author of *Truth, Fiction, and Literature* (1994), editor *Philosophy and Fiction: Essays in Literary Aesthetics* (1983), and co-editor of *Aesthetics and the Philosophy of Art: The Analytic Tradition: An Anthology* (2003).

ANGELA LEIGHTON is Senior Research Fellow at Trinity College, Cambridge. Her critical books include *Shelley and the Sublime* (1984, 2009), *Elizabeth Barrett Browning* (1986), *Victorian Women Poets: Writing Against the Heart* (1992), and *On Form: Poetry, Aestheticism, and the Legacy of a Word* (2007). In addition she has published three volumes of poetry, *A Cold Spell* (2000), *Sea Level* (2007), and most recently *The Messages* (2012). She is currently completing a fourth, while writing a book on the poetics of sound.

ERIC MANDELBAUM is Assistant Professor in the Philosophy and Psychology departments at Baruch College, City University of New York. Prior to Baruch College, he held positions at Oxford University, Yale University, and Harvard University. His essays have appeared in *Behavioral and Brain Sciences*, *Ethical Theory and Moral Practice*, *History of Philosophy Quarterly*, *Philosophical Studies*, *Topics in Cognitive Science*, and *Review of Philosophy and Psychology*.

JESSE PRINZ is Distinguished Professor of Philosophy and Director of the Committee for Interdisciplinary Science Studies at the City University of New York, Graduate Center. His books include *Furnishing the Mind: Concepts and their Perceptual Basis* (2002), *Gut Reactions: A Perceptual Theory of Emotion* (2004), *The Emotional Construction of Morals* (2007), *Beyond Human Nature* (2012), *The Conscious Brain* (2012), and *Works of Wonder: The Psychology and Ontology of Art* (forthcoming). He is the editor of the forthcoming *Oxford Handbook of Philosophy of Psychology* and co-editor of *Mind and Cognition* (2008).

ANNA CHRISTINA SOY RIBEIRO is Associate Professor of Philosophy at Texas Tech University and she is past National Humanities Center Fellow and Mellon/Woodrow Wilson Fellow. She is the editor of *The Continuum Companion to Aesthetics* and her essays have appeared in the *Journal of Aesthetics and Art Criticism, Midwest Studies in Philosophy, Philosophy and Literature*, and in volumes such as *Blackwell Companion to Aesthetics* (2009), *Suffering Art Gladly: The Paradox of Negative Emotions in Art* (2013), and *The Encyclopedia of Aesthetics* (2014). She is currently completing a book tentatively titled *Stealing the Strings of Sappho: Essays in the Philosophy of Poetry.*

ROGER SCRUTON is a philosopher, writer, and political commentator. He is currently quarter-time Professorial Fellow in Moral Philosophy at the University of St Andrews. He has published over thirty-three books, including *The Aesthetics of Architecture* (1980), *Sexual Desire* (1986, 2006), *Aesthetics of Music* (1999), *Perictione in Colophon: Reflections on the Aesthetic Way of Life* (2000), *Death-Devoted Heart: Sex and the Sacred in Wagner's Tristan and Isolde* (2004), *Culture Counts: Faith and Feeling in a World Besieged* (2008), *Beauty* (2009), and *Notes from Underground: A Novel* (2014).

RONALD DE SOUSA is Emeritus Professor of Philosophy at the University of Toronto and is Fellow of the Royal Society of Canada. A leading philosopher of emotion, his research ranges over issues in philosophy of mind, the philosophy of biology, and aesthetics. In addition to many essays, he is the author of *The Rationality of Emotion* (1987), *Why Think* (2007), *Emotional Truth* (2011), and *Love: A Very Short Introduction.*

TZACHI ZAMIR is Associate Professor of English and Comparative Literature at the Hebrew University of Jerusalem. He is the author of *Double Vision: Moral Philosophy and Shakespearean Drama* (2006), *Ethics and the Beast: A Speciesist Argument for Animal Liberation* (2007), and *Acts: Theater, Philosophy, and the Performing Self* (2014). He has published widely in philosophical and literary journals.

Introduction

The Place of Poetry in Contemporary Aesthetics

John Gibson

The title of this volume is *The Philosophy of Poetry*, and if one is unaware of the state of contemporary analytic philosophy of literature, it might seem immodest. When I told a colleague from a department of English about this project, he commented that the title could only work in a discipline as arrogant and cantankerous as Philosophy. I hope few will agree with my colleague's view of our field, but in one respect his opinion was clearly misinformed. He appeared to think that the volume looks at the mass of existing philosophical work on poetry and pronounces it to be in need of a corrective, one which the contributors gathered here heroically produce. The mistake is ironic in the proper sense of the term. Those who work in the philosophy of literature will know that such boastfulness is not possible since no such mass of work exists. Indeed, until *very* recently one could fairly say that poetry is the last great unexplored frontier in contemporary analytic aesthetics, an ancient and central art we have somehow managed to overlook more or less entirely.[1] The title of this volume, then, should be

---

[1] One must here emphasize "analytic" aesthetics because our colleagues in continental aesthetics have a better record with poetry. A fuller version of the story of analytic philosophy of literature's avoidance of poetry would acknowledge that others have tried to bring poetry to its attention. I ignore, for example, all that Richard Eldridge has done on behalf of re-enfranchising poetry. But he is not properly seen as "analytic": his work straddles the boundary between Anglophone and continental aesthetics and is better seen as trying to open up a novel approach to art than as working within one of its established traditions. Eldridge edited *Beyond Representation: Philosophy and Poetic Imagination* (1996), and the

read not as braggadocio but as declaring poetry an object of interest for contemporary aesthetics.

I said that "until very recently" one could speak of an avoidance of poetry in contemporary analytic aesthetics. The watershed moment was in 2009, when Ernie Lepore guest-edited an issue of *Midwest Studies in Philosophy* dedicated exclusively to poetry.[2] In the same year *Ratio* published a special issue on the philosophy of literature with two articles dedicated to poetry.[3] Suddenly there was a small foundation of high-quality work on poetry, and since then a handful of excellent articles on poetry has appeared in *Journal of Aesthetics and Art Criticism, British Journal of Philosophy,* and *Philosophy and Literature,* the journals where the best work in literary aesthetics tends to end up. What has been especially exciting to witness is the kind of philosopher who is drawn to poetry. It is not surprising that luminaries in the philosophy of literature such as Peter Lamarque, Kendall Walton, Richard Eldridge, and Peter Kivy have recently written on poetry (and that in figures such as Anna Christina Ribeiro we see that there are emerging leaders who work almost exclusively on poetry).[4] What is surprising, and what bodes well for the future of the philosophy of poetry, is the number of philosophers who primarily work on mind, language, the self, and ethics who have also taken an interest in the philosophy of poetry. Ernie Lepore is an obvious example, but Elisabeth Camp, Maximilian De Gaynesford, Joseph Stern, John Koethe, Patrick Suppes, and Troy Jollimore are also worth noting.[5] In other words, we suddenly find ourselves with work on poetry and an exciting list of philosophers who have been producing it. What is needed now is a book that organizes and presents contemporary aesthetics' burgeoning interest in poetry in such a way that the shape of a distinct and coherent field may appear: a sense of key issues, of standing quarrels, of centers of argumentative gravity, of new puzzles and paradoxes,

volume has played an important role in creating an alternative to (analytic) philosophy of literature in which is poetry is central.

[2] See *Midwest Studies in Philosophy,* 33/1 (2009).   [3] *Ratio,* 22/4 (2009).

[4] See e.g. Eldridge (2001), Ribeiro (2007), Lamarque (2009), Walton (2011), and Kivy (2011). One should add to this list Rowe (2011), John (2013), and McGregor (2014). It is also worth noting that much of Robert Stecker's work on interpretation is unique in that it focuses on poetry as well as the novel.

[5] All of these authors published on poetry (among elsewhere) in the 2009 issues of either *Midwest Studies in Philosophy* or *Ratio.* See e.g. Lepore (2009), Camp (2009), de Gaynesford (2009), Koethe (2009), Stern (2009), Suppes (2009), and Jollimore (2009).

of people who must be read and positions that must be dealt with. This is the intention behind *The Philosophy of Poetry*.

The chapters of this volume offer an overview of, and so an introduction to, the philosophy of poetry, and thus there is little reason for the Introduction to do so, too. Instead of surveying developing debates in the field, I will try to provide a point of entry to them. I will address my points primarily to the reader new to poetry who needs to be alerted to some of the basic assumptions and views about the history of poetry that inform the chapters here, especially modern poetry, with which the majority of contributors concern themselves. My primary audience is the philosopher of art who needs to understand why her field should take a serious interest in poetry, though my hope is that what I say to her will also be helpful to the philosopher *in genere* who needs to hear why poetry should matter to philosophy at large.

I suspect the philosopher of art already agrees with the spirit of this call to enfranchise poetry in the philosophy of literature. Poetry, obviously, will be a chapter in the story of philosophy of literature. After many years in the woods, the philosophy of art has now made its way back near the mainstream of philosophy, and the philosophy of literature has done so, unsurprisingly, by working on issues adjacent to those in philosophy of language, metaphysics, epistemology, and philosophy of mind. Examples are the marquee debates on interpretation, emotion, imagination, fictional reference, truth in fiction, literary cognitivism, and narrative (if narrative seems the odd duck here, consider its importance to contemporary debates in the philosophy of the self), and the novel has been the literary form of choice for these discussions. No shame here, but it is time to branch out. Indeed, in recent years philosophers of literature have begun to pay serious attention to drama, autobiography, even the graphic novel. The philosophy of poetry should be seen as part of this general turn to the regions of literary production still awaiting our attention.

Philosophers of art of virtually any stripe should find poetry deserving of much more central status in contemporary aesthetics. I will provide a few examples of philosophical challenges poetry offers the philosophy of art, but it is not just the problems poetry raises that make it so interesting. It is that poetry, to a remarkable degree, embodies aspects of the various arts and so a discussion of it will naturally draw upon the interests of almost any philosopher concerned with art. According to an ancient myth, poetry is the mother of the arts: from its rhyme and meter music is born, from its power to conjure up and communicate by way of striking images painting arises, and from its narratological and imaginative dimensions we get stories and the work of fiction. This myth might have things the wrong way round—poetry as a distinct, self-aware art form perhaps came about largely by cannibalizing older, more basic arts (it will be for the art historian to tell us)—but nonetheless we see in much poetry a fusing of elements of many of the arts, comics and gardening perhaps excluded. Whatever one thinks of the myth, it suffices to give one a sense of the extent to which poetry can act as a philosophical hub at which the interests of philosophers of literature, music, and the visual arts can come together and mingle in unexpected and fruitful ways. Other art forms also embody the basic arts in one way or another. Just think of dance or opera. But poetry, a linguistic creature with intense painterly and musical aspirations, does so in unique ways and thus deserves the philosopher of art's full attention.

It is true that there is a certain kind of philosopher of literature who is hostile both to the modern poem and to philosophers who write about it. And since the majority of recent work on poetry concerns itself with twentieth-century poetry, this sentiment needs to be addressed. If one attends enough conferences one will know the sort: the philosopher who sees the value of all modern poetry as summed up, say, in the most blatantly nonsensical line of a weak John Ashbery poem. One should not mince words here: opinions of this sort reveal a huge, and risible, misunderstanding of a philosopher of art's basic professional responsibilities. Whether or not we like poetry of any sort is, strictly speaking, beside the point. Our job is not, or not just, to write about the art we adore. As philosophers of art, it is to make sense of the art world. And poetry is a long-standing and privileged member of that world. Imagine if a philosopher of science tried to justify ignoring physics because he found it difficult, odd, or self-important. Happily, however, those who write on modern poetry do seem to like it very much, and most people, philosophers included, can be made to love it a little, too.

It is worth belaboring this point. Analytic philosophy of literature has produced much work it can be very proud of—research on the nature of fiction is arguably the shinning example—but from a certain vantage-point our work is bound to seem conservative and far behind the work done by our peers in philosophy of music, visual art, even film. Our colleagues who labor in these fields write about Bach, Caravaggio, and Eisenstein, but they also have something to say about atonal music, action painting, cinematic surrealism, and conceptual art. In other words, they have largely done their duty in following their preferred art through its various historical manifestations and up to the present. It is for this reason that they can get away with claiming that they have provided philosophical documentation of their chosen art form *tout court* (a gap here and there notwithstanding). Not so for the philosophy of literature, which has on the whole ignored not just literary modernism but virtually all forms of the avant-garde that have defined the significant literary movements of the past one hundred plus years. If literature had vanished entirely as an artistic practice in the 1880s, it would have little visible effect on the kind of work we produce. A Jane Austen novel, even a Sherlock Holmes story (from which our field seems to draw roughly a third of its examples), could suffice to stage almost all the points we make about fiction, interpretation, ontology, and the nature of our emotional engagement with literature. It may be true that James Joyce's *Finnegan's Wake* or Sylvia Plath's "Daddy" are less than ideal for exploring, say, the metaphysics of fictional worlds, and so philosophers of literature may be excused for focusing on kinds of literature that are better suited for their projects. But the field as a whole pays a great price for this: we can claim no comprehensiveness in our treatment of our field, and to genuine scholars of literature we can seem dabblers. It is on this point that the contributors to this volume are entitled to vaunt: this is the first volume in which analytic philosophers of literature take the modernist, the avant-garde, and the experimental seriously. It takes seriously much else, too. But that is the point: the authors move from Milton to Paul Celan, Wordsworth to Wallace Stevens, and much else in between. The volume as a whole provides a very good reason to think that it will be the philosopher of poetry who will help literary aesthetics attain the expansiveness and openness our friends in other areas of analytic aesthetics have already achieved.

In one sense it is little surprise that many philosophers of art stopped reading poetry. Presumably they stopped taking an interest in poetry at the same time the vast majority of humans did, namely, at some point in the 1910s when modernism reached out across the arts and made them "difficult." Now lest someone draw a silly conclusion, of course there were difficult poems before there were difficult modern poems. The issue is rather how explicit and productive this difficulty becomes in poetry in the wake of, to give a sampling of poets from different traditions, W. B. Yeats,

Rainer Maria Rilke,[6] Guillaume Apollinaire, and, of course, T. S. Eliot and Ezra Pound.[7] Modernists such as Pound implored poets to "make it new"[8] and T. S. Eliot urged that in our age poetry "must be *difficult*,"[9] and the vast majority of poets listened while many casual readers of poetry apparently moved on. Some believe that modernism ended in the 1950s, some believe it has never left us, but since its inception this fabled "difficulty" has stayed with us in one form or another, regardless of whether modernism has as well. For the ocular proof, one need only look at the poetry published in recent issues of *The Paris Review*, *The Kenyon Review*, *Tar River Poetry*, *Poetry*, *The Wolf*, and the many other little or big literary magazines that seek out and showcase new poetry. It is an astonishing, and heartening, thing that such magazines still flourish.

Now explaining just what modernism is and precisely what this difficulty consists in is not something one is advised to attempt in a thousand words or less. But a few words are in order, since this difficulty is so frequently referenced in the following chapters and the reader new to poetry will wish to have a sense of what all this amounts to.[10] The following way of putting it has the virtue of providing the right initial idea, though it is incomplete and should be jettisoned once one knows one's way around modern poetry. Here is the idea: in the wake of modernism poetry can no longer be read naively. Let me explain.

"Naive" here is not meant in an entirely derogatory sense. To say that an artwork of any sort can be appreciated naively is to say that attending only to its surface will repay a non-negligible degree of aesthetic interest. To

---

[6] In the case of both Rilke and Yeats, it would be their later works that have a claim to being modernist, and their poetic careers reflect in miniature the passage from nineteenth-century romanticism to twentieth-century modernism.

[7] However we define poetic modernism—this is no easy task—most scholars acknowledge it is underfoot well before the early 1900s. The birth of poetic modernism is often attributed to the French symbolist poets, and the crucial event is usually thought to be the publication in 1857 of Charles Baudelaire's *Les Fleurs du mal*.

[8] This is the title of Pound (1934).   [9] Eliot (1975, 65).

[10] The reader who wants more than I offer here might consult some of the following studies. For a general overview of the lyric, see Susan Stewart (2009). For studies of modern, largely British and American, poetry, see Pinsky (1976), Altieri (1984), Golding (1995), and Izenberg (2011). Leighton (2007) offers an excellent discussion of how to navigate the aesthetic and philosophical concerns of prominent lines of modern poetry. To read Vendler (2005) and Bernstein (2011) is to see two very different ways of approaching the modern poem that are emblematic of two very different contemporary critical sensibilities and practices. For a popular work on the difficult modern poem, see Orr (2011).

appreciate a literary work of art naively is to find that one can take pleasure in it without concerning oneself with, for example, questions of the artistic project that underwrites a work, the significance of its form, the more clandestine forms of meaning and aboutness it bears, and so on. The great realist novel is a master of providing such surfaces, surfaces that often open up on to an interior of immense complexity. The reader who searches out this complexity will of course attend to the surface, too. But the naive reader may remain there, reading, say, Henry James's *The American* as just a well-told tale of an expatriate in Paris who unfortunately falls in love with a member of the aristocracy, ignoring along the way all of James's grander pursuits in the novel. There is nothing wrong with an artwork that bears a surface that can be appreciated naively. Indeed, bearing such a surface is a tried and true way of forging that crucial initial bond between audience and work. The great romantic poets of the nineteenth century mastered this in their own way, though at this point much pressure was already beginning to be placed on the reader who approaches poetry too naively. Nevertheless, to read, say, Wordsworth's "The World is Too much With Us" naively would be to read it is as a series of mellifluous lines about sleeping flowers and pleasant leas which cumulatively and fairly straightforwardly yield a point to the effect that modern life alienates us from nature. In calling this "naive" there is no implication that the content of my naive reading is wholly unfaithful to the poem or misleads us as to what Wordsworth was really trying to say through it. The surface offers a preliminary encounter with, as it were, meaning and beauty; and what happens in the classroom or in a good work of criticism is that this initial encounter is treated as the first rung of a ladder we are expected to climb if we are to achieve a view of the poem's complexity and so of its full aesthetic and cultural significance. No insult to the surface of the poem is implied, just that the serious reader shall wish to move beyond it at a certain point and that in doing so she will entitle herself to claim that she has fully experienced the poem *as a poem* and not just as a pretty expression of a deep-sounding idea.

Whatever else poetic modernism is, it abandons to a great extent just about everything that makes naive reading possible, and herein lies much of its fabled difficulty. The terms that abound in this volume are *compression, density, abstraction*, and *opacity*, and all are sophisticated ways of marking the basic idea that in the wake of modernism much poetry turns against the standard practice of offering even the semblance of accessible surfaces. We often find a play of images couched in language that revels in its assault on our linguistic and communicative expectations, and frequently we are not even offered an *apparent* preliminary encounter with meaning. Now when speaking of "meaning" in the context of poetry, one likely should not have in mind what a philosophers such as Frege or Davidson mean by "meaning." When speaking of poetry the concept of meaning is used broadly to indicate *whatever* it is that endows a poem with aboutness, with communicative content, with a point: with the capacity, perhaps despite everything, to speak to the reader. And one way of putting what all the talk of density, compression, opacity, and the like gesture towards is the remarkable extent to which we experience meaning as *latent* in so much poetry of the last one hundred years. It tends to hold out meaning as a promise, as a destination rather than a point of departure,[11] and this distinguishes it hugely from most other uses of language, where the goal is usually to wear meaning on the sleeve. To achieve even minimal understanding of much modernist poetry, we very frequently must treat a poem not merely as an object of aesthetic interest but, before this is even possible, as an object of *scrutiny*, which is one thing naive reading will not tolerate. Finally, we find explicit hostility to what may be described as the "narrativising tendencies" of naive reading.[12] It is true that lyric poetry, the dominant form of modern poetry, has always had a hesitant relationship with narrative. But one of the basic habits of naive reading is to approach a poem as always *implying* a narrative, and so as calling on the reader to unearth the story it suggests, and this has a very nasty habit of occluding the more radical, and artistically significant, manners in which poetry can engage with thought, feeling, and life. A lyric can dazzle us simply by exercising its expressive or formal powers, and it need not be expressing a story or have the form of a narrative if it is to so dazzle. These narrativizing tendencies might always be a nuisance when approaching lyric poetry, but the modern lyric often seems to be engaged in a holy war against them, and thus it refuses to let the naive reader employ one of his most basic strategies for approaching literary content of any form.[13]

---

[11] We may never reach the promised destination, but that is another story.

[12] My notion of narrativizing tendencies is heavily indebted to Peter Goldie's discussion of "fictionalizing tendencies" in Goldie (2012, 150–2).

[13] One important difference between the ways an analytic and continental philosopher of literature are inclined to talk about modernist art can be seen here. I've made the

Compare a poem that makes concessions to the naive reader to one that clearly does not.

Emily Dickinson, "Hope is the thing with feathers" (1865, approx.):

> "Hope" is the thing with feathers
> That perches in the soul
> And sings the tune without the words
> And never stops—at all
>
> And sweetest—in the Gale—is heard
> And sore must be the storm
> That could abash the little Bird
> That kept so many warm
>
> I've heard it in the chillest land
> And on the strangest Sea
> Yet—never—in Extremity,
> It asked a crumb—of me.[14]

Wallace Stevens, first stanza of "Sunday Morning" (1915):

> Complacencies of the peignoir, and late
> Coffee and oranges in a sunny chair,
> And the green freedom of a cockatoo
> Upon a rug mingle to dissipate
> The holy hush of ancient sacrifice.
> She dreams a little, and she feels the dark
> Encroachment of that old catastrophe,
> As a calm darkens among water-lights.
> The pungent oranges and bright, green wings
> Seem things in some procession of the dead,
> Winding across wide water, without sound.
> The day is like wide water, without sound,
> Stilled for the passing of her dreaming feet
> Over the seas, to silent Palestine,
> Dominion of the blood and sepulchre.[15]

---

story fundamentally one of meaning whereas for the continental philosophy it would be essentially made a matter of politics. One should suspect that a satisfying account would address both aspects, since they are clearly intertwined (one cannot e.g. explain the difficulty of Celan's language without also, at some point, speaking of the Shoah).

[14] Dickinson (1999, 140). The poem was published posthumously and is assumed to have been written in the mid-1860s.

[15] Stevens (2005, 66–7).

I take it there is no question who the modernist is and which poem is more accessible to naive reading. Both Dickinson and Stevens are, in their own ways, exceptional poets, and one would be very unjust to Dickinson to treat her as an example of guileless romanticism, just in case the reader thinks a value judgment is implied here. But we do see a marked difference, and Stevens is emblematic of a basic form of difficulty one finds in the modernist poem. The nature of the difficulty will change greatly as one moves between, say, Gertrude Stein, Louis Zukofsky, and W. H. Auden. But what I have said should suffice to provide the reader new to poetry with a general sense of what one has in mind when talking about this difficulty.

However radical modernism can at first appear, many (though not all) critics will urge something like a continuity thesis according to which modernism, while surely offering many formal innovations, is on the whole better seen not as breaking entirely with poetry's past so much as finding new, properly *poetic* grounds for inheriting it. Whether or not the continuity thesis holds will likely depend on the poet one is considering. But some version of the continuity thesis surely applies to many modernists, Eliot, Stevens, and even Ashbery included. Think of it in the following terms: in stripping away all that is essential to naive reading, the modernist poet brings us closer to what poetry has really always been.[16] The loss of a surface that can be read naively thus turns out to be no loss to poetry of any genuine sort at all.[17] Consider the old idea that absolute music can train one how to appreciate the *aesthetically relevant* features of music, which the presence of lyric can pollute. In a similar spirit, one might claim that the difficult modern poem gives us that, and only that, which has ever mattered to poetry and thus that through the modern poem we learn something important about how to read poetry in general.

All of this allows me to say very succinctly how poetry presents literary aesthetics with important new philosophical challenges. The point

[16] I ignore what the question of in what, precisely, this core of poeticity common to poems before and after modernism will consist in. This is, expectedly, the point on which the continuity thesis is pressed.

[17] The introduction to Izenberg (2011), "Person, Poetry, and Personhood," offers an excellent overview of competing avant-garde and traditionalist interpretations of poetic modernism.

should be obvious. It turns out that at least one of things the modern poem strips away is the very thing with which contemporary philosophy of literature is essentially concerned. And if a version of the continuity thesis holds, this means that many of our popular theories in the philosophy of literature are at best only awkwardly suited for making sense of poetry of almost any sort. What I hope this discussion of the modern poem motivates is a sense of that we have an entire region of literary art that will call on us to revise and rethink much of what we say when we speak about literature. To have a sense of this, one first must acknowledge how essential the notion of a *fictional narrative* is to so much of our research and indeed to our basic sense of the philosophical problems literature raises. Then one need only ask what happens to our sense of these problems once the notion of a fictional narrative is rendered inapplicable or made of at best secondary importance? One might argue that all poetry is fictional, though there are powerful reasons to be skeptical of this. But no sound argument looms that they are all *fictional narratives*. So what happens, for example, to our theories of imagination, tailored as they are to illuminate the forms of make-believe and pretence that allow us to immerse ourselves in a fictional story? What happens to our theories of the nature of our emotional responses to literature, occasioned as they largely are by the problem of explaining how we can emote over fictional events unfolding in essentially narrative time? More broadly, what happens to our theories of the meaning and interpretation of literary language when we look at an art that seems content to communicate figuratively, imagistically, symbolically, perhaps even prosodically or formally, that is, to communicate *poetically*?[18] My claim is not that poetry will force us to abandon all of our previous work; but since this work is so linked to an interest in fictional narratives and guided by a broadly novelistic conception of literature, our theories will have to be expanded, modified, and made to respect the unique ways in which poetry engages imagination, emotion, and meaning.

There is much more one could say here, and one should expect the list of problems poetry raises for philosophy to extend well beyond the handful of examples just given. But it is best to let the chapters of this volume offer specific details about the ways in which poetry presents

[18] I explore this in Gibson (2011).

unique problems for the philosophy of literature and beyond. While I hope to have said enough to spark the reader's interest, it is the contributors to this volume who provide the richest examples of why poetry matters to philosophy.

The volume opens with Peter Lamarque's probing and wide-ranging "Semantic Finegrainedness and Poetic Value." Though the business of the chapter is to articulate and defend a novel thesis, along the way it offers a fine overview of many basic issues in the philosophy of poetry, particularly those concerning meaning. Lamarque explores a general puzzle about lyric poetry, especially, though not exclusively, the modern short lyric. The often extraordinary linguistic compression of much lyric poetry make these poems, to say the least, resistant to understanding. Why do we value art that pushes language to such extremes? Lamarque's response to this builds on the idea that in poetry we are concerned not just with content but with a "subject-realised-in-just-this-way," and this reveals the extent to which *expression* is the chief object of poetic appreciation and critical scrutiny. Understanding this aright sheds light on long-standing debates concerning the so-called heresy of paraphrase, the supposed identity of poetic form and content, and the idea that poetry bears a uniquely *poetic* brand of meaning.

Ronald de Sousa's "The Dense and the Transparent: Reconciling Opposites" uses a discussion of linguistic density to revisit the ancient feud between poetry and philosophy. The poet embraces suggestion, symbolism, polysemy, and metaphor, and this places the poet's preferred use of language at a pole almost exactly opposite the philosopher's, which privileges clarity of expression, modestly in delivery, and writing that has an apparent subject or point. But there are powerful reasons for thinking that the difference between the creative labor of poet and philosopher is not nearly as pronounced as we might think. Each, de Sousa shows, is concerned with truth, each aims at providing fresh vision, and each has an essential but surprisingly hesitant relationship to language.

Jesse Prinz and Eric Mandelbaum's "Poetic Opacity: How to Paint Things with Words" offers a new framework for approaching the notions of linguistic density and compression so central to discussions of the nature of poetic language. For Prinz and Mandlebaum, semantic density and like features of poetic language turn out to be forms of poetic *opacity*. Indeed, the particular forms of opacity that poetry is apt to produce are the "the mark of the poetic," its distinguishing feature and that upon which a definition, such as poetry will admit of, can be constructed. The chapter identifies various forms of poetic opacity and explains their interrelation and aesthetic significance. Prinz and Mandelbaum conclude by drawing a striking analogy between our experience of poetic opacity and Richard Wollheim's notion of the "twofoldness" of representational painting.

With Sherri Irvin's "Unreadable Poems and How They Mean" we turn to a demonstration of how a poem whose language is evidently senseless can nonetheless bear rich forms of meaning and aboutness. In this way it shows that even poems that rejoice in their attack on sense and syntax cannot so easily be dismissed as nonsense and so impervious to understanding. Interpretation is the primary tool for overcoming the often powerfully felt gap between a reader's understanding and a poem's meaning, and Irvin documents the various techniques we enlist to get a poem that appears meaningless to begin to speak. The meanings we ascribe to poems are not mere subjective projections; they turn out to be, in standard cases, open to intersubjective appraisal and so are publicly available. If this is so, popular ideas that much contemporary avant-garde poetry is meaningless or so "private" as to be inscrutable are bunk.

Simon Blackburn's "Can an Analytic Philosopher Read Poetry?" offers a tongue-in-cheek indictment of analytic philosophy for providing us with philosophical resources too impoverished to be capable of making sense of the poetic use of language and its significance in human life. The contemporary philosopher's Fregean inheritance, concerned as it is with truth and reference—poems can appear to have neither—make it very difficult to acknowledge the philosophical, moral, and cultural value of the poet's labor. Blackburn shows that the matter is not as bleak as it seems, but there are concerns dear to many philosophers that reveal them to have a radically different set of expectations about language than the poet does (he offers the current debate on semantic vagueness as one example of this). In respect to the ancient feud, Blackburn ultimately concludes that it is the poet's sensitivity to language that has the greater claim to being "our best guide to who we are, and even to where we ought to be heading."

In "The Spoken and the Written: An Ontology of Poems," Anna Christina Soy Ribeiro situates the discussion of poetry firmly in contemporary metaphysics, and her chapter offers an excellent sense of the extent to which poetry can raise pressing and unique problems for the ontology of literary works. Unlike, say, the modern novel, poetry is both a written and a *spoken* art, and Ribeiro sets herself the task of offering an ontology of poetic works that respects the diversity of poetic practices old and new. Poems, Ribeiro argues, are abstract artifacts whose existence is essentially dependent on culturally and historically situated practices. These practices are, in the broadest sense, either *inscription-based* or *declamation-based*, and this helps us to acknowledge the role of both textuality and orality in diverse poetic traditions. The upshot of Ribeiro's theory is that philosophers are hugely mistaken to think that one can offer a generic ontology of literary works. The various literary arts each require their own metaphysical attention.

In Roger Scruton's "Poetry and Truth" we turn to a discussion of the notion of poetic truth. Is the form of truth poetry is apt to explore a kind of propositional or discursive truth? Is it a matter of a poem providing a "true representation" of reality? Scruton sees poetry's particular way with truth as more fundamental that any of these traditional conceptions of truth can allow. Poetry does not earn its claim to truth by mirroring an external world or by stating discrete, correct, "facts" about it. Scruton argues that poetry is concerned with truth as a kind of revelation, an "unconcealing" of aspects of existence that lie hidden from us in our everyday encounters with the world. Poetry, for Scruton, *transforms* those aspects of reality it so presents, bestowing value upon them and infusing them with new forms of meaning. In this respect, in poetry we find a genuinely *creative* interest in truth.

In "Poetry's Knowing: So What Do We Know?" Angela Leighton offers an account of knowledge suitable for the poet, whose interest in knowledge is often very different from the philosopher's. The grammar of the phrase "poetic knowing" is important, since the continuous present emphasizes that the poet tends to treat knowledge as a "tentative, unfinished journey, a foray into poetry's difficult thickets of meaning." Leighton's essay reveals the different kinds of cognitive interest we can take in the affairs of life, and she compares philosophical and poetic works to highlight how the forms of writing and thinking distinctive of each open up or preclude ways of knowing. This chapter does not take a side in the ancient quarrel, but it does offer powerful reasons against thinking that the descendants of Socrates have a greater claim to the pursuit of knowledge than those of Sappho.

Alison Denham's "Ethical Estrangement: Pictures, Poetry, and Epistemic Value" explores the cognitive and moral significance of the kind of imaginative experience poetry offers. She identifies two forms of imaginative experience that are especially important to poetry: "experiencing-as" and "experience-taking." Experiencing-as is "inherently first-personal, embodied, and phenomenologically characterized," while in experience-taking one "takes the perspective of another, simulating some aspect or aspects of his psychology as if they were his own." Through a sensitive and probing reading of Paul Celan's *Psalm*, Denham shows the role these two forms of experience play in producing the unique form of ethical and epistemic value poetry can bear. Denham's argument for this has important implications for our understanding of the poetic imagination and nature of our experience of meaning in poetic contexts.

With the concluding two chapters we see the importance of close reading. In "The Inner Paradise" Tzachi Zamir turns attention away from the lyric and to the epic poem, using *Paradise Lost* to structure a discussion of the philosophical and epistemic value of poetry. Zamir calls into question the habit of explaining the relationship between philosophy and literature in terms of a "compensatory" thesis according to which literature is able to bring to perfection and so complete the forms of understanding philosophy pursues. Zamir argues that literature is often hostile to the compensatory thesis, and he offers a close reading of *Paradise Lost* to demonstrate that poetry's pursuit of insight, even knowledge, often takes a distinctly aesthetic and literary, rather than philosophical, form. It is not a completion of the philosopher's project but a distinctly poetic manner of pursuing and articulating knowledge. In this respect, there is a unique form of poetic knowledge, and we should not expect philosophy to take us very far in coming to possess it.

The volume concludes with Richard Eldridge's " 'To Think Exactly and Courageously': Poetry, Ingeborg Bachmann's Poetics, and her Bohemia Poem." His reading of Ingeborg Bachman's "Böhmen liegt am Meer" explores the extent to which the poem is exemplary of the distinctive achievements of lyric poetry. The poem provides an object study in how the lyric allows the human voice to pursue, and at times acquire, expressive freedom. The various sonic, affective, rhythmic, figurative, and expressive devices of poetry account for why its products are not merely lovely aesthetic objects but exemplary of the "imaginative economy of human life." What lyric that aspires to this status shows us is the unique claim poetry has to providing what Stendhal called the *promesse de bonheur.*

References

Altieri, Charles. 1984. *Self and Sensibility in Contemporary American Poetry.* New York: Cambridge University Press.

Bernstein, Charles. 2011. *Attack of the Difficult Poems: Essays and Inventions.* Chicago: University of Chicago Press.

Camp, Elisabeth. 2009. "Two Varieties of Literary Imagination: Metaphor, Fiction, and Thought Experiments." *Midwest Studies in Philosophy,* 33/1: 107–30.

de Gaynesford, Maximilian. 2009. "Incense and Insensibility: Austin on the 'Non-Seriousness' of Poetry." *Ratio,* 22/4: 464–85.

Dickinson, Emily. 1999. *The Poems of Emily Dickinson.* Ed. R. W. Franklin. Cambridge, MA: Harvard University Press.

Eldridge, Richard. 1996. *Beyond Representation: Philosophy and Poetic Imagination.* Cambridge: Cambridge University Press.

Eldridge, Richard. 2001. *The Persistence of Romanticism: Essays in Philosophy and Literature.* Cambridge: Cambridge University Press.

Eliot, T. S. 1975. *Selected Prose of T. S. Eliot.* New York: Harcourt Brace Jovanovich.

Gibson, John. 2011. "The Question of Poetic Meaning." *Nonsite,* 4. <http://nonsite.org/article/the-question-of-poetic-meaning>, accessed January 2, 2012.

Goldie, Peter. 2012. *The Mess Inside: Narrative, Emotion, and the Mind.* Oxford: Oxford University Press.

Golding, Alan C. 1995. *From Outlaw to Classic: Canons in American Poetry.* The Wisconsin Project on American Writers, Madison: University of Wisconsin Press.

Izenberg, Oren. 2011. *Being Numerous: Poetry and the Ground of Social Life.* Princeton: Princeton University Press.

John, Eileen. 2013. "Poetry and Directions for Thought." *Philosophy and Literature,* 37/2: 451–71.

Jollimore, Troy. 2009. "'Like a Picture or a Bump on the Head': Vision, Cognition, and the Language of Poetry." *Midwest Studies in Philosophy,* 33/1: 131–58.

Kivy, Peter. 2011. "Paraphrasing Poetry (for Profit and Pleasure)." *Journal of Aesthetics and Art Criticism,* 69/4: 367–77.

Koethe, John. 2000. *Poetry at one Remove.* Ann Arbor: University of Michigan Press.

Lamarque, Peter. 2009. "The Elusiveness of Poetic Meaning." *Ratio,* 22/4: 398–420.

Leighton, Angela. 2007. *On Form: Poetry, Aestheticism, and the Legacy of a Word.* Oxford: Oxford University Press.

Lepore, Ernie. 2009. "The Heresy of Paraphrase: When the Medium Really is the Message." *Midwest Studies in Philosophy,* 33/7: 177–97.

McGregor, Rafe. 2014. "Poetic Thickness." *British Journal of Aesthetics,* 54/1: 49–64.

Orr, David. 2011. *Beautiful and Pointless: A Guide to Modern Poetry.* 1st edn. New York: HarperCollins Publishers.

Pinsky, Robert. 1976. *The Situation of Poetry: Contemporary Poetry and its Traditions.* Princeton: Princeton University Press.

Pound, Ezra. 1934. *Make it New.* London: Faber & Faber.

Ribeiro, Anna Christina. 2007. "Intending to Repeat: A Definition of Poetry." *Journal of Aesthetics and Art Criticism,* 65/2: 189–201.

Rowe, Mark. 2011. *Philip Larkin: Art and Self: Five Studies.* Basingstoke: Palgrave Macmillan.

Stern, Josef. 2009. "The Maimonidean Parable, the Arabic Poetics, and the Garden of Eden." *Midwest Studies in Philosophy,* 33/1: 209–47.

Stevens, Wallace. 2005. *The Collected Poems of Wallace Stevens.* 1st Vintage Books edn. New York: Alfred A. Knopf.

Stewart, Susan. 2009. "Lyric." In Richard Eldridge (ed.), *Oxford Handbook of Philosophy and Literature.* Oxford: Oxford University Press, 45–70.

Suppes, Patrick. 2009. "Rhythm and Meaning in Poetry." *Midwest Studies in Philosophy,* 33/1: 159–66.

Vendler, Helen. 2005. *Invisible Listeners: Lyric Intimacy in Herbert, Whitman, and Ashbery.* Princeton: Princeton University Press.

Walton, Kendall. 2011. "Thoughtwriting—in Poetry and Music." *New Literary History,* 42/3: 455–76.

1

Semantic Finegrainedness and Poetic Value

Peter Lamarque

I

It is characteristic of a certain kind of poem—notably the short lyric—to compress language in a way that resists initial easy comprehension. Examples abound. Consider the two opening stanzas of a recent poem, 'Waves', by Giles Goodland:[1]

> The sea is a misunderstanding
> we have to go through in order to make sense,
> like the word for a loss of a word.
> It leaves a sense of having left,
> through which silence leaks.
>
> What waves are reopening nightly is
> the senseless apparatus of an eye.
> If you live in a house made of thought
> you nod in the silence the sea makes.

This compression of meaning is undoubtedly a mark of, but is not peculiar to, modern or modernist poetry. It can also be found in other periods

---

[1] Giles Goodland, 'Waves', in Roddy Lumsden (ed.), *The Best British Poetry 2011* (London: Salt Publishing, 2011), 36. This choice of example is fairly arbitrary but it seems suitably typical of a certain style of modern poetry, it well illustrates the kind of difficulty that interests me, and it was selected as among the 'best British poetry' for 2011.

including the nineteenth century. This is the beginning of Algernon Charles Swinburne's poem 'Hertha':[2]

> I am that which began;
>> Out of me the years roll;
>> Out of me God and man;
>> I am equal and whole;
> God changes, and man, and the form of them bodily; I am the soul.

On the face of it, writing of this kind is puzzling. The words themselves are not technical or obscure, the subject matter not especially recondite, at least in the former poem, yet the meaning is difficult to grasp, the syntax irregular, there is no obvious point (to inform, to advance knowledge), and standard discursive norms of clarity are bypassed. Nevertheless, such writing is immediately recognizable as poetry and often admired, not in spite of, but because of the semantic complexity it exhibits.

My principal question is this: why should writing of this kind that is dense, complex, and resistant to ready understanding have value, specifically poetic value, when in other contexts it might be censured for its wanton lack of clarity? Why does poetry license, even encourage, such compression of meaning?

There are of course certain stock answers to these questions and it might be thought they are sufficient: for example, that the complexity of poetic language simply reflects the complexity of the thoughts and emotions being expressed; or that the complexity rests on the fact that poems characteristically use metaphor and figurative speech; or simply that poets like to play with language, push it to its limits, explore its possibilities, that's what poets do. There's truth in all of these answers, without doubt, but none of them quite explains why such uses of language should be highly valued. Perhaps poets do push language to its limits—and use metaphor more than usual—but what is the value in that? Why should readers get pleasure from having to struggle to understand poetry? And is it really the case that complex language in poetry is always the expression of complex thoughts? Giles Goodland writes this about his poem 'Waves':

Staying at a beach chalet with the kids, I was playing with the idea that the humours in the eyeball have a similar composition to seawater, and I read somewhere that

---

    [2] Algernon Charles Swinburne, 'Hertha', in Arthur Quiller-Couch (ed.), *The Oxford Book of English Verse 1250–1900* (Oxford: Clarendon Press, 1931), 974.

this is a relic from our very distant evolutionary past. We all carry a little bit of ocean with us, and use it to look with. This combined with being on a beach with my children and thinking about the various meanings of waves. Sound also is very important in the poem and I allowed myself to get carried away with some slightly outrageous sound-alike words and phrases . . . Something about the sea always seems to loosen me up in my use of words . . . So I let the words play around, as the children were doing, in my notebook. Language is like the sea, as a whole it is form-less, but it can form localised shapes called sentences or even poems. The poem ends with the children, and that feeling of having the ground pulled under you when a wave rolls back into the surf. Sitting on the beach watching them, I got the idea for the poem: we are like waves, we carry sea with us, generation after generation.[3]

The thought itself—about eyes and sea water—is intriguing but hardly complex and the circumstance of children playing on a beach seems not to demand semantic contortion. The stock answers, then, seem only to rein-force the urgency of the original question. For 'Waves' is a pleasing poem, fun to read and repeat, not overly profound, not perhaps one of the great works, but typical in its complex word-play. Here are the last few lines:

> Poe-lipped polyps lens and tense
> to sense the same body inside this one.
> Their homeland is brine,
> the gull-lulling greys of its waves.
>
> Lip-read the sea rolling in pain. See
> such children it sucks like a sweet.
>
> The pebbles are frantic under them.

We hear and enjoy what the poet calls the 'slightly outrageous sound-alike words and phrases'. But more needs to be said to explain poetic value than appeal to word-play alone.

II

To get more deeply into the discussion it will help to reflect on four sup-posed commonplaces about poetry. These provide a clearer focus, at least at a philosophical level, into the nature of poetic meaning and its value.

(1) The Experiential thesis. *The core value of a poem lies in the experience(s) the poem affords when read as a poem.*

---

[3] Lumsden, *Best British Poetry 2011*, 126–7.

(2) The Heresy of Paraphrase thesis. *The precise meaning of a poem is unparaphrasable.*

(3) The Form-Content Unity thesis. *The form of a poem is indivisible from its content.*

(4) The Semantic Density thesis. *Poetic language affords a peculiar kind of 'semantic density'.*

Each of these theses is closely connected to the others; in a sense they are mutually supportive. Furthermore, as often repeated commonplaces, they seem to possess more than a grain of truth. But of course they need a great deal of unpacking. All are puzzling from the point of view of standard theories of meaning. What should be so peculiar about poetic language that, unlike nearly any other usage, it should be resistant to paraphrase? Part of the answer no doubt lies in the Experiential thesis but that itself is problematic because it is not obvious why any piece of discourse should be valued primarily for the 'experience' it affords rather than, say, the proposition(s) it expresses or the information it conveys. And what kind of experience is at issue? The supposed indivisibility of form and content will only make sense when the ideas of 'form' and 'content' are amplified but it would be a marked peculiarity of poetic usage—again setting poetic language apart from other usages—if it should be the case that in poetry *how* something is said should be so integrally related to *what* is said that there should be only one possible way in which a certain content could be expressed. If the Semantic Density thesis is right—that poetic language somehow generates a depth of meaning not found in other linguistic modes—then this too needs explanation. After all, most of the 'devices' characteristic of poetry are familiar elsewhere: metaphor, simile, imagery, alliteration, onomatopoeia, rhyme, repetition, etc.

We need to fill out the theses and explore how they are related. The Experiential thesis, that the value of a poem lies in the experience(s) the poem affords, is defended by A. C. Bradley in his 1901 inaugural lecture 'Poetry for Poetry's Sake'. Bradley argued that 'an actual poem is the succession of experiences—sounds, images, thoughts, emotions—through which we pass when we are reading as poetically as we can'.[4] Taken

---

[4] A. C. Bradley, 'Poetry for Poetry's Sake', in *Oxford Lectures on Poetry* (London: Macmillan, 1926), 4.

literally, that is a strong claim as it appears to identify a poem with a succession of experiences; if it is a genuine identity claim, an ontological claim, it seems on the face of it implausible.[5] However, Bradley qualifies his remark by saying he is not 'aiming here at accuracy' or offering a 'definition of poetry' and the Experiential thesis as I present it is not a thesis in ontology, rather a thesis about value. This too is the core of Bradley's view, for the experience of reading poetry, he states, 'is an end in itself, is worth having on its own account, has an intrinsic value ... *poetic* value is this intrinsic worth alone'.[6] So the value of a poem, its poetic value, is for Bradley the intrinsic value of the experience the poem affords. A similar view is expounded by Malcolm Budd: 'what matters in poetry is the imaginative experience you undergo in reading the poem, not merely the thoughts expressed by the words of the poem'.[7]

What more can be said about this experience? Can anything substantial be said about it, in abstraction from particular cases? The first point to make is that the experience of each poem is unique to the poem: no two poems afford qualitatively the same experience, at least at the level of specificity which the relevant experience demands. No doubt there are shared generic experiences associated with poems on broadly similar themes or in similar poetic styles. But that is not the level of generality at which poetic value lies.

Second, the experience in question is the experience of *readers*, not the experience of poets themselves. Poetic value does not reside in the quality of any psychologically real state of mind manifested in a poet as either the cause or subject of a poem. Where a poem expresses an emotion it is the expressed emotion itself—expressed in just this form—that is the subject of an attentive reader's experience and thus the source of the poem's value.

Third, the experience is normative: not any experience that a poem elicits in a reader can be considered an appropriate measure of the poem's value. For Budd the relevant experience involves 'interacting with [the work] in whatever way it demands if it is to be understood' and must be

---

[5]   However, the idea that the identity of a work is essentially bound up with responses to the work has been defended by others. Derek Attridge e.g. identifies a literary work with an *event* of reading: see *The Singularity of Literature* (London: Routledge, 2004), 59.

[6]   Bradley, 'Poetry for Poetry's Sake', 4.

[7]   Malcolm Budd, *Values of Art: Pictures, Poetry and Music* (London: Penguin Books, 1995), 83.

'imbued with an awareness of (all) the aesthetically relevant properties of the work'.[8] No doubt, quite legitimately so, there will also be more purely subjective experiences (responses) leading to subjective judgements of value. However rational or dispassionate we are in our judgements it would be absurd to expect that we all enjoy the same poems. But a judgement of the poem itself should, as far as possible, be grounded in the experiences that the work elicits on its own terms, rooted in its own objective properties.

Fourth, the experience is multi-faceted; it is not just, if at all, a sensation or feeling of pleasure, nor is it to be classed as a sui generis 'aesthetic experience'. What we shall see later is that it is an experience of a subject through a mode of presentation. It involves, as Bradley remarked, such elements as 'sounds, images, thoughts, emotions' and it is a temporal process, not a state. It is a process of thought, constrained by the linguistic medium that gives it both its character and its identity.

We shall come back to the Experiential thesis when we have explored the three other theses. It is significant that, in highlighting experience in relation to the value of poetry, the thesis places poetry naturally in the context of other arts. That experience should be prominent in accounts of music, painting, film, sculpture, or dance is not especially remarkable. But poetry is a language-based art and language is indissolubly associated with meaning, so an important shift has occurred when a thesis on the value of poetry makes no explicit reference to meaning and indeed highlights experience over meaning. Our other theses, on paraphrase, form and content, and semantic density, do seem more directly connected to meaning but it will be a theme of the argument to follow that an overemphasis on meaning can be misleading in capturing what is of value about poetry.

The Heresy of Paraphrase thesis, that the precise meaning of a poem is not paraphrasable (i.e. expressible in other terms), is a commonplace about poetry, in the sense that lip-service is paid to it in general reflections on the subject, but is nevertheless controversial under closer examination. There are those who simply deny that resistance to paraphrase is an integral or even interesting feature of poetry. Peter Kivy, for example, has argued that for the most part paraphrasing poetry does not present

---

[8] Budd, *Values of Art*, 4.

an insuperable problem once we are clear on a 'criterion of success'.[9] We must not, he insists, set such a criterion unreasonably high, so high in fact that it couldn't possibly be fulfilled. Significantly, he suggests that one such criterion is too high and unfulfillable, namely that paraphrase capture the *experience* that the poem affords.

No one who sets out to say in prose the content of what a poem says in poetic form intends as the goal of the task to provide an alternative way of experiencing the poem. And to fault the interpreter for failing to do what is not the point of interpretation in the first place is plain nonsense.[10]

Three brief preliminary comments on this.[11] The first is that Kivy is readily conceding that there is indeed a relevant experience uniquely associated with the poem yet, on his view, it is not to be identified with the poem's content, nor in any essential way connected to interpretation. The second is that Kivy is associating paraphrase with interpretation, as if the goal of interpretation is to paraphrase a poem's meaning. That assumption needs to be challenged for it is far from clear that a good interpretation of a poem seeks simply to say in other words what the poem itself says. Poetic interpretation, I suggest, is better conceived as a way of encouraging, enhancing or developing precisely the experience a poem affords, as described in our discussion of the Experiential thesis. The third point is that Kivy, in setting apart paraphrasable content, on the one hand, and experience, on the other, is falling into just that dualism that Cleanth Brooks, who coined the expression Heresy of Paraphrase, warned against: a dualism between some kind of 'statement' that the poem makes and the eloquence, or beauty, or clarity with which it does so.[12] In fact Brooks is quite happy to concede just the kinds of loose paraphrase that Kivy defends: 'the point is . . . not that we cannot describe adequately enough for many purposes what the poem in general is "about" and what the general effect of the poem is'. Indeed he allows that '[w]e can very properly use paraphrases as pointers and as short-hand references' as long

---

[9]   Peter Kivy, 'On the Unity of Form and Content', in *Philosophies of Arts: An Essay in Differences* (Cambridge: Cambridge University Press, 1997), 104.

[10]   Kivy, 'On the Unity of Form and Content', 105.

[11]   For further discussion, see Peter Lamarque, 'The Elusiveness of Poetic Meaning', *Ratio*, 22/4 (2009), 398–420.

[12]   Cleanth Brooks, 'The Heresy of Paraphrase' (1947), in *The Well Wrought Urn: Studies in the Structure of Poetry* (London: Methuen, 1968), 160.

as 'we know what we are doing and that we see plainly that the paraphrase is not the real core of meaning which constitutes the essence
of the poem'.[13] That so-called 'essence', for Brooks, resides only in the
total 'structure' of the poem and cannot itself be captured in other
formulations.

Philosophers of language are rightly wary of claims of unparaphrasability. The thought that there could be only one way in which something
could be said goes against basic principles of semantics, including what
Ernie Lepore (after Donald Davidson) has called 'semantic innocence',
the idea, at its simplest, that 'what an (unambiguous) word means it
means everywhere it occurs'.[14] The Heresy of Paraphrase violates semantic innocence to the extent it holds, as Lepore puts it, that 'what the
words of a poem mean is contingent upon where in a poem they occur'.[15]
Lepore, however, ingeniously offers a defence of the Heresy of Paraphrase
while retaining semantic innocence. To do so he introduces the idea of
hyperintensionality, which claims there are 'linguistic environments in
which replacing an expression with its synonym changes meaning'. The
prime example in natural language is quotation. Lepore illustrates this
as follows:

'bachelor' is the first word in 'bachelors are unmarried men'
'unmarried man' is the first word in 'bachelors are unmarried men'

The former is true, the latter false, yet 'bachelor' and 'unmarried man' are
synonymous. He goes on:

Likewise, try replacing 'sheen' with 'luster' in Coleridge's poem *The Rime of the
Ancient Mariner* (1797):

> And through the drifts the snowy cliffs
> Did send a dismal sheen;
> Nor shapes of men nor beasts we ken
> The ice was all between.

The change sufficiently alters the rhythm and rhyme to break the bind between
the lines, and thereby alters the poem itself. Since synonym substitution in a

---

[13] Brooks, 'Heresy of Paraphrase', 160.
[14] Ernie Lepore, 'The Heresy of Paraphrase', *Midwest Studies in Philosophy*, 33
(2009), 181.
[15] Lepore, 'Heresy of Paraphrase', 182.

poem can change metre or rhyme, etc., and thereby change the topic, poems too create hyperintensional contexts. The right conclusion is *not* that expressions carry unique meanings inside and outside of poems.[16]

Behind the idea that poems create hyperintensionality, indeed a partial explanation of that idea, is a further claim that 'poetry, like quotation, doesn't support substitution of synonyms because it harbours devices for being literally (partly) about their own articulations'.[17] Because a poem is 'partly constituted by its own articulation . . . it is not re-articulable in another medium'.[18] Lepore's suggestion is ingenious and, if correct, has the merit of taking some of the mystery out of the semantics of poetry. However, what the account does not do is answer our initial question about the *value* of the compression of meaning in some lyric poetry. Why should it be of value or afford an intrinsically valuable experience that a poem should be somehow about its own articulation? If this is just another way of saying that pleasure can be had in attending to the modes in which thought in poetry is presented then so be it, for that is surely right, but there seem to be additional factors at work because there is no particular pleasure to be had in the hyperintensionality of quotation. And is it true that poems are even partially *about* their articulation? That seems doubtful in itself, quite apart from the worry that it doesn't explain their value. What a poem is about, I will suggest, is its finegrained content identified by, certainly, but not equivalent to, its particular mode of articulation.

Other philosophers have appealed to metaphor to explain unparaphrasability in poetry. Two lines of thought are evident here. The first says that it is in the nature of live or poetic metaphors to be inexhaustible in their connotations so no precise literal equivalent is possible. The second, following Davidson, denies there is any such thing as metaphorical meaning, so there is nothing, as it were, to paraphrase. What a metaphor means is simply what the words mean in their literal application and the rest is merely effect. Neither view is especially illuminating about the supposed unparaphrasability of poetry. Perhaps the direction of explanation is the wrong way round. Might it not be that an adequate theory of metaphor could benefit from an account of the value of poetry rather than the value of

---

[16] Lepore, 'Heresy of Paraphrase', 195.
[17] Lepore, 'Heresy of Paraphrase', 195.
[18] Lepore, 'Heresy of Paraphrase', 193.

poetry being explained through a theory of metaphor? The idea that metaphor is inexhaustible might be true in some cases but the nature of, and constraints on, that inexhaustibility, if relevant here, will only be determined in the light of some wider conception of poetry and its aims. As for the Davidsonian account of metaphor, it might seem in principle promising in the context of poetry if only for its focus away from meaning and its admission of non-propositional elements in responses to metaphor. However, there is an unruliness in relying exclusively on unconstrained effects which is not true to the kind of normative experiences demanded by poetry.

So what remains of the Heresy of Paraphrase thesis? At one level the resistance of poetry to paraphrase follows simply from the thought that it matters in poetry, more so than in other forms of language use, exactly how something is expressed. The form of expression is not distinct from what is expressed, a point we shall return to. The idea that there might be some other way of saying precisely what the poem says contradicts the very nature of poetry, which is to draw attention to, give salience to, its modes of expression. That is the truth behind the hyperintensionality view.

The Form-Content Unity thesis, that the form of a poem is indivisible from its content, expands on, but is not identical to, the Heresy of Paraphrase thesis. The latter might be true but not the former. Resistance to paraphrase, in a milder version, might be judged just a contingent fact about the complexity of poetic language; the less complex a poem the more open it is to paraphrase. But if form-content unity is true then unparaphrasability is not contingent but necessary for if paraphrase captures content, and content is indivisible from form, then form too must be retained. That is hyperintensionality again. A. C. Bradley rarely mentions paraphrase but argues explicitly for form-content unity: 'this identity of content and form . . . is no accident; it is of the essence of poetry in so far as it is poetry'.[19]

Clearly to assess the Form-Content Unity thesis the ideas of 'form' and 'content' must themselves be clarified. That in itself is not straightforward given the multiple ways the terms are used. However, it is fairly clear what kinds of features count as formal in poetry: rhyme, metre, rhythm, alliteration, repetition, etc. The 'etc' might be difficult to cash in but some preliminary points about indivisibility can still be maintained. One is

---

[19] Bradley, 'Poetry for Poetry's Sake', 15.

that form-content unity in poetry is holistic: the content of the whole is indivisible from the form of the whole. But (holistic) form-content unity does not imply that for any individual formal feature it is legitimate to ask what feature of content it is equivalent to, even if a rough and ready account might be available for the contribution made to the whole by each of the parts. Also it would be wrong to think of 'form' in the relevant sense just as the sum of individual formal features. Form-content unity is stronger than that in insisting that the total surface configuration of a poem is indivisible from its total content. This is more like what Brooks means by 'structure'. Total content, whatever that might mean, is in a sense supervenient on the structural base.

The idea of 'content' is equally problematic. In the light of the Experiential thesis it should not automatically be identified with meaning. Perhaps better is to think of it in terms of 'aboutness', while recognizing that aboutness is interest-relative.[20] Specifications of what a poem is 'about' come in degrees of finegrainedness according to the interests served in making the specification. In some contexts it might be enough to say of Giles Goodland's poem that it is about waves or the ocean or a day out at the sea or a hypothesis about eyes and sea water. But these descriptions do not do justice to finegrained content. Ultimately the most finegrained specification of the content—the 'total' content—is that which incorporates the precise form in which the content is presented: in other words the poem itself. This level of finegrainedness is anticipated in hyperintensionality and in the Heresy of Paraphrase. The interest served at this level is an interest in the poem, as Bradley would say, 'for its own sake'. It is at this level, but only here, that content becomes indivisible from form.

Form-Content Unity now takes on a different complexion. It need not be thought a merely contingent fact about (some) poems that their content is indivisible from their form. Form-content identity is not something that one discovers in a poem but rather something one *demands* of a poem when bringing to it a certain kind of interest: an interest in the poem for its own sake. This is not to deny other kinds of interest in a poem which might focus on more abstracted features of content or indeed form. One might, for example, be interested in commonalities across poems, perhaps metrical or thematic similarities.

---

[20] This idea is also developed in Lamarque, 'Elusiveness of Poetic Meaning'.

But it is not an eccentric interest to attend to form-content indivisibility in a poem.[21] Attention to finegrained content—a subject-realized-in-just-this-way—is essentially attention to expression. The philosopher W. M. Urban in *Language and Reality* (1939) defends form-content identity like this: 'The artist does not first intuit his object and then find the appropriate meaning. It is rather in and through his medium that he intuits the object.'[22] Such a view is familiar also from R. G. Collingwood for whom the very act of expressing an emotion gives a clear identity to that emotion: the expression both characterizes and discovers the emotion, which would remain unknown without that mode of expression.[23] So it is that the specificity with which Giles Goodland characterizes his thoughts on the ocean and seaside in the poem is not a way of capturing thoughts that pre-existed the expression, except in the most general terms, but crystallized and brought into being the thoughts themselves.

Before we begin to tie our theses together and draw out some general conclusions about poetic value, we must attend briefly to the fourth thesis, Semantic Density, which is most explicitly about meaning. For the New Critics of the 1930s and 1940s what distinguished literary language, by which they primarily meant the language of poetry, from ordinary or non-literary language is a kind of 'density' of meaning characterized by 'ambiguity', 'tension', 'irony', 'implicit meaning', 'connotation', etc., these being favoured terms of art.[24] It was with examples of just such density or compression of meaning that we started so it is hard to deny that such qualities can be exhibited in poetry. Again,

---

[21] Peter Kivy has charged that the view that poetry, read as poetry, *demands* form-content identity is unduly 'essentialist'; he prefers a 'pluralism' that countenances different equally valid ways of reading poetry. Of course it is right that readers are ultimately free to read as they like but that there are conventional norms even in reading is suggested by what might be called the teaching test; if you are teaching someone how to read poetry it is important to make clear early on that 'finegrainedness' of expression is important, that those words in that order matter and should be attended to as such. Note that this is not the way that reading in other forms of discourse must be taught, where it is allowable that the very same meaning could be expressed in different ways. See Peter Kivy, 'Paraphrasing Poetry (for Profit and Pleasure)', *Journal of Aesthetics and Art Criticism*, 69/4 (2011), 367–77.

[22] Quoted in Brooks, 'Heresy of Paraphrase', 163.

[23] R. G. Collingwood, *The Principles of Art* (Oxford: Clarendon Press, 1947), 111, 122.

[24] Monroe C. Beardsley uses the expression 'semantical thickness' to characterize literary discourse: Monroe C Beardsley, *Aesthetics: Problems in the Philosophy of Criticism*, 2nd edn (Indianapolis: Hackett, 1981), 129.

though, caution is needed in grasping the significance of this. The trouble with semantic density is that if you look for it—anywhere—you are likely to find it. All words are rich in connotation. In conversational discourse nuances of meaning are sometimes picked up but more often than not transparency is aimed for and achieved in the imparting of information. Connotations, implied meanings, and potential ambiguities are overlooked or viewed as distractions. And that is the point. In most contexts language is treated as a transparent medium for communication. Getting an idea across in some way or other is the goal. In poetry, given form-content indivisibility, transparency is replaced with opacity. The very forms of expression draw attention to themselves. Richness of meaning is not an obstacle but a medium. Connotations, allusions, symbolic meanings, resonances, add to the pleasures of the poetic experience. Semantic density, then, like form-content unity, is not discovered in poetry but demanded of it. It is striking that Cleanth Brooks in *The Well-Wrought Urn* finds tension and irony not only in John Donne and W. B. Yeats, where you might expect it, but also in Gray's 'Elegy', Pope's 'Rape of the Lock', and Tennyson's 'Tears, Idle Tears', which seem, on the face of it, deceptively uncomplicated.

III

Again, going back to where we started, the mere presence of semantic density or multiple meaning does not explain poetic value. Indeed its own value is what needs explaining. But I think now we have the elements to offer an explanation. It is wrong to think of the pleasure of reading poetry, especially difficult poetry, as centred on the deciphering of meaning, somewhat like doing a crossword puzzle.[25] Pleasure might be had in that activity but it cannot be at the heart of the value of poetry. Issues about meaning of course crop up—a word or phrase might need explication—but often where help in interpretation is needed what matters is grasping the *point*, a kind of contextualization. Indeed this is what Giles Goodland offers in his comments on his poem, drawing our

[25] Both William Empson and Aldous Huxley have noted parallels between obscure poetry and crossword puzzles, both in positive terms: see John Press, *The Chequer'd Shade: Reflections on Obscurity in Poetry* (London: Oxford University Press, 1963), 41.

attention to the theme that connects eyes and sea water. But grasping the point in this way—like noting word-meaning—is not an end but a mere preliminary for a deeper appreciation. Here meaning gives way to experience. If Bradley is right the value of a poem as a poem lies in the intrinsic value of the experience the poem demands. What is this experience? In brief, it is the experience of a form-content unity. And what exactly is that? It is the experience of a subject matter partially defined by the very modes of expression through which it is presented. The language of a poem is not a vehicle for conveying a thought that is independently expressible; it conveys a thought that is encapsulated in the vehicle. Poems create hyperintensional contexts, with content that is unparaphrasable, not just because synonyms cannot be substituted but because, given the interests brought to the poem, the content demands the most finegrained identity conditions; it is a content given in just this way, inseparable from the form of its presentation.

Why should the experience of finegrained content be valuable? Sometimes of course it is not valuable—not all poems succeed and they can fail in many directions but always in the end because of weaknesses in the form-content unity, in diction, thought, originality, wit, and so on. To criticize a poem as a form-content unity is to criticize at one and the same time both what is expressed and how it is expressed. The poem for whatever reason doesn't work, it doesn't capture our attention, it is flat and lifeless. Maybe in the end we just abandon the attempt to read it as a poem. Where poems do succeed it is because of the pleasures to be had in adopting a unique (finegrained) perspective on a subject whether, in broad terms, familiar or unfamiliar. Of difficult poems we should not ask 'why could it not have been put more simply?' because there is no reference for 'it', the content, such that this way—the difficult way—of expressing the content is but one alternative among others. To use a different form of expression would have been to express a different content. We might not like the content so presented but we couldn't ask that that very content be presented differently.

What a poem offers is not, usually, a single thought on its subject but a thought-process. The value of poetry is at least partially the value of following a thought-process through the perspective of the poetic speaker.

In the Goodland poem we follow the speaker's ruminations from his general observations at the beginning:

> The sea is a misunderstanding
> we have to go through in order to make sense,
> like the word for a loss of a word

to the specific images at the end:

> Lip-read the sea rolling in pain. See
> such children it sucks like a sweet.

Through this process of thought and imagination we ponder what kind of misunderstanding the sea might provoke—connected perhaps to what we think of our own eyes—and conjure at the end the image of the waves like lips sucking sweets, roaring with a kind of muted pain.

More common in lyric poetry is a journey from the specific to the general. The Edinburgh poet Norman Kreitman offers nice reflections on 'Clearing the Loft'.[26] The first stanza takes us into the loft:

> Dismay is waiting behind that door,
> where across the floor footprints like hieroglyphs
> chronicle the history of past defeats.
> Dead clothes, the skins of our former selves,
> still tumble from broken cases, crates
> split their sides with books, a three-legged chair,
> bewildered, leans in that corner where a viper's nest
> of jerseys entwines a broken lamp—
> all the high spume and flotsam
> washed up by the long ebbing decades.

The second stanza speaks of the memories prompted by the cluttered objects:

> . . .
> They resurrect absurdly youthful passions
> exploring marvels of what might have been

---

[26] Norman Kreitman, 'Clearing the Loft', *Dancing in the Dark: New and Selected Poems* (Edinburgh: Clydesdale Press, 2010), 17. Reprinted with the permission of Susan Kreitman. I have chosen this poem by Norman Kreitman (1927–2012) not because it exemplifies the kind of difficulty in poetry with which we started (on the contrary it is notably accessible) but because it well illustrates a familiar kind of movement of thought in the short lyric. My choice is also a tribute to a fine poet and friend with whom I had fruitful discussions over many years on the theory and practice of poetry.

> but for a word misplaced or not spoken,
> a touch delayed a moment too long. . . .

The third and final stanza broadens out the reflections, as it were cashing in the symbolic weight of the loft as a store of memories and lost desires:

> Yet knowing so little and understanding less
> was all the wit I had. Besides the play was different
> when all these ghosts were living hands and eyes,
> when hopes and desires which can barely be recalled
> were as urgent as a trumpet. Or perhaps those scruples
> were not so foolish, since every season
> has its proper logic: sufficient unto its time
> the reasons thereof. . . .

A key to the experience the poem affords is not the grasping of a summative proposition, the idea of memories prompted through a visit to the loft. It is rather that the thoughts are pervaded by the mood evoked—the tint of melancholy, time past, age, loss, lessons learned. The darkness of words like 'dismay', 'past defeats', 'dead clothes', 'broken cases', 'broken lamp', 'flotsam', pervade the experience; the perspective of sadness gives the content its special character, it gives shape to the process of thought as it develops.

I said earlier that form-content unity and semantic density are not *discovered* in a poem but *demanded* of poems when read 'poetically' (in Bradley's term). The fundamental idea here is that of broadly marked conventions of reading or at least expectations brought by readers when approaching a piece of writing as a poem. Poetry is constituted by a practice, which is grounded in convention-governed expectations among poets and readers. To write a poem is to engage the practice and invite (one hopes also reward) certain kinds of interests and responses among readers; to read a poem 'poetically', seeking its poetic value, is to deploy the relevant interests and responses thereby making appropriate demands and one hopes achieving the valued experience on offer.

A simple and familiar example of how conventional expectations in poetry can shift the focus of interest might arise from Noam Chomsky's famous sentence 'Colorless green ideas sleep furiously', which he introduced (in 1957) as an example of a sentence syntactically well-formed but semantically without meaning. In the context of semantics the sentence, with its multiple category violations, lacks evident truth conditions, but there have been numerous attempts to find meaning in it through contextualization. The most telling comes from the poet John Hollander who incorporated the sentence into a short poem, nicely titled 'Coiled Alizarine' (alizarine being a red dye), and dedicated to Chomsky:

> Curiously deep, the slumber of crimson thoughts:
> While breathless, in stodgy viridian,
> Colorless green ideas sleep furiously.[27]

Whether or not the poem finds meaning where before there was none is a moot point, but there is no doubt that the context of the poem elicits a specific kind of interest in the famous line. The category violations are no longer merely semantic anomalies; they are now given salience, they become suggestive, they resonate round the metaphorical core of sleeping thoughts. The colours too come to life; colourless green and stodgy viridian contrast with the brightness of crimson. So while the crimson thoughts can sleep deeply or soundly, the colourless green ones, anaemic and stodgy, sleep furiously and breathlessly. When we read the lines as a poem we look for semantic density, for resonances and internal connections, for connotations, for metaphorical and symbolic interpretations, for unity of form and content. We attempt to adopt a perspective on the whole—an unfolding process of thought—that might issue in an experience we can value. We set aside any initial, natural recoil from surface unintelligibility. Now we take pleasure in it.

IV

So what conclusions can we draw from this discussion? Perhaps poetry is not an easy subject for philosophy of language. It is sometimes thought that all that philosophers need to cope with poetry is a theory of metaphor. That seems patently inadequate. Indeed, as suggested, it might be, in contrast, that metaphor could be better understood through attention to how poetry works and what values it yields. My own emphasis has been to shift the focus away from meaning as somehow the key to the peculiarities of poetry. There is no poetic language as such. Linguistic usage in poetry is as varied as poetry itself and the presence of poetic 'devices' is never sufficient for a stretch of discourse to count as a poem. To understand what

---

[27] John Hollander, *The Night Mirror: Poems* (New York: Atheneum, 1971).

poetry is it is no good merely cataloguing formal features. We need to understand the very practice that makes poetry possible, a practice characterized by the expectations and interests of its practitioners, readers and poets alike. To use a different idiom, we must look at the 'game' of poetry, in the Wittgensteinian sense, its rules and norms.[28] The immense variety of poetic forms and genres should not distract us from the thought that there is something distinctive about poetry, that classifying a piece of discourse as 'poetry' is not merely vacuous or uninformative. The classification gives us a clue to what kind of interest might be appropriate, what kind of value might be sought. There is no implication that in calling something a 'poem' it will reward the attention we bring to it. It tells us, minimally, only the kinds of value we might seek, not what we will find.

The four commonplaces about poetry that we have explored all serve to characterize some of the fundamental rules of the poetry game. In their simple formulations they pick out truths about poetry that most practitioners at least pay lip-service to. More interestingly, although each is true in a rough and ready sense, under closer inspection none turns out to be quite as it seems. The Heresy of Paraphrase, Form-Content Unity, and Semantic Density are not, as sometimes depicted, mere facts about particular uses of language, something we find *here* but not *there* given sample stretches of discourse, as if, in some objective sense, *these* sentences are unparaphrasable, have form-content unity and semantic density, while *these* do not. They are better seen as very loosely defined conventions of reading, not something we discover but something we demand when we approach discourse as poetry. Poets of course know the conventions too—they know the game they are playing—so they will tend to adopt usage, in their own way and for their own purposes, which will reward the attention they invite of their readers, both of the conventional kind associated with poetry per se and the more specific kinds associated with their own aims. It is important to stress just how broad-based these 'conventions' are and how neutral they must be to different styles, genres, and periods of poetry. Poets who pioneer new styles of poetry often seek to distance themselves from conventions of the past. William Wordsworth, for example, makes much of this in his Preface to

---

[28] For more on the 'game' analogy in the literary context, see Peter Lamarque, 'Wittgenstein, Literature, and the Idea of a Practice', *British Journal of Aesthetics*, 50 (2010), 375–88.

the *Lyrical Ballads* (1800), even to the point of worrying that his readers might not acknowledge his works as poetry:

I will not take upon me to determine the exact import of the promise which by the act of writing in verse an Author in the present day makes to his Reader: but I am certain it will appear to many persons that I have not fulfilled the terms of an engagement thus voluntarily contracted.[29]

But these are not the conventions we are concerned with. Our interest is with those that characterize the very enterprise of poetry itself. It is certain that Wordsworth would grant the more general species; after all we can be assured he would not settle for paraphrases of his poems as somehow substitutable for them, nor be indifferent to the form in which they are expressed, nor be unreceptive to resonances of meaning found in them. In this regard he is no different from those poets, like Donne or Cowley or Dryden or Pope, from whom he wants to distance himself.

Finally, what about the experiences we value in poetry, according to the Experiential thesis? Again the commonplace view must be handled with care. Certainly experience is at the core of what gives poetry value but it is not merely passively received so much as sought after under relevant modes of attention when the poetry game is engaged. The definitive experiences are not sensations or even emotions—there is no determinate phenomenology of poetic experience across all genres (the very idea is absurd)—but are processes of thought precisely shaped by the form-content unities that are their focus of attention. Of course there might be accompanying emotions or sensations in particular cases but these are contingent and context-dependent. So, returning to our initial question, why do we value the complexity—and difficulty—of (some) poetry when we spurn it elsewhere? The answer at its simplest is: because it is part of the poetry game that in poetry we attend to the finegrainedness of language, its textures and intricacies, its opacity, in conveying thought-processes, and we find value in the experience that affords, in precedence over the more humdrum norms of communication, such as transparency, the imparting of information, and the assumption of paraphrasability.[30]

---

[29] William Wordsworth, 'Preface to *Lyrical Ballads* (1800)', in D. Wu (ed.), *Romanticism: An Anthology*, 3rd edn (Oxford: Blackwell Publishing, 2006), 497.

[30] I am grateful to audiences at Birkbeck College and the Universities of Stirling, Essex, and York for constructive and helpful feedback on this chapter.

2

The Dense and the Transparent
Reconciling Opposites

Ronald de Sousa

I Introduction

In one of the plays of Jean Anouilh, a character remarks that since the works of "primitive" or "naïf" painters sometimes fetch the highest prices, it would seem only fair to accord some value to the opinions of primitive and naïve critics. I did passionately want to be a poet when I was a child, but no *production* of mine ever strayed very far from the very limited and certainly dated dialectic between the ironic and the sentimental. I am now only an occasional and always a highly prejudiced reader of poetry, and I am, in particular, almost completely unable to see the point of much of what is currently published as poetry.

That one confession out of the way, what follows is another, in which I tell how I lost my grip on a cherished conviction.

First, to explain that conviction and its charm. I had long thought it obvious that philosophy and poetry are perfect antagonists. That view did not stem from the sorts of reasons adduced by Plato in his self-undermining rhetorical excesses about art's deficient degree of reality. Assuming, as Plato did, that art is meant to represent something, a work will not only evoke its subject but also draw attention to its own concrete reality as paint, or as shaped bronze, or as plot and character on the stage. In that way, works of art present both something else and themselves. We might infer that such works have more, not less, reality than what they represent. In any case, Plato's reasons were disingenuous. Although he made it look as if the contrast between them was about the priority of truth over appearance, it was really more about the purposes served by the devices exploited both by himself and the poets. The emotional power of Plato's great myths is not really different in kind from the emotional power of the rhetoric he despised. The difference lies in the doctrines they were used to sell.

If what follows is as much a narrative of my changes of mind as a sustained argument, perhaps this is not inappropriate, insofar as it constitutes a partial repudiation of the conception of philosophy that values argument above all.

Two factors might encourage the view that poetry and philosophy are antagonists. One rests on a consideration of the ideal use of language in each domain. The second relates to the standards we intuitively appeal to when we ascribe *truth* to a philosophical thesis or a passage of poetry, or say of either that we find it "compelling." The connection between the two will, I hope, emerge as I proceed. I begin with a sketch of the first contrast.

Poetry welcomes polysemy, metaphor, allusion—in short, everything likely to concentrate the greatest load of meaning into as few words as possible. I shall refer to this quality as *density*. By contrast, analytic philosophy[1] aims to make things plain: its use of language is intent on purifying language of ambiguity in the pursuit of the explicit and the transparent. Transparency in this sense is the antagonist of density. My own adoption of the ideal of transparency was undoubtedly influenced by something philosophy teachers like me often tell our nervous students: it's not agreement with this or that view that counts, but the clarity and quality of your arguments. So proclaims no less a master than Robert Nozick: "A philosopher's seriousness is judged by the quality of his arguments" (Nozick 1981, 4). After a lifetime of reading and writing philosophy, however, I am unable to evade the embarrassing fact that

---

[1] Not every philosopher aspires to density. One wag observed that asking a continental philosopher to come straight to the point would be like expecting the matador to shoot the bull as it enters the ring. Much of the mutual incomprehension between analytic and "continental" styles of philosophizing may be ascribed to deep differences between their conceptions of the role of language and the place of the ineffable in philosophy. I make no attempt here to shed light on these differences; by "philosophy," I shall henceforth refer exclusively to what is broadly known as "analytic" philosophy.

arguments seldom convince anyone of anything non-trivial, and hardly ever settle anything of philosophical importance. How good can an argument be if it fails to convince? A bold new hypothesis recently propounded by Mercier and Sperber (2011) holds that reasoning is an evolutionary adaptation geared to persuading rather than to establishing the truth. That is supposed to explain why our arguments are often so bad at guiding us to the discovery of truth; but it hardly explains why arguments so seldom succeed in persuading anyone of the truth of a philosophical thesis. This might be a clue that formulating straightforward truths is not, contrary to appearances, the sole aim of philosophical discourse. And since it probably seems obvious to anyone that poetry does not aim to establish the simple truth of any propositions, philosophical or otherwise, it might also suggest that poetry and philosophy are not as far apart as the bald statement of their antagonism implies.

Independently of that thought, I have found myself, for several decades now, describing philosophy to undergraduates as aiming (among other things) to change our vision, in the broadest sense of that word. My favourite way of illustrating this involves a "droodle": a simple circle with two short line segments sticking out of it on opposite sides. When given the appropriate caption, almost anyone can *see it as* "a Mexican on a bicycle seen from on top." I find two lessons in this example. First, it affords a compelling yet simple counterexample to the widely accepted doctrine, first propounded by Jerry Fodor, that our perceptual systems are "informationally encapsulated" (Fodor 1983). Fodor's claim is often supported with an allusion to the well-known Muller-Lyer illusion (though I prefer the less familiar but much more captivating McGurk effect[2]). Such illusions illustrate the fact that what we perceive can remain remarkably impervious to what we know. But the Mexican droodle shows that this claim must be qualified, because words affect experience in non-standard ways. Priming phenomena, for example, affect our behavior and our emotional responses without even having been the object of awareness.[3] The mechanisms of these effects are mysterious and probably

---

[2] See <http://tinyurl.com/cvygnpa> for a short BBC documentary explaining this effect, in which the same actual sound is heard as "ba" or as "fa," depending on the sight of the speaker's mouth as it is uttered.

[3] See e.g. a number of experiments by John Bargh (Bargh et al. 1996; Bargh and Ferguson 2000).

akin to some of the ways poetry works on us. Second, the droodle is a metaphorical illustration of the way that philosophy, when it works as it should, can change our vision of life. The way it does so also depends on language, but philosophical discourse typically provides arguments rather than captions.

This suggests a conception of philosophy as aspiring not to lock in true beliefs, but to provide a fresh overall vision. Much classical philosophy is friendly to that view. Plato, Nietzsche, Wittgenstein, and many others, can plausibly be thought to aim at inducing in their audience a more fitting vision of human nature and its place in the universe.

The foregoing sketch should be enough to indicate the main lines of my argument in what follows. It is time to explain the antagonism between philosophy and poetry as I originally conceived it. But first, a surprising parallel needs to be noted, namely that *both poetry and philosophy are reluctantly bound to language.*

II I Gotta Use Words When I Talk to You (But I Wish I Didn't)

One might describe a piece of music, landscape, or plastic art as "poetic," but these uses are metaphorical, or *poetic,* and are therefore best eschewed while trying to elucidate what that term might mean. Poetry in the literal sense can hardly do without language, though it has often been enhanced by music. Indeed, it has sometimes aspired to the condition of music. Witness Verlaine:

De la musique avant toute chose / . . . / Tout le reste est littérature.[4]

Poetry's music-envy might be regarded as a wish to return to the womb, if scholars are right in surmising that early poetry was sung or chanted rather than spoken or read. In several poetic traditions and styles, there is an affinity between poetry and spells, incantations, and prayer:

> May she be granted beauty, and yet not
> Beauty to make a stranger's eye distraught
> Or hers before the looking glass . . . [5]

[4] "[Poetry should be] music, above all else . . . All else is but literature." Paul Verlaine, "Art poétique." From *Jadis et naguère* (1884).
[5] "Prayer for my daughter," in Yeats 1996, 188.

The ineffable is sometimes posited as the ultimate unattainable but guiding ideal of poetry. This is sometimes expressed in the prescription that what is at the core of a poem, its true "meaning," should never be made explicit but only be suggested. According to Nico Frijda and Louise Sundararajan, this is an essential part of Chinese poetics. They quote the following example, in which the emphasis is on the enhancement of poetic experience by "savoring" (*pin wei*), allowing the experience to mean much more than is being said. Such experiences

occur under attitudes of detachment and restraint, their experience involves reflexive second-order awareness, they result from and contain extensive elaboration of appraisal of the eliciting events that may invest the events with meanings far beyond their immediately given aspects, and they include virtual states of action readiness rather than states that manifest in overt acts or suppressed action impulses. (Frijda and Sundararajan 2007, 227)

A similar idea is embodied in the Japanese concept of *yugen*. The *Stanford Encyclopedia* entry on Japanese aesthetics characterizes it as instantiating "a general feature of East-Asian culture, which favors allusiveness over explicitness and completeness" (Parkes 2011).

In Indian theory, too, suggestiveness or *dvhani* is central to poetry. As Keith Oatley describes it:

Dhvani is what the words do not explicitly say. Sometimes, as if to emphasise the point, it can be the opposite of what the words say. Lalita Pandit (1996) offers an example from Shakespeare's Macbeth. The eeriness of the play is created beginning with the witches who hail Macbeth and say that he will become king, apparently joyous tidings. But what the witches' appearance implies and what their words suggest, but do not say, is the opposite. Macbeth's will is propelling him towards a region of evil and anguish. (Oatley 2006, 27)

Insofar as poetry pursues the ineffable, then, poetry's bond to language is reluctant. Since common sense would normally take poetry to be "about" language rather in the way that painting is "about" paint (the more self-consciously so as one progresses from primitive representational art to modern more abstract styles), that is paradoxical. But it is not eccentric. And it illustrates an aspect of the density of poetic language, in that the more is suggested by language without being explicitly said, the richer is the experience of meaning evoked by that use of language.

There is an obvious similarity with philosophy here in the reliance on language to transcend language. The philosophical tradition, beginning before Plato, does not lack examples of esoteric doctrines, secret unwritten teachings that could be comprehended only by devotees of a practice. Still, philosophy is evidently a mode of *discourse*: it is as difficult to conceive of a work of philosophy as it is to think of a work of poetry that altogether does without language. Difficult, but perhaps not altogether impossible: after all, as John Cage has shown with his "4′33″" for solo piano (in which the pianist is instructed not to play any notes for the piece's entire three movements, totaling four minutes and thirty-three seconds), one can even conceive of music without sound—though it must be conceded that as a genre, silent music is likely to suffer from a certain monotony. Similarly, then, we might take as either a poetic or a philosophical statement the silence of the sage. It was reported that "the Buddha has not uttered a single word from the time of enlightenment to the time of his death" (Masson 1977, 12). The silence could be described as expressing, if perhaps not exactly paraphrasing, the proposition, *After enlightenment, there is nothing to say.*

Just as silence constitutes a sort of limiting ideal of music, then, conveying something beyond words seems to be a limiting ideal for both poetry and philosophy. That is the reason for qualifying as reluctant the commitment of both to language.

That attitude may carry a trace of philosophy and poetry's common origins. The founding texts of the Judeo-Christian, of the Chinese, and of Indian traditions are frequently expressions of world views, with religious and metaphysical implications that have traditionally been classed as philosophical.[6] Often, if not invariably, they were expressed in poetic forms. The explicit blending of philosophy and poetry survives in Lucretius's sophisticated and pointedly anti-religious philosophical poem, *De Rerum Natura*. Doubtless many would want to include Dante's and Milton's great poems as both philosophical and poetic. But while historians of philosophy still take Lucretius seriously, it would be unusual in an analytic philosophy course to assign Dante or Milton. Poetry and philosophy, like science and religion, may have the very same ultimate source; but each has drawn apart from the other in quest of its own

---

[6] Some philosophers have found it frustrating that what they know as "analytic philosophy" still carries the same name as those ancient forms of "wisdom." One has gone so far as to propose that we give up the name "Philosophy" entirely, replacing it with "Ontical Science" (McGinn 2012).

singular relationship to—or compromise with—language. In the case of philosophy, the feeling that language constrains or shackles us reflects the ambition to understand the world at the deepest level. While that may be a self-serving formulation philosophers will be eager to endorse, it is sometimes buttressed by the idea, less congenial to analytic philosophers, that language hints at some more primal, non-linguistic experience of reality.

However overblown philosophy's ambition may seem, one must at least grant that it begs the question to assume that philosophical tasks can be accomplished *only* in the medium of language, or, for that matter, that any properly philosophical task can be accomplished with language *at all*. How reasonable that assumption is, depends on one's stance regarding an important bifurcation in philosophy. On the one hand, the philosophical tradition has been associated with wisdom, and with the pursuit of insight into the nature of the human condition. On the other hand, it has been associated with a *method* which puts *argument* at the centre of its pursuit of truth. In this latter perspective, the central enterprise is a pursuit of *truth,* and philosophical truth is pretty much defined as what can be made, from the raw material of experience, by reason and argument. We can't argue without language. Philosophy remains essentially tied to language, at least in its "analytic" incarnation.

In the next section, I will give a reason for thinking that, while silence might conceivably be a limiting case of poetic speech, it could never count as even a limiting condition of philosophical speech. The reason for this lies in the characteristic which, in my view, or at least in the view that I am about to moult partly free of in this chapter, demands that we regard philosophical and poetic language as opposite extremes on a continuum of what I will call *density* of language.

III Density, and the Meanings of "Meaning"

Anna Christina Ribeiro has argued that three features are, if not necessary and sufficient to define a poem, at least "broadly typical":

(1) most poems are lyric poems written in the first person;
(2) most poems are formal; indeed, most are highly formal; and

(3) most poems use figurative language—metaphors, similes, imagery, and so on, to a greater, often much greater, extent than other literary forms (Ribeiro 2009, 66).

I shall return to (1) in a moment. (2) partly explains why it is better, when learning a new language, to read and memorize poetry than prose. Given their formal characteristics, poems are easier to learn by heart, which means you have big chunks learned at one go and pleasure too. But there is more to it, and that additional factor is not quite exhausted by Ribeiro's reference to tropes. Spending an hour on a page of good poetry is more rewarding than spending an hour on a page of good prose. As a direct function of the density of poetic meaning, there is more to savor on each page, and savoring is best done slowly.

My intuition that poetry and philosophy are antagonists, then, was driven by the thought that poetry strives for density, while philosophy aspires to transparency, which is equivalent to the lowest possible density. But what exactly do these terms mean?

Density is in part the result of the sort of "suggestiveness" praised in the theories of poetry I have cited, for wherever something is suggested, it is present without taking up space. This ideal is not confined to the East. Western poetry also commonly strives to evoke something beyond prose, and even beyond words. These lines of Wordsworth express this well:

> A presence that disturbs me with the joy
> Of elevated thoughts; a sense sublime
> Of something far more deeply interfused,
> Whose dwelling is the light of setting suns,
> And the round ocean and the living air,
> And the blue sky, and in the mind of man.

> (Wordsworth, "Tintern Abbey")

In their feeling of reaching for something beyond what can be described, these lines seem to me in tune with what, according to Jeff Masson, "many Sanskrit critics consider . . . to be the most beautiful poem in the Sanskrit language":

> glimpses something
> or a hair of sound touches him
> And his heart overflows with a longing
> he does not recognize

> then it must be that he is remembering
> in a place out of reach
> shapes he has loved
> in a life before this the print of them still there in him waiting.

(Merwin and Masson 1977, 33).

At the same time as the quest for something beyond language, there is often an emphasis on the concrete particular. We can find it in Wallace Stevens's "Blue Guitar," for example:

> the man replied things as they are
> are changed upon the blue guitar
> And they said then, "but play, you must,
> a tune beyond us, yet ourselves."

(Stevens 1964, 165)

Simon Critchley comments: "Such is the whole enigma of modern poetry: to say something 'beyond us, yet ourselves'" (2005, 53). But it applies not only to modern poetry, as attested by the following lines from another Sanskrit poem:

> a poet should learn with his eyes
> the forms of leaves
> you should know how to make
> people laugh when they are together
> he should get to see
> what they are really like
> you should know about oceans and mountains
> in themselves
> and the sun and the moon and the stars
> his mind should enter into the season
> he should go
> among many people
> in many places and learn their languages[7]

So at one level this notion of density seems to come from the power of poetic language to evoke more than they say. But I think the notion of density can be explained more clearly and schematically, in terms of more mundane conceptions of meaning.

---

[7] Tr. W. S. Merwin from the *Kavikanthabharana,* vv. 10 and 11, ed. Pandit Dhundhiraja Sastri (Masson 1985, 5–6).

I have in mind the essentially structuralist notion that meaning is a matter of potential contrasts. It is an ancient idea, of which the germ is already present in the medieval slogan (itself ultimately traceable to Parmenides) that "every predication is a negation." It is basic to the structural linguistics inaugurated by de Saussure (1966), and it is neatly expressed in Paul Ziff's book, *Semantic Analysis* (1964), which defines the meaning of a word as *the set of contrastive sets in each member of that word's distributive set*:

> The significance of what is said depends on what is not said. The utterance actually uttered stands in contrast with and takes its shape from what is not but could without deviation be uttered. The fact that "excellent," "splendid" and the like are available and yet not employed serves to determine the significance of "That is a good painting." (Ziff 1960, 147)

Here is a simple application of this idea. What is the meaning of the word "cat"? The first part of the answer is given by the set of frames it can fit into: its distributive set. Members of that set include *The ____ is on the mat; What a nice tabby ____; It's raining ____s and dogs*; etc. The second part of the answer is given by specifying, for any member of the previous set, what else could go into the same frame: *The BIKE is on the mat; The DOG is on the mat; The TURD is on the mat*. But it does not include *The THOUGHT is on the mat*, or *The GONE is on the mat*.

To be a little more realistic about how the word affects us, however, we need to weight every member of a set with a probability. "Time" and "monkey" could both appear in the context *What's the best ____?* But the former is very much more probable. That measure of probability is doubtless correlated with the strength of the association between the frame and its alternative fillers. These associations, in turn, can be thought of as an aura of connotation, and the richer they are, the more dense the meaning of the passage that includes them.

Notice that this approach to meaning doesn't necessarily say anything about what is *true*; the criterion of membership in a set may be only that the set be somehow acceptable, or as Ziff cryptically writes, "nondeviant." The question of what counts as deviant is highlighted by Chomsky's famous example of a syntactically acceptable but semantically deviant sentence: *Colourless green ideas sleep furiously*. That last sentence, however, might not strike us as deviant if we thought it had been composed by a surrealist poet, or perhaps by John Ashbery.

Here we come to a major cleavage between the philosopher's and what I will refer to as the poet's conception of meaning. In one of the master texts of analytic philosophy, Gottlob Frege distinguishes two objective properties of meaningful units: reference (the actual object or class of objects designated by an expression) and sense (the set of specifications that allow us to identify the reference). Both are contrasted with "colouring and shading," which "are not objective, and must be evoked by each hearer or reader according to the hints of the poet or the speaker" (Frege 1980, 55). Subjective colouring and shading, or connotations, are not pertinent to the determination of truth value, but are of crucial importance in the context of rhetoric or therapy. Given that distinction, the question arises as to whether those connotations should be regarded as part of meaning.

Analytic philosophers have taken a firm stand for the negative. Donald Davidson, for example, insisted that the meaning of any linguistic unit just *is* no more and no less than its contribution to the *truth conditions* of any sentence in which it figures (Davidson 1978, 1982 [1967]). But for the poet, any difference that makes a difference contributes to meaning in the broad sense, even if the difference it makes doesn't affect truth conditions. This could be merely a difference in sound, between two synonyms, as between "Greek" and "Hellene," making no difference to the truth value of any sentence containing them.[8]

This shows that the contrasts involved in contrastive sets must be defined in terms of what can make a relevant difference. But relevant to what? Grant (quibbling aside) that (1) and (2) have the same truth conditions:

(1) The raven is still sitting without moving on top of the white bust of Athena, just above the door of my room. And his eyes look like those of a devil having a dream. And the lamp's light behind him

---

[8] Unless they appeared in indirect speech, in which case almost any difference can annul synonymy. A paper by Benson Mates (1952) sparked a lengthy correspondence in *Analysis* (ably summarized yet perhaps not wholly resolved by Tyler Burge 1978) about whether, given the synonymy of "Greek" and "Hellene," anyone could doubt that whoever believed that whoever is a Greek is a Hellene, while not doubting that whoever is a Greek is a Greek. If the answer is that someone could, then it seems *any* difference even between strict synonyms could in *some* contexts of indirect discourse make a difference in truth value.

casts a shadow on the floor, and my soul is lying there and will not be lifted ever again from that position floating on the ground.

(2) And the raven, never flitting, still is sitting, still is sitting
On the pallid bust of Pallas just above my chamber door;
And his eyes have all the seeming of a demon's that is dreaming,
And the lamp-light o'er him streaming throws his shadow on the floor;
And my soul from out that shadow that lies floating on the floor
Shall be lifted–nevermore!

If only differences of truth conditions count, alliteration, rhyme, and rhythm make no relevant difference, and (1) and (2) will not differ in meaning. For the poet, on the contrary, those features are crucial.

IV   Why Do They Do It?

Although the creative process is mysterious and protean, we can be fairly confident that the impulse most likely to issue in a poem will differ from the process of writing a philosophy essay. A philosopher will start with a thesis, or at least hope to end up with one. Poets are liable to say that they first heard a certain rhythm, an assonance, or an image. A thought too trivial to express in prose seems irresistibly to shape itself into verse (or a few lines of verse pop into one's head, expressing a truth too banal to be worthy of prose). At other times, a form might offer a challenge, giving rise to a conscious intention to write a sonnet, or a ballad, or a limerick. Occasional poems, *poèmes de circonstance*, generally pass for one of the lowest forms of verse, as puns are often held to be the lowest form of wit. Still, many poems remain close to occasional verse, as an impulse to give form, or merely draw attention, to some particular thing, something that doesn't need to be argued or established. Many lyrical poems are of this sort. Think, for example, of Byron's "So we'll go no more a-roving / By the light of the moon / Though the heart be still as loving / and the moon be still as bright." Lyrical poetry as a genre is a kind of elevated occasional poetry. It is intended to be taken by the reader as having some universal import, but also seems focused on a specific type of situation. This is true not only of romantic lyrics. It applies to many Shakespeare sonnets, and to Donne's or Marvell's erotic poetry such as "On going to bed," or "To his Coy Mistress." As Ribeiro has noted, "The personal mode of expression invites a personal mode of engagement with the content of the work, so personal indeed that the ideal engagement involves identification, on the part of the listener or reader, with the impressions, thoughts, or feelings expressed in the work, something evinced in the phenomenon of appropriation" (Ribeiro 2009, 73).

How then, in these cases, do the results turn out to be poems rather than something else? Why are they not essays, or descriptive fiction? Prose poems raise the question most acutely. As Ribeiro observes, the prose poem is a peculiarly French invention, and although it appears to be a form that "cannot decide what it wants to be," there is never the slightest doubt, when reading a prose poem by Baudelaire, Rimbaud, or Francis Ponge, about its being a poem and nothing else. Take the brief *chosiste* poem, *Le cageot*, a favorite piece by Francis Ponge:

A mi-chemin de la cage au cachot la langue française a cageot, simple caissette à claire-voie vouée au transport de ces fruits qui de la moindre suffocation font à coup sûr une maladie. Agencé de façon qu'au terme de son usage il puisse être brisé sans effort, il ne sert pas deux fois. Ainsi dure-t-il moins encore que les denrées fondantes ou nuageuses qu'il enferme. A tous les coins de rues qui aboutissent aux halles, il luit alors de l'éclat sans vanité du bois blanc. Tout neuf encore, et légèrement ahuri d'être dans une pose maladroite à la voirie jeté sans retour, cet objet est en somme des plus sympathiques–sur le sort duquel il convient toutefois de ne s'appesantir longuement. (Ponge 1942)[9]

On the surface, this is in fact a simple description. It could be an "essay" of the sort that English schoolchildren used to be asked to compose for oral presentation in "just a minute," as in the classic BBC game show of that name. But Ponge's piece, which holds easily within the minute when read aloud, is clearly a poem. Why? In part it is because it stresses the sensual quality of language, as an impasto painting might stress the relish of paint, starting and ending with meta-level observations that frame its scrupulous descriptive core. The first is a comment on the sound of the word for a light produce crate, and it is the word that is first described as being "midway"

---

[9] "Midway between *cage* and *cachot*, a dungeon, the French language has *cageot*, a simple open-slatted crate designed for the transport of the sort of fruit that is sure to sicken at the slightest hint of suffocation. Constructed so as to be easily destroyed after use, it never serves twice. Thus it lasts not even as long as the melting or ethereal delicacies it encloses. Thus, at the corners of every street leading to the market, it gleams with the unassuming lustre of white pine. Still brand new and somewhat aghast and awkward at being dumped irretrievably on the public thoroughfare, this is really a most appealing object—on whose fate, however, it would not do to dwell too long." (My translation.)

between *cage* (cage) and *cachot* (dungeon). As a sort of pun, it is thus literally untranslatable. The striking difference between the effect of the English paraphrase and the direct enjoyment of the original vividly illustrates one of the contrasts between philosophy and poetry. Much the same is true of the awkward phrasing in the first clause of the last sentence, which conveys just the feeling that it comically ascribes to the produce crate itself. The last thought is also a meta-level comment, this time about the very idea of dwelling on the thought of produce crates. In between, there is much discreet subterranean play with traditional "poetic" themes such as death and passion, with the suggestion of the "sickness unto death" that fruity flesh is heir to; the virginal character of its "gleaming white wood"; and the enduring theme of evanescence. In short, "Le cageot" confirms Ribeiro's claim that we don't confuse prose poems with real prose.

Does "Le cageot" make a philosophical point? In a sense, it does. But at the risk of seeming wantonly paradoxical, the philosophical point it makes is due precisely to its being perfectly anti-philosophical. Philosophy is abstract and general. As Peter Lamarque (2009) has pointed out, poetry, no less than philosophy, necessarily makes use of abstraction, simply by dint of using language. Ponge's prose poem is concerned with a very specific concrete object of no significance at all. The philosophical point it makes is about the importance of the unimportant particular.

Like the focus on the particular, the emphasis on the personal in lyric poetry brings it paradoxically closer to philosophy. That is because the rhetorical power of poetry immediately confronts me, the reader, with the question of whether or not the vision conveyed is one that I can appropriate. Take, for example, two short poems by Fernando Pessoa. One is quoted and translated by Anna Cristina Ribeiro and reads, in part:

> I love everything that was,
> Everything that no longer is,
> The ache that no longer hurts,
> The old and erroneous faith,
> The yesterday that left pain,
> Or that left happiness
> Just because it was, and flew away
> And today is already another day.
> (Ribeiro 2009, 67)[10]

[10] "Eu amo tudo o que foi, / Tudo o que já não é, / A dor que já me não dói, / A antiga e errônea fé, / O ontem que dor deixou, / O que deixou alegria / Só porque foi, e voou / E hoje

Here, Pessoa expresses the idea that pastness is of value in itself. This could be one definition of the emotion of nostalgia, or perhaps *saudade,* the national emotion of the Portuguese. But when it is put this bluntly my own inclination is to resist. Pastness is not a value. So while I apprehend the thought and appreciate it, I ask myself whether or not I can *endorse* it. In the end, it is part of my experience of the poem that I do not. As a philosopher, it then occurs to me that I might want to *argue* about it, that I might want to confront it with a different view of nostalgia, such as that elaborated by Scott Howard, who argues that nostalgia is about transience, and the longing for some specific quality in the past, not about pastness as such (Howard 2012). I want, in short, to bring it into the realm of what is *true* or *not true*, rather than leaving it in the realm of what is merely *experienced*. When confronted with the Pessoa poem, I transition more or less gently from the experiential mode to a mode of judgment.

My second example from Pessoa is about the importance of being ridiculous. The poem goes (in part) like this:

> all love letters are
> ridiculous.
> They would not be love letters if they were not
> ridiculous.
> I too have written love letters in my time,
> like all the others
> they were ridiculous
> love letters—if there is love—must be
> ridiculous
>
> But in the end,
> It's only those that have never written
> love letters
> who are
> ridiculous[11]

é já outro dia." (Retrieved from <http://www.luso-poemas.net/modules/news03/article.php?storyid=558#ixzz1x1akzxou>.)

[11] The poem published under Pessoa's "heteronym" Alvaro de Campos is widely anthologized. This extract came from <http://www.citador.pt/poemas/todas-as-cartas-de-amor-sao-ridiculas-alvaro-de-camposbrbheteronimo-de-fernando-pessoa> and <http://www.releituras.com/fpessoa_cartas.asp>. The translation is mine.

Here again, I seem to be invited to endorse or to reject a certain vision of how I should be. And in this case I say Yes, I want to write ridiculous love letters; I would feel ridiculous not to let myself be ridiculous. And I can even buttress my endorsement with a recent article in a serious journal, showing experimentally that self-deception inhibits humour (Lynch and Trivers 2012). Laughter, particularly at oneself, is inimical to self-deception. And since self-deception is an unprepossessing trait, the determination to allow oneself to be ridiculous is an ideal worth emulating—a better way to be human. The fact that humour is not a traditional Aristotelian virtue illustrates the subtlety of poetry's philosophical force. Humour presupposes a number of appraisals of what matters and what doesn't matter in human life; in that respect, it is linked to traditional virtues such as modesty, a sense of proportion, and a sense of the importance of seeing the unimportance of things transient even as they are savored. Such traits have been the subject of praise, aspiration, and meditation on the part of people traditionally called philosophers. But it would be pedantic, not to say bizarre, to insist on dragging all of this into one's appreciation of Pessoa's poem. The vision here is much more specific, much closer to the model of the "occasional poem" sparked by a particular moment in which someone reflects on the risk of being thought ridiculous for daring to write a love letter.

Both the poet's method of work and the reader's intended response are marked by the personal character of lyric poetry. But this is precisely what brings them back, in the end, to an unexpected reconciliation with philosophy. To explain this, I first return to the notion of density.

V   The Excesses of Density

To be sure, the notion of density fits some kinds of poetry better than others. It reaches an extreme level in surrealist poetry. But it can go further. In much of John Ashbery's poetry, for example, there is a dreamlike disconnection between the elements found in any particular sequence of words in a randomly chosen poem. In a fascinating interview with A. Poulin, Ashbery expresses surprise that anyone has trouble understanding his poetry. "It seems to me that the poetry is what's there and there are no hidden meanings or references to other things beyond what most of us know" (Poulin 1981, 244). And again: "it doesn't particularly matter about the experience; the movement of experiencing is what I'm trying to get down . . . Most of my poems are about the experience of experience." This sounds good, but does nothing to mitigate the baffling character of many of Ashbery's poems. In terms of the formula I derived from Paul Ziff, what seems to be happening in Ashbery's poetry is that words are deliberately located in highly improbable contexts. This should enrich their potential for meaning; but it does so only in a technical sense, derived from the mathematical or "Shannon" theory of information. In that sense, a sequence of digits or letters carries maximum information if it is completely random. The reason is that information is inversely related to probability: the least probable event adds the most to your existing store of belief. But it is not informative in the common understanding of that term, which requires new information to be not only unexpected but *interesting*.

VI Stylistic Progress

A high degree of unpredictability due to randomness is not in general likely to make things particularly interesting to creatures looking for human significance. Nevertheless, it is, by definition, something that is likely to arouse surprise. That is at the root of an intriguing investigation. On the basis of computerized analysis of changes in word usage, Colin Martindale undertook to explain the course of changes in poetry (among other arts) from Chaucer to Larkin. His two basic variables are "arousal potential" and "primordial content." The former includes "complexity, surprisingness, incongruity, ambiguity, and variability." These, in turn, are operationalized with measures of "polarity (a measure of semantic intensity or strikingness)," mean word length, potential for ambiguity in words used, and three different coefficients of variation: in word frequency, word length, and phrase length (Martindale 1990, 121–2). He divided the period in question (from 1290 to 1949) into thirty-three successive twenty-year periods. The impressive graphs that resulted seem to support his general "evolutionary theory of artistic change," which posits successive waves, separated by radical changes of style, in which there is a steady rise in both arousal potential and primordial content. Periodically, those two parameters reach a peak (which gets steadily higher over the long haul), until they are reset at a lower level, when the quest for novelty is temporarily satisfied by stylistic innovation instead of further escalation of arousal and primordial content.

Martindale's conception of primordial content derives from the psychoanalytic concept of "primary process thought." In its contrast with "secondarily process cognition," which is "abstract, logical, and reality oriented . . . the thought of everyday waking reality . . . concerned with problem solving, logical deduction and induction, and so on," primary process thinking is "free associative, concrete, irrational, and autistic. It is the thought of dreams and reveries" (Martindale 1990, 56).

Nowadays, philosophers with an interest in cognitive science are more likely to think of the distinction between the two systems of "dual processing theory." Daniel Kahneman's recent intellectual autobiography has recast half a century of his research in terms of this dual processing perspective (Kahneman 2011). But it is not the same distinction. "System 1" in modern dual processing theory consists in extremely efficient mechanisms for dealing with the real world. Freudian primary process thinking, by contrast, ignores the limitations of actual reality, and is innocent of logic and language (Freud 1911). We need to make room for a kind of thinking more dreamlike, driven by associations, emotions and wishes, a type of consciousness uncommitted either to practical ends or logical process. Such states would recall those described by Frijda and Sundararajan. Rather than being purposive, they would include, at most, "virtual states of action readiness rather than states that manifest in overt acts or suppressed action impulses" (Frijda and Sundararajan 2007, 227). This contrasts not only with secondary process thinking which, of course, includes all the manifest content of analytic philosophy, but also with "system 1" processing as it is understood by most dual process theorists. If we are to believe recently published reports indicating that we are more creative when tired out, and more likely to solve hard problems (Wietha and Zack 2011), states of unguided daydreaming may indeed be shown to have particular importance for creativity.[12]

Martindale's research—anathema though it be to literary theorists—does seem to provide empirical evidence that a progressive pursuit of incongruity in poetry affects the choice of words, themes, and syntax in different periods, and also of a poet's production in the course of a single

[12] I am indebted to Zachary Irving for drawing my attention to the importance of such "wandering states" of the mind.

life. It illustrates one aspect of the sort of density that a certain conception of philosophy generally strives to avoid.

VII   Reconciliation?

My argument so far may seem to ignore examples of poems that are incontrovertibly intended to convey a philosophical idea. I have already mentioned Peter Lamarque's observation about the inevitability of abstract content in any genre of which the medium is language. John Koethe (1984) has given a number of examples, including these two, respectively from Wallace Stevens and from T. S. Eliot, of overtly philosophical lines of poetry:

> Death is the mother of beauty, mystical,
> Within whose burning bosom we devise
> Our earthly mothers waiting, sleeplessly.[13]

> There are three conditions which often look alike
> Yet differ completely, flourish in the same hedgerow:
> Attachment to self and to things and to persons, detachment
> From self and from things and from persons; and, growing
> between them, indifference
> Which resembles the others as death resembles life,
> Being between two lives . . .[14]

But here is the large difference, which appears particularly clear from the point of view of the reader. In neither of these cases am I, as reader, seriously tempted to *argue*, as I would if I were to receive it as philosophy: Why are our earthly mothers waiting "sleeplessly"? Our mothers are either dead or alive, and if alive, then why are they "in the bosom of death"? Well, it's a trope, of course. But could it be right or wrong? Surely it could, when it engages directly in a philosophical dispute. Such is Larkin's rejection of the Epicurean view of death as not to be feared, decried as "specious stuff that says No rational being / Can fear a thing it will not feel, not seeing / That this is what we fear." This comes after Larkin's contemptuous dismissal of religion as a "moth-eaten musical brocade / Created to pretend we never die."[15] But the two attacks are

---

[13] "Sunday Morning" (Stevens 1964, 68–9).
[14] From "Little Gidding" (Eliot 1968, 55).
[15] Philip Larkin, "Aubade" (Larkin 2012, 123).

very different: against religion, Larkin offers brilliant sarcasm; against the philosopher, a rather prosaic argument with which the partisan of Epicurus seems challenged to take issue.

Koethe seeks to disarm impertinent cavils about facts or opinion by noting the difference between truth and truthfulness. The latter is what matters here, and it would be uncouth to confuse them. The truth of a poem, I would be happy to concede, is akin to the truths of an emotion. Elsewhere, I have argued that the sense of truth appropriate to emotions is a "generic" one, differing in two ways from the specific kind of truth ascribed by standard semantics to propositions. First, the sort of generic truth that can be ascribed to an emotion admits of degrees; secondly, it is relative, in every case, to standards specific to the emotion in question.[16] Similarly, what we are asked to endorse in a poem is not some universally valid truth, but a picture of a certain kind that is convincing in its own terms, while we are contemplating the poem. To a large extent, the truth we are invited to endorse is a local one, fitting standards that are set by the poem itself.[17]

One of Koethe's own examples will serve to make the point. He quotes, from not quite accurate memory, a sentence from Proust's *Remembrance of Things Past*: "What is love but the heart grown conscious of separation in time and space?"[18] and comments:

I had that familiar feeling of assenting to a striking insight we often experience in reading great literature ("How true!"), but then it occurred me that the same feeling of assent could also be prompted by the near negation of that sentence, "What is love but the heart grown unconscious of separation in time and space?" While the latter is more banal than, and not strictly the negation of, the former, clearly the two observations are in tension with one another. (Koethe 2009, 55)

Actually I was brought up to believe that this feature defines a Profound Truth quite generally: a Profound Truth is one of which the negation is also a Profound Truth. There's nothing especially poetic about this, but on the standard philosophical criteria of univocal meaning as

---

[16] For more on this conception of generic truth, see de Sousa 2011, 55–6.

[17] I am side-stepping a large literature on the question of what "truth" might mean when applied to literature. For an enlightening approach to this problem, focusing on fiction rather than poetry, see Gibson 2007.

[18] The original is "l'amour, c'est l'espace et le temps rendus sensibles au cœur" (Proust 1966, iii. 385), which actually says nothing explicitly about separation. It is better rendered as "love is time and space rendered perceptible to the heart."

truth conditions, profound truths are indeed defective as philosophical pronouncements. As the philosopher-poet Leonard Cohen has put it, however, "there is a crack in everything; that's how the light gets in."[19] Although irritating to the analytic philosopher, profound truths are not always devoid of insight.

I have stressed two contrasts in the foregoing reflections. One is that poetry pursues meaning density, while philosophy eschews it. The other is that what passes for truth in philosophy is more strictly tied to propositions as truth-bearers, capable of being sufficiently insulated from their context of origin to be held true universally. Unsurprisingly, given the quasi-biological diversity of what has been called poetry, I have had to make a number of concessions along the way. None of the claims I have made is nomologically valid either about philosophy or about poetry. But as a picture of how things stand in philosophy in comparison to poetry, I remain convinced of the truthfulness, if not of the truth, of a conception of poetry as aspiring to meaning density, and as susceptible of generic rather than conventional truth. At the same time, I have found much to weaken the case for pure transparency as an invariable demand of philosophy.

Note, incidentally, that the cultivation of transparency does not preclude the pleasures of style. One has only to think of some of philosophy's famous sentences to remember that some philosophers can still write. Consider just two examples:

> Good sense is the best distributed thing in the world, for everyone thinks himself to be so well endowed with it that even those who are the most difficult to please in everything else never deem themselves to need any more of it than they already have.

The incorrectness of rendering "Ctesias is hunting unicorns" in the fashion:

> $(\exists x)(x \text{ is a unicorn. Ctesias is hunting } x)$

is conveniently attested by the nonexistence of unicorns, but is not due simply to that zoological lacuna.

Neither of these fine sentences, however, allows the slightest doubt as to its unique meaning. And if they did admit of anything more distracting

---

[19] Leonard Cohen, "Anthem."

than a shade of irony, each of their authors would regard that as a defect. So in some philosophy, at least, the demand for transparency seems well established. Nevertheless, this doesn't hold true for all those who would regard themselves as doing philosophy. More importantly, insofar as it seems incontrovertible that the aims of philosophy legitimately include a new vision, a "re-gestalting" of the world, I must concede the potential for a convergence.

Most of what I have said to soften the antagonism between poetry and philosophy has been designed to bring poetry closer to philosophy. Something more should be said about the convergence as it might be seen from the other side. A spirited defense of the claim of "lyrical" uses of language to be incorporated into the language of philosophy itself has been made by Jan Zwicky—a musician, poet, and philosopher (Zwicky 1995, 2003). In a recent summary describing her two books of philosophy, Zwicky describes the contrapuntal method according to which her own reflections occur on pages facing contributions culled from others: "there is a second, parallel, text composed of excerpts from other authors, excerpts from musical compositions, photographs, mathematical proofs, etc. That second text, in combination with my own, attempts to trace a multi-dimensional polyphonic structure" (Zwicky 2013, 15).

She goes on to distinguish analytic from lyric philosophy in two ways:

To read analytic thought sympathetically is to be favourably disposed towards the presupposition that meaning is essentially a linguistic phenomenon although, in any given case, the exact words may not matter. The reading of lyric compositions presupposes that, in significant ways, meaning exists prior to and independently of language—but that if language is to bear its trace, the choice of words must be exact. (Zwicky 2013, 2)

If we read "lyric compositions" as referring to poetry, it is not contentious that "the choice of words must be exact." But it is puzzling to find this claim tied to the idea that meaning "exists prior to and independently of language." For if language strains, as we have seen many poets feel, to express something that is beyond the reach of words, there is no reason to believe that just one form of words will qualify. If none really succeeds, several might come equally close. On the other hand, if one takes all meaning to be linguistic—or more modestly, if our best chance of constructing a clear conception of meaning is to take linguistic meaning as a paradigm—I don't see why it would follow that the choice of words "may not matter." I would expect precisely the reverse. The compromises required in "translations" of poetic texts afford an obvious illustration: to convey the meaning of a text in another language, there are sure to be several alternatives, precisely because none might be quite right. Insofar as no extra-linguistic source of meaning exists, there will be no true synonyms. Surely it is when language is all there is, when words are not intended to transpose anything from some non-linguistic reality, that "exact words" will matter supremely.

Nevertheless, Zwicky seems right in suggesting that an aim of philosophy is to effect a change of vision. Since that formula fits the aim of much poetry, the original contrast I drew between philosophy and poetry is all the weaker. Nevertheless, I balk at regarding philosophy as so inclusive as to encompass every approach to what we might broadly call "understanding," including not only poetry but music, art, and mathematics. For while every discipline, from science to poetry (and perhaps even, if tolerance is indulged to the point of laxity, religion), contributes to understanding in the broadest sense, it seems confusing to call it all philosophy.

There remains, furthermore, a crucial difference in the role of truth, and the kind of truth that we expect in philosophy and in poetry. We apply the word "compelling" both to a philosophical argument and to a poem (or even a few lines of poetry). But what we mean when we say a poem is compelling is not the same as what we mean when we say an argument is compelling.[20] Even in the most philosophical of poems, we don't apply the standards of conviction that prevail when assessing a philosophical text. A philosophical poem might be presenting a new way of seeing things, as in the examples of the two Pessoa poems; or it might even present itself as an argument, like those slightly annoying early Sonnets in which Shakespeare is *arguing* that his friend should have a child. But in either case, the kind of truth we are looking for is quite different from the kind of truth we look for in philosophy. Even when a philosophical text is not one of those that rely entirely on argument, we find it compelling only if it leads us to believe its conclusion to be *true*, or the picture it presents to be the *right* picture of how things stand in a very general way. By contrast, to find an argument or a position taken in

---

[20] Robert Nozick once offered a third alternative definition of a compelling argument: "if the person refuses to accept the conclusion, *he dies*" (Nozick 1981, 4).

a poem incredible does not necessarily remove its virtue as a "compelling" presentation of a certain sort of *possible* way to be. Because a poem is most likely rooted, as Ribeiro suggested, in a personal experience, a poem doesn't need to claim universality to ring true or be truthful.

In sum, I now see my original conviction that poetry and philosophy are inherently polar opposites in their relation to language as simplistic. In its modest and limited way, I regard this as a "vision" of the relation of philosophy and poetry. It is not poetic; it is philosophical; and I was led to it by a mix of arguments and animadversions, of which this is the last.[21]

References

Bargh, J. A., and Ferguson, M. L. 2000. "Beyond Behaviorism: On the Automaticity of Higher Mental Processes." *Psychological Bulletin*, 126: 925–45.

Bargh, J. A., Chen, M., and Burrows, L. 1996. "Automaticity of Social Behavior: Direct Effects of Trait Construct and Stereotype Activation on Action." *Journal of Personality and Social Psychology*, 71(2): 230–44.

Burge, T. 1978. "Belief and Synonymy." *Journal of Philosophy*, 75(3): 119–38.

Critchley, S. 2005. *Things Merely Are: Philosophy in the Poetry of Wallace Stevens*. London: Routledge.

Davidson, D. 1978. "What Metaphors Mean." *Critical Inquiry*, 5: 31–47.

Davidson, D. 1982 [1967]. "Truth and Meaning." In *Inquiries into Truth and Interpretation*. Oxford: Clarendon Press, 17–42.

de Saussure, F. 1966. *Course in General Linguistics*, ed. C. Bally and A. Sechehaye, with A. Reidlinger, tr. W. Baskin. New York: McGraw-Hill.

de Sousa, R. 2011. *Emotional Truth*. New York: Oxford University Press.

Eliot, T. S. 1968. *Four Quartets*. Orlando, FL: Harcourt Brace.

Fodor, J. 1983. *The Modularity of Mind*. Cambridge, MA: MIT Press.

Frege, G. 1980. "On Sense and Reference." *Mind*, 65(259), 51–78.

Freud, S. 1911. "Formulations on the Two Principles of Mental Functioning." In *Standard Edition of the Complete Psychological Works*. London: Hogarth Press, 213–26.

Frijda, N., and Sundararajan, L. 2007. "Emotion Refinement: A Theory Inspired by Chinese Poetics." *Perspectives on Psychological Science*, 2(3): 227–41.

Gibson, J. 2007. *Fiction and the Weave of Life*. Oxford: Oxford University Press.

Howard, S. A. 2012. "Lyrical Emotions and Sentimentality." *Philosophical Quarterly*, 62: 546–68.

---

[21] I am indebted to Scott Howard for helpful comments on an earlier draft.

Kahneman, D. 2011. *Thinking, Fast and Slow*. New York and Toronto: Farrar, Straus & Giroux; Doubleday Canada.

Koethe, J. 1984. *The Late Wisconsin Spring*. Princeton: Princeton University Press.

Koethe, J. 2009. "Poetry and Truth." *Mid-West Studies in Philosophy*, 33: 53–60.

Lamarque, P. 2009. "Poetry and Abstract Thought." *Mid-West Studies in Philosophy*, 33: 37–52.

Larkin, P. 2012. *Poems, Selected by Martin Amis*. London: Faber & Faber.

Lynch, R. L., and Trivers, R. F. 2012. "Self-Deception Inhibits Laughter." *Personality and Individual Differences*, 53(4): 491–5.

McGinn, C. 2012. "Philosophy by Another Name." *New York Times* (Mar. 4). <http://opinionator.blogs.nytimes.com/2012/03/04/philosophy-by-another-name>.

Martindale, C. 1990. *The Clockwork Muse: The Predictability of Artistic Change*. New York: Basic Books.

Masson, J. M. 1977. "Introduction." In W. Merwin(ed.) and J. M. Masson (tr.), *The Peacock's Egg: Love Poems from Ancient India*. San Francisco: North Point Press, 1–35.

Masson, J. M. 1985. *The Assault on Truth: Freud's Suppression of the Seduction Theory*. Harmmondsworth: Penguin.

Mates, B. 1952. "Synonymity." In B. Linsky (ed.), *Semantics and the Philosophy of Language*. Urbana, IL: University of Illinois Press, 111–36.

Mercier, H., and Sperber, D. 2011. "Why do Humans Reason? Arguments for an Argumentative Theory." *Behavioral and Brain Sciences*, 34(2): 57–74.

Merwin, W., and Masson, J. M., eds. 1977. *The Peacock's Egg: Love Poems from Ancient India*. San Francisco: North Point Press.

Nozick, R. 1981. *Philosophical Explanations*. Cambridge, MA: Harvard University Press.

Oatley, K. 2006. "Simulation of Substance and Shadow: Inner Emotions and Outer Behavior in Shakespeare's Psychology of Character." *College Literature*, 33(1): 15–33.

Pandit, L. 1996. "Dhvani and the 'Full Word': Suggestion and Signification from Abhinavagupta to Jaques Lacan." *College Literature*, 23(1): 142–63.

Parkes, G. 2011. "Japanese Aesthetics." In E. N. Zalta (ed.), *The Stanford Encyclopedia of Philosophy*. <http://plato.stanford.edu/archives/win2011/entries/japanese-aesthetics>.

Ponge, F. 1942. *Le Parti pris des choses*. Paris: Gallimard.

Poulin, A. Jr 1981. "The Experience of Experience: A Conversation with John Ashbery." *Michigan Quarterly Review*, 20(3): 241–55.

Proust, M. 1966. *A la recherche du temps perdu*. Paris: Gallimard, Bibliothèque de la Pléiade.

Ribeiro, A. C. 2009. "Towards a Philosophy of Poetry." *Midwestern Studies in Philosophy*, 33: 61–77.

Stevens, W. 1964. *The Collected Poems*. New York: Alfred A. Knopf.

Wietha, M. B., and Zack, R. T. 2011. "Time of Day Effects on Problem Solving: When Non-Optimal is Optimal." *Thinking and Reasoning*, 17(4): 387–401.

Yeats, W. B. 1996. *The Collected Poems*. Ed. R. J. Finneran. New York: Scribner.

Ziff, P. 1960. *Semantic Analysis*. Ithaca, NY: Cornell University Press.

Zwicky, J. 1995. *Lyric Philosophy*. Toronto: University of Toronto Press.

Zwicky, J. 2003. *Wisdom and Metaphor*. Kentville, NS: Gaspereau Press.

Zwicky, J. 2013. "What is Lyric Philosophy?" *Common Knowledge*, 20(1): 14–27.

3

Poetic Opacity
How to Paint Things with Words

Jesse Prinz and Eric Mandelbaum

I Looking for the Essence of Poetry

Analytic aesthetics, like analytic philosophy more broadly, has had an appetite for definitions. Textbooks and syllabi give disproportionate space to the question, "What is art?" It is no surprise, then, that analytic philosophers of poetry might ask, "What is poetry?" and we will follow suit. Our goal is to say something about the nature of poetry—something general enough that might capture a unifying feature of items that fall in the extension of that term. To contemporary readers, this might sound like a quaint, or perhaps even hopeless, endeavor. "Haven't we moved past the days of definitions?" To address this anxiety, we will begin with some general remarks about why it's not completely hopeless to search for a properly constrained search for the essence of poetry. We will then move on to our proposed analysis. To anticipate, we will argue that poetry has a characteristic form of opacity—a form that distinguishes it from other kinds of writing, and forges an analogy with painting.

The gripe about definitions is not merely an expression of boredom: been there, done that. There are substantive worries about definability here. These worries were most influentially instilled by Wittgenstein, who got generations of philosophers in a tither about "games"—a term, he claimed, has no set of individually necessary conditions (nor any unifying or fixed set of sufficient conditions). This did not go unnoticed in aesthetics. Within an eye-blink of the *Philosophical Investigations*, several talented authors expressed skepticism about defining art (Ziff 1953; Weitz 1956; Kennick 1958). No set of features unified art, they said, and offering such a list would belie the "open texture" of the category: art is about innovation, not essence. The crusade against definitions continued in semantics and psycholinguistics (Fodor et al. 1980), before it was subsequently taken up by cognitive psychologists inspired by Wittgenstein (see Smith and Medin 1981), who showed that people classify things using features that are statistically typical and salient, but not necessary; such features are called "prototypes." In a similar spirit, post-Wittgensteinians have proposed "cluster" theories of art (Gaut 2000; Dean 2003). Gaut's cluster theory is inspired by Wittgenstein's account of proper names, and Dean's is inspired by prototype theory in psychology. Contemporary critics of cluster theories sometimes note that concepts that are *understood* by means of clusters of features may nevertheless refer to categories that have unifying essences, which can be discovered by natural science. But this response to skepticism about definitions—which replaces mentally represented definitions with scientifically discoverable ones—will offer little solace to would-be definers of art. It would be highly contentious to suggest that art is a natural kind. Likewise, one might think, for poetry.

We summarize these initial concerns by presenting three claims that seem to jointly exclude anything like a defining analysis of poetry:

(1)   There are no definitions in the head, except perhaps for some "nominal concepts," as technical terms, whose definitions are stipulated.

(2)   There are definitions out there to be empirically discovered in the world, but only for natural kind concepts.

(3)   Poetry is neither a nominal kind nor a natural kind.

It seems to follow that there is no definition of poetry in the offing.

All this might make one a bit queasy about asking, "What is poetry?" But we think that this question can be pursued without trepidation or embarrassment, much less an upset stomach. The trio of premises ignores that poetry may have a definition (or an essence—we will use the terms interchangeably) that is neither in the head nor out of the head. This is no plea for paraconsistency. Rather, we think that the idea that a definition must either be in the head or empirically discoverable *à la* natural kinds offers a false dichotomy and excludes a possibility. The trio of premises entails that there is no definition of poetry mentally represented in the mind, or waiting for science to discover it in the world. But between these two alternatives, there is a third: one can construct a definition of poetry by systematizing our classification procedures. Presumably, we use a variety of different features to recognize something as a poem, such as rhyme, repetition, line breaks, and metaphor. None of these features is necessary, so they can be said to comprise something like a prototype. But they may share something in common—not a natural property, like a chemical microstructure, but rather something that we humans, as the inventers of poetry, have tried to cultivate with this art form. Perhaps the features in the prototype have something like a common end. If so, then even if we have a disjunctive set of features we look for in deciding whether something is a poem, it would still turn out that all of these coalesce around a unifying property, which is implicit in our classification procedures, not explicit. This would constitute a definition of poetry, but not one that is in the head or in the world, as the dichotomy forces us to assume, but rather in the practice of making, classifying, and listening to poems. In what follows, we will try to make good on this possibility by advancing a specific proposal.

II The Mark of the Poetic

1 Three Forms of Opacity

We will approach our account in stages. The basic strategy is to try to identify a "mark of the poetic"—some feature that poetry has across a range of styles and forms. A hint about this mark, we think, comes from the fact that a lot of people detest poetry. On the face of it, that is very strange. It wouldn't make sense to hate many other aspects of language. It would be bizarre to declare a hatred for paragraphs or dependent clauses. It is also unusual to hate specific uses to which language is put: like speeches, or stories, or essays. Poetry meets with greater resistance than these things. The question is, why? One possible answer is that people resist poetry, because poetry resists them. Consider the second and third stanzas of Wallace Stevens's "Bantams in Pine-Woods"

> Damned universal cock, as if the sun
> Was blackamoor to bear your blazing tail.
>
> Fat! Fat! Fat! Fat! I am the personal.
> Your world is you. I am my world[1]

---

[1] The full poem can be read at the website of the Academy of American Poets: <http://www.poets.org/poetsorg/poem/bantams-pine-woods>.

What could the meaning of a poem with such lines be? It has one, but it's not readily evident. As this example illustrates, poetry, in comparison to conventional prose, can be a challenge to read. The poem resists easy interpretation because the allusions in it are hard to detect without serious background knowledge. The "Pine-Woods" referred to in the title alert the reader that Stevens is addressing Emerson, by way of Emerson's essay "The Poet" (Emerson 1903), where they serve as the pastoral setting for the poet to find universal truths (D'Avanzo 1977). The poem is filled with the intricacies of sound, fat with alliterations, assonance, and consonance. These sounds can delight, but also distract the reader. Even the seasoned reader of poetry can be perplexed by this short work. Without knowing an essay of Emerson's, and some background of Stevens, the revolutionary tone of the poem is lost. Stevens is railing against the robust canonical tradition in poetry ("Fat! Fat! Fat! Fat!"), and announcing that he is to follow Whitman in creating a truly American poetry (Bloom 1980). Stevens is announcing that the true American poet will break with tradition.

Although this is an exceptional poem, it displays many of the qualities that make reading poetry so difficult for so many. Poetry can be flowery, obscure, metaphorical, rich with allusion, ambiguous in narrative voice, and constructed in metric schemes that depart away from ordinary linguistic usage. In a word, these things tend to make poems seem *opaque*. We take this as our starting place.

We think poetry is actually opaque in at least four different, but interconnected ways. By presenting these in turn, we can approach our analysis in a series of steps. The first form of opacity was just mentioned: poems are often difficult to read. They do not wear their meaning on their sleeves; they take extra effort. The second form of opacity is a property that falls under that term in the philosophy of language. A linguistic production (such as an utterance of a sentence) is said to be opaque when it is subject to substitution failures. Such substitution failures are sometimes understood epistemically: one can know or grasp a sentence stated in its original form without knowing or grasping a sentence which has been replaced with some synonymous or co-referential terms. Epistemic substitution failures become semantic (failures of substitution *salva veritate*), when an epistemically opaque sentence is placed in an opaque content, such as the that-clause of a *de dicto* propositional attitude report. This is true of poetry, we want to suggest, but there is also a further form of opacity, which is even more important.

Poetic productions, like sentences in general, are epistemically opaque, in that substituting synonyms can change comprehension. But the standard truth test—embedding in an attitude report—seems out of place with poetry, since it is odd to report beliefs using poetic language. Consider Romeo's claim that, "Juliet is the Sun." From this we can infer that, "Romeo believes that Juliet is the Sun." This fails substitutivity *salva veritate*: Romeo doesn't believe that Juliet is the star around which Earth orbits. The example shows the applicability of the truth test, but note how odd it is to say, "Romeo believes that Juliet is the Sun." It's not just odd because it's a metaphor. Generally, we attribute metaphors within belief reports without much hesitation (e.g. Jane believes that there was a collapse in the price of housing, that we shouldn't go down that road again, that what comes around goes around, etc.). But consider the oddity of saying, "Juliet believes that that which we call a rose by any other name would smell as sweet." We don't conventionally ascribe beliefs in iambs. More to the point, the standard truth test distracts away from a third form of opacity that may be crucial for understanding the nature of poetry. Suppose we substitute "the Sun" in Romeo's belief report with a phrase that he would understand, "the brightest celestial body as seen from Earth." Here we might preserve comprehension and truth, but something else is lost. We lose the forceful simplicity of his original words, and the forthright feelings they express in the context in which they are embedded. We also lose the meter and the sound of the poem (cf. Frost (1925) who says, in poetry, "The tone-of voice element is the unbroken flow on which [other senses] are carried along like sticks and leaves and flowers"). Putting aside the truth test, which uses attitude reports, there is a further sense in which verbal substitution would alter a poetic work. Changing a line in a poem is a bit like changing a line in a painting: it alters artistic content, not just semantic content, if semantic content is affected at all.[2] Call this "aesthetic opacity."

Aesthetic opacity goes beyond the kind of identity change that would take place if one substituted a synonym in ordinary speech. There one

[2] Note what would happen if one substitutes "overweight" (or "mildly obese," or "portly" or some such) for "fat" in the Stevens poem. Such a switch would do irreparable harm to the poem's artistic content.

would end up with a different sentence type, but any aesthetic alteration that ensued would be accidental. Ordinary sentences do not vie for aesthetic assessment. With aesthetic objects, such as sentences in a poem, an alteration in form can impact aesthetic worth. Since aesthetic objects do vie for aesthetic assessment, such impact amounts to a change in both the identity of the work (which is also true of ordinary sentences), and what might be called its aesthetic identity, which are the features of the work that are used in making aesthetic assessments. Ordinary sentences may have aesthetic properties, but they lack aesthetic identity at least in a teleological sense: they do not have the ordinary function of being aesthetically evaluated. Thus, a paraphrase of an ordinary sentence may stand in for the original without violating any aesthetic rule on preservation of form. One might say that paraphrase does not diminish the value of the original. But paraphrasing a poem alters its original value. This is also why poetic translation is, in some sense, impossible. We tolerate translations because they are necessary for comprehension across monolingual populations, but we recognize that translations inevitably lose something that was essential to the aesthetic role played by the original. We don't regard translations as different works from the originals, but perhaps we should think of them as such, or as representations of originals, rather than as tokens of the same aesthetic type. Translations of ordinary sentences can retain aesthetic type identity for the trivial reason that ordinary sentences are not typed aesthetically. Except for extreme cases where aesthetic features become unignorably salient, we tend to ignore this dimension of ordinary sentence. Ignoring the aesthetic features of a poem, in contrast, would be, to put it lightly, an error.

The three forms of opacity that we have introduced so far are all true of poetry, but none qualify as a mark of the poetic, since all are also true of other kinds of discourse. Being challenging to read (the first kind of opacity) is true of technical prose, such as philosophy; semantic opacity is true of all sentences in *de dicto* attitude contexts; and aesthetic opacity is true of any writing that has aesthetic pretentions—a same-language paraphrase of a novel would qualify as a different work. To find the mark of the poetic, we must move beyond the constructs thus far introduced but, we now want to suggest, there is a construct in the vicinity that might deliver what we need.

2 Poetic Opacity

The three forms of opacity thus far adduced normally arise independently. The obscurity of technical writing derives from the use of jargon and the need for background knowledge. The semantic opacity of ordinary sentences derives from the existence of a gap between reference and cognitive significance. When ascribing attitudes *de dicto*, we aim to comment not just on what fact a person has before her mind, but her way of thinking about that fact, which can be intimated, at least in some cases, by the choice of words. Aesthetic opacity stems from our conventions for individuating artworks. As Goodman (1968) observes, every form of art comes with implicit norms for tolerable variation. With artworks that allow for multiples (such as musical performances or prints), there are conditions on what can be a token of the same type. One can play Bach's *Mass in B Minor* on modern instruments, but one can't change the melodies; a group of any number of musicians with any type of instruments can play Terry Riley's *In C*, replaying each musical phrase any number of times, but it wouldn't count as a rendition of *In C* if one didn't play the phrases on the score (or didn't play it in the key of C for that matter); one can reprint a Goya etching on modern paper, but one can't increase the size and regard it as a token of the same print, as opposed to a mere reproduction. With literature fonts and even spellings can be tinkered with, but wordings cannot be. To account for these norms, one would have to delve into the histories of these different art forms.

Though normally orthogonal, these forms of opacity may be more closely related in poetry than they are in other forms of writing. To begin with, consider why poetry is opaque in the sense of being obscure or difficult. An obvious answer is that poets typically choose words (and word orderings) very carefully. In poetry words are objects of attention in their own right, independent of what they express. To achieve this end, poets often avoid using words or phrases that are so familiar as to be habitual. For ordinary forms of address, listeners ignore the words (and semantically unimportant changes in word orderings) and move straight away, as it were, to what those words express. Poetic norms greatly differ from other communicative practices. Compare: did we just write that the norms of poetry greatly differ from other communicative practices or that the norms of poetry differ greatly from other communicative practices or that poetic norms greatly differ from other communicative practices? The difference in word ordering matters little here as long as the content was properly conveyed; since each construction conveyed the same idea, substituting one in for the other doesn't matter one whit. The situation is drastically different in poetry. Changing word order can erase the emotional impact of a line (to say nothing of its aesthetic quality, meter, and rhyme scheme). The famed standalone couplet from Eliot's "The Love Song of J Alfred Prufrock" ("In the room women come and go / Talking of Michelangelo") would be mortally wounded if we changed it to a synonymous construction: "The women come and go in the room / Talking of Michelangelo."

Words, in non-poetic contexts, are like windows that aim for transparency, delivering the world without interference. In communicative contexts clarity is king. Poetic words are usually intentionally chosen to resist this kind of transparency—they are supposed to be noticed en route to the world (assuming the world is to come up at all). Thus, the difficulty or obscurity of poetry typically derives from this intentional effort to introduce a verbal filter between mind and world.

Next consider semantic opacity. Ordinary sentences are semantically opaque in that they resist substitution *salva veritate* in intentional contexts. It is sometimes pointed out that opacity of this kind is an unfortunate feature of language or human psychology. One might expect that an ideal language would have no co-referential terms, so that so-called Frege cases (never mind Mates cases) would not arise. Kripke (1979) argues that Frege cases can arise even for tokens of the same word type, suggesting that the problem is not with language, but arises because of a regrettable gap between linguistic meaning and a speaker's understanding. Fodor (1994) goes so far as to say that people who fail to realize that co-referring terms co-refer are irrational, and should be excluded from ordinary psychology. On these accounts, semantic opacity is a bad feature, which we are stuck with but would be better off without. For the poet, almost the opposite is true. The fact that there are different ways to express the same thing is crucial for poetry.[3] For the poet, the precise word choice, even

---

[3] This idealization is not meant to imply that the goal of poetry is to express the same exact semantic content with different modes of presentation. Rather, the idea is that poets play with the ability of expressing quite similar ideas through vastly different constructions.

among (putative) synonyms, matters a great deal. The task of the poet is not to use words that would, under ideal circumstance, collapse the gulf between mode of presentation and reference. It would be absurd to say that an ideal *poetic* language would have no co-referring terms. The mode of presentation is tremendously important. The medium may not always be the message, but it's certainly not orthogonal to the poet's artistic endeavor. Thus, semantic opacity in poetry is linked to the same ambition that underlies the first form of opacity. Poets are interested in ways of expressing things, not just in what gets expressed.

Turn finally to aesthetic opacity. This, we said, stems from the conventions associated with different art forms. In the case of poetry, we can ask, why do the words typically matter even though the font (almost always[4]) does not? The answer is that poets conventionally select words and word placement (such as line breaks) with utmost care. It is a central aspect of their creative process. Words are not arbitrary, or even just instrumental, in a typical poem. They are a locus of aesthetic choice—part of what a poet might revise and revise again while keeping other aspects fixed. Indeed, it might be said that there are many poems with more or less the same content, but presumably none with the same word forms.[5] Words are central to the art of poetic writing. Why? It's because of the nature of the poet's task. Poets are not just presenting facts, nor even fictions. They present contents in a specific way, and the way of presenting is supposed to be a dimension on which their work is evaluated. The words are not just ladders to be kicked away once readers have arrived at understanding.[6] The words are supposed to be primary objects of the reader's attention.

These three forms of opacity, then, can be said to be integral to the aims of poetry, and integral for roughly the same reason. Each is integral because poetry is characteristically a form of writing in which words are intended to be noticed as objects unto themselves—they are

---

[4] We say "almost always" because some concrete poets make font choice part of their art, and font choice affects the aesthetic experience of reading any poem. This is one reason why it can be less satisfying to read poems in the drab typefaces used by some digital reading devices.

[5] Furthermore, some poems may just repeat the same content in each verse, with the difference in word forms supplying the difference in aesthetic content from verse to verse (see e.g. Stevens's "13 Ways of Looking at a Blackbird").

[6] Sometimes the goal is less doxastic than "understanding" implies; a certain emotional reaction is often the desired end of the words' effects.

no longer just mere vessels for delivering content but are an integral constituent in their own right. Words are a veil through which content is delivered—a veil that is (or is at least intended to be) salient to the reader. Notice that this is another form of opacity. We will call it poetic opacity. To a first approximation, we will say that text is poetically opaque if the author intentionally constructs it in such a way that readers' attention is drawn to the words used and not just to what those words represent.

Poetic opacity is one of the most strikingly obvious features of poetry. To see this, we need only consider some of the most standard poetic devices. Here are a few instructive lines from Christina Rossetti's "Goblin Market":

> She dropped a tear more rare than pearl,
> Then sucked their fruit globes fair or red:
> Sweeter than honey from the rock,
> Stronger than man-rejoicing wine,
> Clearer than water flowed that juice;
> She never tasted such before,
> How should it cloy with length of use?
> She sucked and sucked and sucked the more
> Fruits which that unknown orchard bore,
> She sucked until her lips were sore;

Here Rossetti uses rhyme and repetition to create a sense of rhythm. She also uses meter (iambic tetrameter), but mixes it up with three trochees for emphasis. These devices ensure that we pay attention to form, and not just content, though the two also interact: the poem sounds like a nursery rhyme but concerns adult themes about sexuality, which creates a sense of dissonance.

In the twentieth century, meter went out of vogue, but formal experimentation increased. Consider this familiar passage from e. e. cummings:

> —the best gesture of my brain is less than
> your eyelids' flutter which says
>
> we are for each other: then
> laugh, leaning back in my arms
> for life's not a paragraph

The mere presence of line breaks introduces poetic opacity, but cum-mings goes much farther. Every line is enjambed,[7] including an ambigu-ous break (the word "then" first looks like it modifies "we are for each other" but is actually a temporal adverb modifying "laugh"), and there is a confounding stanza break after "says." There is also internal rhyme ("laugh" and "paragraph"), alliteration ("laugh, leaning"), consonance ("best" and "just"; "flutter" and "each other"), word-play ("than" and "then"), and metaphor (the final line). Other twentieth-century poets create lines that are hard to parse syntactically. Here's one from John Berryman, "Dream Song 14": "Life, friends, is boring." Correlatively, Surrealists and Dadaists create poems that are semantically anomalous. Tzara's *Chanson Dada* instructs readers thus, "drink some bird's milk / wash your sweets." Throughout the centuries, poets have also made use of unusual words or unexpected imagery; here's a couplet from Amy Lowell's "The Taxi": "I call out for you against the jutted stars / And shout into the ridges of the wind." On the face of it, these poetic devices have little in common. One might wonder why they are all called "poetic." Our answer is that they are all instruments of poetic opacity. They all draw attention to the text.

   Poetic opacity also makes sense of the fact that poetry can take on some startlingly unusual forms. Consider concrete poems. Here is one of Apollinaire's calligrammes, taken from his poem "2e Canonnier Conducteur":

```
J'ENTENDS CHA
L                    N
E                    TER l'oiseau
B                    E
EL OISEAU RAPAC
```

The poem translates: "I hear the bird singing / the beautiful bird of prey." The phrasing is colloquial (notwithstanding the chilling irony), but the physical form of the poem forces readers to focus on the words in new ways. The two phrases must be read in different directions (left to right, and then top to bottom, and right again), and then they converge at their

---

[7] Here's a creative (if cloying) use of hyphenated enjambment from Willard Espy's, "The unrhymable word: orange": "The four eng- / Ineers / wore orange / brassiers."

tail ends. The convergence forces the words for singing and for prey to converge on common letters, and the overall shape of the poem is designed to resemble a cannon shell. This invites readers to read "bird" as a euphemism for a cannon shot, flying overhead. Concrete poems were popular among modernists (such as Morgenstern and Marinetti) and post-modernists (such as Susan Howe), but they actually instantiate a feature quite universal in poetry: tactics for making words and positioning impossible to ignore. One might ask, why are there concrete poems and not concrete novels? Answer: manipulating the physical arrangements of words on a page makes them poetically opaque. We can't ignore words that have been unusually configured.

Also consider nonsense poems. Nonsense words lend themselves to poetry precisely because they block the move to content, and draw attention to themselves. Here is an excerpt from Elsa von Freytag-Loringhoven's "Klink—Hratzvenga (Deathwail)":

> Arr—karr—
> Arrkarr—barr
> Karrarr—barr—
> Arr—
> Arrkarr—
> Mardar
> Mar—dóórde—dar—

Like an abstract painting, form trumps content here, though the term "Deathwail" in the title tips us off that this is a chant of mourning, penned after the author's husband committed suicide. The use of meaningless words, dashes, consonance, and line breaks forces us to ineluctably and ostentatiously attend to the form of this poem, even if we also care about the content which it expresses.

Notice that though concrete poems and nonsense poems are recent inventions, we easily recognize them as poems. Poetic opacity can help explain this, and it allows us to imagine new poetic devices, such as poems written using words that all have the same number of letters. Poetic opacity can also explain why we find poetry in things that are also named using different terms. Limericks, some prayers, and song lyrics all qualify and they are all poetically opaque. Rhyme, rigidly fixed forms, and musical setting make the words in each of these categories poetically opaque.

Poetic opacity may even shed some light on content-based poetic devices, such as metaphor and metonymy. Though strictly speaking, these do not depend on form, the fact that poets depart from literal meanings forces readers to regard familiar words in new ways, and this may draw attention to the words themselves. We have already seen metaphors from Shakespeare and Apollinaire, and examples are pervasive. Here's another from Dylan Thomas: "Your mouth, my love, the thistle in the kiss?" This conveys the dark side of love by forcing readers to reconstrue kissing in a negative light. This reconstrual is based on content, but Thomas also makes sure to highlight form: he uses iambic pentameter, rhymes "kiss" with "*this*tle," and ends on a question mark, calling his key term into focus through punctuation and lifting intonation. The result is a kind of doubling of experience in which the conventional meaning of kiss comes through, but the context calls that meaning into question and thus forces readers to grapple with the word itself.

These examples suggest that many of the staggeringly varied techniques used in poetry may have a common consequence. They force readers to pay more attention than they ordinarily would to words and word arrangements. Many uses of language aspire for transparency. Newspaper articles, email messages, clothing catalogues, instruction manuals, and even literary novels, are usually in the business of transmitting information clearly, so they avoid techniques that create a verbal barrier between reader and meaning. Poems do the opposite. They deliver meanings and often use poetic devices to do so, but those devices also make form more salient and important than it is elsewhere, and thus impose a form of attention that operates at two levels: form and content. This is what it means to be poetically opaque.

3 Twofold Reading

The concept of poetic opacity relates to the idea of twofoldness, which Wollheim (1980) develops in his theory of painting. For Wollheim representational paintings afford a kind of double seeing: viewers see both what they represent and how they represent. Viewers see paint and painted. It is central to most traditions of painting that there be a distinctive style. In the modern period artists took this in highly individualistic directions, developing styles unique to each creator. When we view paintings, we pay special attention to how paintings look, and we praise painters not just for what they paint, but for how they paint—the latter often being more important.

Poetic opacity is not (or need not be) visual, so it is not exactly the same as twofoldness, but it is probably a kindred concept. Both poets and painters want us to notice their choice of forms, even when content is also important. Indeed, this is a common theme in the arts. Dance, for instance, or vocal music, can have both content and form, but form is a primary focus of attention. Thus, poetic opacity may be related to what makes poetry like other forms of art, especially like painting, where form and content have historically both been vitally important (in dance and music, content has more frequently been absent). We can think of the poet as someone who paints with words. She presents contents using words that have characteristics, including style, that make them objects of our attention.

Notice that other forms of prose do not characteristically have poetic opacity. Ordinary speech and even much story telling have far more to do with content than form. People may notice form, but the primary intention is typically to deliver content—to inject it, one might say, into the mind. We would not deny that this is sometimes done in a colorful way in order to make the ideas stick (note the metaphor, "inject"), and we often praise story-tellers for great writing. We think great writing and colorful turns of phrase can be distinguished from poetic opacity, however. Colorful wording is often used to accent non-poetic discourse, but it is neither integral to nor pervasive in non-poetic discourse. Indeed, one might say, it adds poetic accent, suggesting that non-poetic writing can have poetic elements, even though it is not poetic throughout. As for "great writing" outside the poetic context, we might say it is great when we pay attention to it, but it normally allows one to read and understand it without immediately noticing its eminence, or at least without doing so all of the time. Great writing is there to be seen when we step back and look at word forms. Or, in some cases, it does not depend on word forms, but instead on inventive narrative techniques, engaging characterization, carefully constructed imagery, and so on. With poetry, words and phrases almost function as a barrier to content—pervasive and impossible to ignore. One might even say that poetic words distract—it is harder to immediately grasp the basic word meanings because of the cognitive load brought on from the poetic presentation. But whereas poetic words distract, prose words deliver. Of course, some bad writing also distracts, but unintentionally. Poets distract us intentionally with their words. We will consider some apparent counter-examples below, but for now we want to suggest that the intentional introduction of pervasive poetic opacity is characteristic of poetry, and not other forms of writing.

If poetic opacity distinguishes poems from other forms of writing, it may be a mark of the poetic. The similarity to twofoldness, however, raises the worry that poetic opacity doesn't adequately distinguish poetry from painting, or other arts. But this worry can be quickly dismissed, since poetic opacity derives from words, and twofoldness derives from styles of painting. There may also be a difference in the temporal qualities of the two forms of twofold phenomenology. In his early formulations of twofoldness, Wollheim (1980) supposed that form and content alternate, like the two aspects of an ambiguous figure, when we look at painting. He later revised this proposal to claim that the two aspects, form and content, are experienced simultaneously (Wollheim 1990). Neither seems exactly right when it comes to the two aspects of poetic reading. When poems are difficult to interpret, form may present itself prior to content, and independent of it. This counts against simultaneity. Once meaning is ascertained, we do not alternate back and forth, because it is hard to experience the meaning without keeping the words in view. At that point, there may indeed be a simultaneous experience of form and content, but, as already noted, that need not occur right away. In the case of noise poems or poems that are incomprehensible, it may never occur. But there is, nevertheless, a deep similarity between Wollheim's concept of twofoldness and the duality entailed by poetic opacity, a similarity that goes beyond the fact that both involve form and content. Wollheim's concept of twofoldness is introduced in a discussion of "seeing-in," which refers to the phenomenonology of seeing the meaning of a representational painting. Seeing-in contrasts with ordinary seeing, in that the later is, in some sense, transparent; it doesn't require seeing anything other than the object. For Wollheim, some forms of hyper-realistic art, such as *trompe l'œil*, are also transparent in this way. But art that is not generates illusions of reality that tend to evoke twofoldness. In such cases, we see the work itself, and we see something "in" the work. Poetic opacity invites a similar analysis. We see meaning in poems. This is not literally seeing-in, because it is not visual, but, as with painting, it is a kind of indirect disclosure. Where ordinary seeing gives us objects transparently, reading ordinary prose does the same with respect to meaning. Poetic opacity, when poems are meaningful, involves a process of finding meaning in the work. Thus we think reading poems may be a twofold process in a way that relates to the kind of twofoldness that Wollheim introduced.

The fact that both poetry and painting evoke experiences that can be described as twofold may help to explain why they are often co-classified as belonging to the system of we know as the arts. We don't mean to deny that the system of the arts is a historical construct. Kristeller (1951, 1952) and Shiner (2001) point out that painting is not even included as an art in early taxonomies. For the ancients, poetry was king and plastic arts were more associated with craft. But one might wonder why painting came to be included among the arts, and one partial answer may involve this dimension of similarity with poetry. We have described poems as word paintings, but equally painting might have come to be seen as visual poems—a possibility we won't pursue here.

In summary, we think that poetic opacity may be a mark of the poetic. Perhaps there are other marks, but poetic opacity may even prove to be *the* mark of poetry. It is quite extraordinary to discover that this one construct can subsume so many dramatically different devices, styles, and forms. It explains why blank verse sonnets hang together with nursery rhymes and punk rock lyrics, and why metaphysical conceits belong in the same category as acrostics. There is a dizzying and perhaps open-ended range of ways we can achieve poetic opacity, and that range seems to coincide remarkably well with the range of things we consider to be poems or poetic. Poetic opacity is a unifying feature of a highly diverse art form.

III Objections and Replies

1 Against the Necessity of Poetic Opacity

A skeptical reader might object that poetic opacity is not a necessary condition for something to be classified as poetry. For example, the Imagists made it part of their credo to not include any "unnecessary" words and traditional meters (Pound 1958). One might think that the crux of Imagism is to present an image as clearly as possible, with no unnecessary words to obscure the readers' attention from the objects. On this reading the words themselves are otiose, and are only there to convey the image as clearly as possible to the reader.

We are unmoved by such an objection. No doubt, many Imagists prided themselves on using an economy of words. However, the words used were important in and of themselves, and not just for supplying the reader with the referent. Picking particular poems out and using them as one-off examples will make for a difficult dialectic, but the discussion runs the risks of an impotent abstractness without examining some poems. Thus, we will hesitatingly discuss some very canonical poems in the hope that they serve as instructive exemplars of their genre.

Take, for example, perhaps the most famous Imagist poem, Ezra Pound's "In a Station of the Metro":

> The apparition of these faces in the crowd;
> Petals on a wet, black bough.

The use of "apparition" is important to the poem and would-be synonyms would not suffice. If all that Pound was trying to convey was a certain scene, any near-synonym should do. However, "apparition" is irreplaceable in the text. Much ink has been spilled on the use of "apparition"; indeed one critic has called it "the single word which lifts the couplet from bald statement to poetry" (Bevilaqua 1971). The word creates a sound to be doubled in the first syllable of the second line. Its connotations create a feeling of the otherworldliness, and this feeling is then used as a set-up for the clash delivered in the second line. Moreover, as Bevilaqua notes, "apparition" can be interpreted as (and perhaps was intended as) a false cognate. In French "apparition" sometimes conveys a meaning of how something appears upon its first being seen. (The reading is enhanced by the fact that Pound wrote the poem while in France and its subject is a French subway; moreover, the immediacy of the perception would be in line with the influence haikus and, in particular, their use of clashing images had on Pound.)

Imagist poems may at first appear to be a challenge for the poetic opacity view, but we think it in fact helps to display our point. The more stripped down the words are, the more stark they become; the poet's choice of words becomes that much more severe when a single wrong word would stick out. An economy of usage demands that the author choose her words carefully, which in turn makes the reader that much more aware of the words. Likewise, the form of a poem is heightened as the poem's length decreases. This can be observed in William Carlos Williams's famous Imagist poem "The

Red Wheelbarrow."[8] The first line, "so much depends / upon," calls the readers' attention to the potential gravity of the poem, and acts as a contrast to the seemingly mundane subject of the poem. The use of "glazed" in the third stanza, "glazed with rain / water," brings up associations with the other art forms, particularly painting. This is not accidental: Williams is presenting the poem almost as an example of twofoldness: Williams wants to reader to form the image of the wheelbarrow, but not at the expense of the form of words. The structure of the poem acts as part of its meaning, presenting the wheelbarrow in its component parts. The use of enjambment heightens the readers' attention to the component parts of the objects to be formed in mental imagery. One encounters "wheel" before being able to complete "wheelbarrow"; likewise, one reads "rain" before encountering "water." Note how there are no hyphens in the line, so that the reader cannot suspect that the image of the object is not yet completed. This use of enjambment turns the readers' attention to the particularities of the object, but it also forces the reader to encounter the words as a surprise in themselves.

The reader may protest that Imagist poems are too stripped down to use for the objector's purpose. If so, prose poems may be a better place to look for counterexamples to opacity as a necessary condition. After all, many prose poems are there to convey a specific message. One of the most famous prose poems, Carolyn Forche's "The Colonel," is particularly politicized, letting the reader catch a glimpse of the atrocities that were occurring in late 1970s El Salvador. The poem isn't written in any canonical poetic style; rather, it is just presented as a journalistic paragraph. In fact, that was the intent of the poet: Forche claims that she wrote it as a diarist memoir—it was a reminder of the encounter that she could use for journalistic purposes (Haba 1995). Yet for all that it still strikes readers as poetry. We submit that this is the case because the work contains poetic opacity. For example, the poem is rife with the use of bodily imagery, which heightens the readers' attention to sensation. The poem begins by offhandedly mentioning the relative mundanities of everyday gustatory experience: coffee, sugar, dinner, mangoes, salt, and bread. This sets the reader up for the shock of equating the truly startling

---

[8] The full poem can be read at the website of the Academy of American Poets: <http://www.poets.org/poetsorg/poem/red-wheelbarrow>.

desiccated ears with ordinary dried peach halves. Forche needn't (and probably didn't consciously) use perceptual verbs ("What you heard is true") and tropes ("My friend said to me with his eyes") but the word choices aid the readers' identification of the piece as a poem. Moreover, the individual sentences of the poem tend to be anapestic. Were this merely a journalistic piece, then switching out (e.g.) the perceptual verbs for synonyms wouldn't change the meaning nor the work's identity—an editor could do so without even informing the author and yet it would still be the author's work. However, any such change to "The Colonel" and the identity of the piece would be destroyed. It's part of its essence that it uses perceptual idioms to heighten the sensual feel and changing the diction would change the poem (and probably destroy the anapests).

2 Against the Sufficiency of Poetic Opacity

Other readers may object that poetic opacity does not suffice for a text to be categorized as a poem. Great prose and oration can also appear to be so specifically worded that attention is drawn to the form as much as the content. If poetic opacity is the mark of the poetic, then how can the identity of these other non-poetic texts also crucially depend on word choice? To use a concrete example, let's return to Emerson's essay "The Poet."

The poet's habit of living should be set on a key so low that the common influences should delight him. His cheerfulness should be the gift of the sunlight; the air should suffice for his inspiration, and he should be tipsy with water. That spirit which suffices quiet hearts, which seems to come forth to such from every dry knoll of sere grass, from every pine stump and half-imbedded stone on which the dull March sun shines, comes forth to the poor and hungry. . . . If thou fill thy brain with Boston and New York, with fashion and covetousness . . . with wine and French coffee, thou shalt find no radiant wisdom in the lonely waste of the pine woods. (1903)

This essay is identifiable as an essay though it is rife with poetic imagery. It may strike one as more oratorical than essay-like. Similarly, great novels can have long passages that read poetically. However, as we have mentioned, such colorful wording is used as accent in a larger work. Great novels are often rife with poetic passages, but they are also rife with the prosaic. We submit that in the places where word choice is of the utmost importance, in places where the novelists are drawing attention to the specific words themselves, the reader will interpret the text as having poetic elements. Were a novel, or say a speech, to only consist of such elements, the work would cease to be one that fit neatly in any genre—it would strike the reader as being e.g. both a speech and a poem.[9]

It is important to see what we are and are not claiming. Non-poetic writing may indeed contain poetic elements by employing poetic opacity. Our claim is that, if the work itself is infused poetic opacity throughout, then it will strike the reader as poetry and in fact be poetry. For comparison, imagine someone writing a conventional novel without noteworthy writing and declaring that it was a poem. This would surely meet with resistance. On the other hand it would clue readers into how the work should be read. To read a novel as if it were poetry would involve paying special attention to words, treating them as if they were a decorative barrier interposed between mind and meaning. This would be hard to do with an ordinary novel, of course. Our point is that the mere mandate to view something with poetic regard involves a shift in reading style— a shift to the surface, as it were. In poems, as opposed to conventional novels, the work itself usually contains elements that force this kind of reading upon the reader.

The opponent of our proposal may also object to sufficiency by focusing on less artistic endeavors, such as logos and taglines. It is difficult to deny that the typography used in consumer product logos is designed to get our attention. Likewise for taglines. They are supposed to catchy and attention-grabbing, and advertisers take special care to pick just the right words.

Nevertheless, we persist in thinking that poetic opacity separates poetry from these other modes. Doubtlessly, word choice and logo design is of great import to marketers. These items do vie for our attention. But it is unlikely that advertisers want taglines and logos to be the primary objects of focus, much less barriers between consumers and what that the items represent. The words in taglines are often evocative, but they are rarely distracting. Rather they serve to instill positive beliefs as attitudes

---

[9] No doubt there may be such works that are generally classified as novels, but appear to have as much poetic opacity as, say, narrative poems. Perhaps some of the works of Michael Ondaatje (e.g. *Coming through Slaughter*), Marilyn Robinson (e.g. *Housekeeping*), Don Delillo (e.g. *Ratner's Star*), or Paul Harding (e.g. *Tinkers*) seem to fall in this class. We haven't the space to examine any of these authors' individual works in detail, but suffice to say that we have two options with these putative problem cases: either we need to show how the opacity inherent in these works is secondary to the works (either in purpose or in fact) or we need to argue that these works shouldn't be so neatly categorized as novels *tout court*.

about products. Logos are often eye-catching, but there is a difference between noticing a graphic design and allocating attention to a word. Poets impress us by their choice of words; designers impress by visual appeal.

One might still worry that our characterization of poetic opacity is too inclusive: there are many devices that draw attention to words that are not considered poetic. Consider quotations, italics, puns, or dictionary definitions, to name a few. Each of these uses of language makes words into objects of focus in some way. Given our informal characterization of poetic opacity, it might seem to follow that each of these is poetically opaque, and, thus, each qualifies as a kind of poem.

We think this is a serious objection at it suggests that much work is still needed to refine the concept of poetic opacity so it can be distinguished from other uses of language that draw attention to words. Fortunately, we think there are four differences between poetic opacity and what is found in these other phenomena. First, there are differences in what can be called primary aims or primary functional roles. The primary role of quotation is, typically, to inform readers exactly what someone said. The primary role of italics is to emphasize a single word or phrase within a larger linguistic context. The primary role of a pun is to amuse by exploiting the fact that the same word form can have different meanings. The primary role of a dictionary definition is to convey the normal usages (and sometimes even meanings) of a word. All these things draw attention to words, but in very different ways and toward different ends. Crucially, none of them has opacity as their ultimate goal. They draw attention to words, but they do so as a means to some other end. Italics make words salient, but their ultimate goal is to emphasize a concept. A good definition informs readers how to understand a word, so it will not be as opaque in the future. A quotation gets at what was said, but normally what interests readers is the meaning conveyed or proposition expressed, not the exact words. Notice that quotations are rarely seen as untranslatable, while poems are, and when quotations are difficult to translate that is because some words lack cross-linguistic synonyms, not because the actual form of the words is so important. Puns resist translation for similar reasons, but they too are not intended to introduce a formal veil blocking smooth passage to content. Poems, by contrast, aim at this kind of opacity. Those who engage in writing poems explicitly or implicitly engage in a practice that involves assembling words that will interpose themselves. Poetic opacity is not just a matter of drawing attention words, but doing so as a primary end.

This brings us to another difference, which can be expressed in terms of the phenomenology of twofoldness. We've granted that the other phenomena under consideration engender experiences that have two aspects: form and content. But the poetic variant of twofoldness is not simply a matter of experiencing two things at once. As with painting, it is a kind of seeing-in. We keep the words in view and try to find meaning in them, if there is meaning to be found. Dictionary definitions involve a quest for meaning, of course, but nothing like seeing-in. We don't discover meaning *in* the defined word, but rather learn the meaning from the definition and then assign it to the defined word. There can be a quest for meaning in reading quotations, especially if they are obscure, but here interpretation is not a twofold experience. We try to restate the content of an obscure quote, and once we have found one the original quote is dispensable; it serves only as evidence that this content came from a certain source. With puns and italics, there is nothing like seeing-in.

Third, in these other cases, the words that become salient are situated in contexts that are otherwise comparatively transparent. In a dictionary definition there is a single word whose form is salient, but the words in the definition are not, if the definition is understood. In a pun, again, there is normally one salient word, and the rest is not. Italics emphasize a word or phrase, but the surrounding sentence is transparent. Quotes can make whole sentences salient, but they are embedded in texts whose non-quoted sentences are intended to be transparent by comparison.

Fourth, poems are aesthetic objects. They are the kind of things about which aesthetic assessment is appropriate. Moreover, the language chosen by a poet is generally one of the central loci of evaluation, often the main locus. So, poetic writing is writing that brings words into attention in a way that we characteristically evaluate aesthetically. Consequently, the phenomenology of verbal salience differs from the other phenomena under consideration. Our experience of the words in a poem intermingles with aesthetic engagement. This may include the application of aesthetic norms, and feelings of appreciation. This suggests that poetic opacity is best understood as something more than mere salience. It might be better described as aesthetic salience. Salience of forms for aesthetic scrutiny. Aesthetic opacity makes words and their arrangements candidates for aesthetic assessment as a matter of course, unlike ordinary definitions, italics, quotations, and puns.

This last point about aesthetics brings us to a final sufficiency objection. If aesthetic capacity is a matter of bringing words into a position of salience that invites aesthetic evaluation, what are we to say about words that appear in paintings? Juan Gris, for example, has several cubist still life paintings that include a newspaper masthead, with the words "Le Journal." In pop art, Andy Warhol painted consumer packages with words on them, and Roy Lichtenstein painted comic-book portraits replete with word balloons containing dialogue. Conceptualists, such as Lawrence Wiener and Joseph Kosuth, painted words and phrases as a central part of their practice, in an effort to abandon the standard subject matter of painting and move towards an art based on ideas. The words in these paintings seem to satisfy our characterization of poetic opacity. They draw attention to words in a way that invites aesthetic assessment.

In response, we will simply point out a familiar fact about paintings that contain linguistic elements. In most cases, these paintings are best described as depicting words, rather than containing works. Cubist newspapers and pop icons are representations of real-world objects that happen to have words printed on them (newspapers, packages, comic-books). Thus, the opacity here is just the ordinary kind of twofoldness associated with painting. We are aware of a form (the painting of a word) and what that form represents (a word out there in the world). With conceptual art, things are a little different. Conceptualists might be said to use words in their work, rather than depicting words. To that extent, however, they do not want these words to be opaque in any sense. Conceptual art often opposes formalism, and intentionally involves the production of works that lack formal aesthetic properties. In this case, it is not the form of the words that matters, but the ideas that they express.

This brings us to our conclusion. We have been arguing that a mark of the poetic, perhaps the mark, is poetic opacity. In poems there are two foci for attention: what is represented and how it is represented. The form of a poem is salient and central to its aesthetic value, and the experience of content characteristically involves seeing (or more accurately interpreting) something in that form while keeping the form in view. In these respects, poetry is much like painting. Poems paint with words. But we also drew some contrasts with painting. Poetic opacity may be unique to poetry. It distinguishes poetry from other uses of language and other arts. Our goal here has been programmatic and the concept of poetic opacity would, no doubt, benefit from further exploration and refinement. We are content to conclude that poetic opacity deserves its place in a discussion of poetry's essential features. It offers an explanation of why so many different techniques and devices are all recognized as belong to a single class. All these devices introduce a duality into our experience of language, a duality that forestalls the habitual leap from word to world, keeping both in view.

References

Bevilaqua, R. 1971. "Pound's 'In a Station of the Metro': A Textual Note." *English Language Notes*, 8/4: 293–6.

Bloom, H. 1980. *The Poems of our Climate*. Ithaca, NY: Cornell University Press.

D'Avanzo, M. 1977. "Emerson and Shakespeare in Stevens's 'Bantams in Pine-Woods.'" *American Literature*, 49/1: 103–7.

Dean, J. 2003. "The Nature of Concepts and Definitions of Art." *Journal of Aesthetics and Art Criticism*, 61/1: 29–35.

Emerson, R. 1903. "The Poet." In *The Complete Works of Ralph Waldo Emerson*. Cambridge: Riverside Press.

Fodor, J. 1994. *The Elm and the Expert: Mentalese and its Semantics*. The 1993 Jean Nicod Lectures. Cambridge, MA: MIT Press.

Fodor, J., Garrett, M., Walker, E., and Parkes, C. 1980. "Against Definitions." *Cognition*, 8: 263–367.

Frost, R. 1925. "Letter to John Freeman, November 5 1925."

Gaut, B. 2000. "'Art' as a Cluster Concept." In Noël Carroll (ed.), *Theories of Art*. University of Wisconsin Press, 25–44.

Goodman, N. 1968. *Language of Art: An Approach to a Theory of Symbols*. Indianapolis: Bobbs-Merrill Co.

Haba, James. 1995. *The Language of Life: A Festival of Poets*. New York: Doubleday.

Kennick, W. 1958. "Does Traditional Aesthetics Rest on a Mistake?" *Mind*, 67/267: 317–34.

Kripke, S. 1979."A Puzzle about Belief." In A. Margalit (ed.), *Meaning and Use*. Boston: Reidel, 239–83.

Kristeller, P. 1951. "The Modern System of the Arts: A Study in the History of Aesthetics (I)." *Journal of the History of Ideas*, 12/4: 496–527.

Kristeller, P. 1952. "The Modern System of the Arts: A Study in the History of Aesthetics (II)." *Journal of the History of Ideas*, 13/1: 17–46.

Pound, Ezra. 1958. *Pavannes and Divagations*, vol. 397. New York: New Directions.

Shiner, L. 2001. *The Invention of Art: A Cultural History*. Chicago: University of Chicago Press.

Smith, E., and Medin, D. 1981. *Categories and Concepts*. Cambridge, MA: Harvard University Press.

Weitz, M. 1956. "The Role of Theory in Aesthetics." *Journal of Aesthetics and Art Criticism*, 15/1: 27–35.

Wollheim, R. 1980. "Seeing-as, Seeing-in, and Pictorial Representation." In *Art and its Objects*, 2nd edn. Cambridge: Cambridge University Press, 1980, 205–26.

Wollheim, R. 1990. *Painting as an Art*. Princeton: Princeton University Press.

Ziff, P. 1953. "The Task of Defining a Work of Art." *Philosophical Review*, 62/1: 58–78.

4

Unreadable Poems and How They Mean

Sherri Irvin

I

Several years ago, the poet and critic Joan Houlihan offered a scathing indictment of some contemporary poetry for using words in a way that treats them as meaningless.[1] Of the words making up one offending poem, she asks, "Why are they printed in a journal someone paid to produce, for someone else to pay to read[,] instead of being spoken by a stroke victim in a rest home?"

She proposes, further, that the particular words of such poems are, in fact, inessential to them: massive substitutions can be made while preserving the poem's identity. She even goes so far as to transform a particular poem, Christina Mengert's "*."[2] The original reads as follows:

> Is an axle's excavation
> an axiom's inversion

---

[1] Houlihan's series of nine essays, *How Contemporary American Poets are Denaturing the Poem*, was published by *Web del Sol* from 2000 to 2005. All remarks quoted in this chapter are taken from Part VII (2003), "Post-Post Dementia," <http://www.webdelsol.com/LITARTS/Boston_Comment/bostonc7.htm>, accessed Sept. 2011.

[2] Reprinted with the permission of the author. Houlihan cites a version of the poem, titled with an asterisk, that appeared in issue 17 of *Slope*, winter/spring 2003. As Christina Mengert indicated to me in correspondence, it is an excerpt of a longer poem, "It Was, As They Say, A Threaded Body," that appeared in the second of six undated issues published by the online magazine *Castragraf* from 2000 to 2003. The full poem remains available here: <http://www.castagraf.net/pdf/issue2.pdf>. For the purposes of this chapter, I will follow Houlihan in treating the *Slope* version as an independent work.

> that muzzles
> the ventriloquist breath
>
> of a nipple. The revolving door
> of its throat.

In revenge, Houlihan offers this:

> Is an axiom's evacuation
> an axle's inversion
> that snubs
> the ventriloquist bread
>
> of a testicle. The spinning jenny
> of its lashes.

"I would argue my poem *is* the original," she says. "It is exactly the same poem, albeit with different words—but neither set of words makes any difference to the meaning."

We can reasonably take Houlihan's claim regarding the equivalence of the two poems as hyperbolic. There are serious questions here, though: can Mengert's poem, and other poems that use language in oblique, nonstandard, and ungrammatical ways, have actual meanings? Or are they susceptible only of a "chaotic democracy of 'readings'" (Hirsch 1967, 5) imputed by readers who project idiosyncratic associations onto them? Moreover, if they can't have meanings, or if any meanings they do have are very difficult to access, does this undercut their value?

I will suggest that the meaning resources available to such seemingly unreadable poems are more extensive than Houlihan's charge might lead one to believe, and that one can gain access to them through practices of reading poetry that are already well established. At the end, I will offer a tentative apology for unreadability: the poems we are most likely to find unreadable are those that seem alien to us, and the appearance of alienness is often the product of gulfs of identity and experience that we have a duty to bridge.

II

Central to Houlihan's complaint is that it is impossible to tell what an unreadable poem is trying to do. There is, thus, no way of knowing what would constitute success, no way of knowing whether the substitution of a word would make the poem worse, improve it, or leave its quality untouched.[3] This is why substitutions are acceptable: they don't make any difference to how well the poem achieves its (nonexistent) aims.

I agree that we evaluate artworks, in large part, based on an understanding of their aims. Following Stein Haugom Olsen (1978, 94–5), Peter Lamarque (2009, 412) mentions the Principle of Functionality, a principle of reading according to which "what is there (in the poem) is there for a purpose[;] things are not just accidentally as they are." In reading, then, we attribute to the poem purposes or aims that allow us to make sense of its features. Some of these aims may be given by the art form, while others are particular to the work and are ascertained by inference from the work's features. Works of lyric poetry have, by virtue of belonging to that form, the aim of expressing the states of mind of the narrator. Particular lyric works have more specific aims: A. R. Ammons's poem "Mansion," for instance, aims to propose a vision of mortality.[4] (This is a crude but, I hope, uncontroversial characterization of a central aim of the poem.) We know this straightforwardly, through its content:

> So it came time
> > for me to cede myself
> and I chose
> the wind
> > to be delivered to
>
> . . .
>
> When the tree of my bones
> > rises from the skin I said
> come and whirlwinding
> stroll my dust
> > around the plain

We can ask, of Ammons's poem, how interesting and original is this vision? How rich and revelatory is it? How rewarding is the experience of immersing oneself in it?

---

[3] "Since we don't know what original effect was intended, and since the only one we can experience directly is bafflement, *we don't know how the line, or the poem for that matter, could be improved.* What does improvement mean here? Or damage for that matter?" Houlihan (2003, emphasis in original).

[4] Ammons 1957, 41. I excerpt two of the poem's five stanzas in this chapter.

What does Mengert's poem "*" supply by way of aim that can allow us to focus our assessments? Clearly, we will not be able to answer this question by reading off its manifest sentential content, in the way that we are able to do with "Mansion." For, as Houlihan observes, "*" may not have any sentential content. She reads the poem as beginning with a question, and that question is either aborted at the extra line break or ill punctuated: "Is an axle's excavation an axiom's inversion that muzzles the ventriloquist breath // of a nipple[?]" If this is a question, it is very difficult to know what is being asked (though one strongly suspects, nonetheless, that the answer is "no").

The situation is, in fact, even less clear than this. For there are at least two more ways of understanding the structure of the first sentence. First, it may be that the asterisk of the title serves as the sentence's grammatical subject. It is, after all, not unprecedented for the title to figure in the poem, to count as its beginning. The sentence may, then, be an assertion about the asterisk ("* is an axle's excavation[,] an axiom's inversion[,] that muzzles the ventriloquist breath of a nipple.") rather than a question about an alleged equivalency between an axle's excavation and an axiom's inversion.

A further possibility is that titling the poem "*" is meant to position the body of the poem as some sort of footnote to another text which is not made available to the reader: the poem might, for instance, serve to elucidate some term in the unavailable text. This would make the opening sentence an assertion rather than a question, but with an unknown subject: "_____ is an axle's excavation ... "

If these possibilities are all in play, we don't even know what the first sentence of the poem is; and even if we could select one of these options over the others, the meaning of the sentence would remain entirely unclear.

But then, the poem is telling us something, isn't it? "Don't look for my point or purpose in manifest sentential content." Of course it isn't in this poem's personality to say that so bluntly, but it seems very reasonable to see this as a message that emerges out of our thwarted attempts to read the poem in the standard way. The poem does invite us to make such attempts—it doesn't, after all, completely eschew grammar—but once we realize that our search for sentential meaning isn't working out, we know that we have to try something else.

We could give up, of course. If the poem wants to be so obnoxious in its tantalizing quasi-grammaticality and ultimate refusal of meaning, then we should treat it the way we would treat an obnoxious person: walk away (perhaps giving it a good scolding first, as Houlihan does).

I can understand the attraction of this response. In fact, as I was searching out poetic illustrations for this article, I often found myself caught in the introductions of books, fearful of venturing into the actual poems. I would flip back to the center of a book, read a few lines, and then balk. If I made it through a poem it was because the ending caught me by surprise. "What have I gotten myself into?" I thought. "Why did I choose a topic that would force me to consort with so many unfriendly poems?"

But it is also true that, since first seeing it reprinted in Houlihan's article several years ago, I have come to find "*" rather evocative. This is why I want to explore the meaning and function of such poems, as well as the duties we as readers might have to engage seriously with them.

So, back to the question of the poem's aim. The poem does not, as we have seen, have sentential content that will point us in the direction of its aim. Smaller units of content, below the sentential level, don't help much either: the pairings of "axle" and "excavation," of "axiom" and "inversion," perplex more than they inform. Is the axle being used to dig? Is it "excavating" the wheel into which it is inserted? And if so, what does this have to do with the inversion of an axiom (whatever that means), or with nipples or throats? We are not going to find the aim of the poem by first identifying some subject that the poem is about.

One option, here, is to revert back to an understanding of the aims of poetry more generally. Of course, one traditional aim of poetry is to convey a comprehensible meaning, and we already know that the poem has eschewed this aim. But there are other traditional aims that it seems to embrace. There is clear attention to meter and consonance (the repetition of the "x" sound), especially in the first two lines, which have an intricate metrical structure that satisfies standard expectations about the rhythms of poetry. The metrical structure changes, and the consonance is dropped, when the poem reaches the line "that muzzles." This line, as we shall see, is a sort of fulcrum for the poem. The structure of sounds, then, has been carefully designed.

Houlihan's substituted poem fails to preserve many of these relationships. Her first two lines clearly lack balance, by comparison to Mengert's. Here are scans of the two poems using the ictus and x system, in which the ictus (slash) indicates a stressed syllable and the x an unstressed syllable:

Mengert:
   xx/x xx/x
   x/xx x/x
   x/x
   xx/xx/

   xx/x xx/x/
   xx/

Houlihan:
   xx/xx xxx/x
   x/x x/x
   x/
   xx/xx/

   xx/xx x/x/x
   xx/x

Houlihan's first line has five unstressed syllables crammed in between the stressed syllables of "axiom" and "evacuation" respectively, but only two unstressed syllables between the two stressed syllables of the second line. As a result, on arriving at the end of the second line one has the feeling of being forced to pull up short after a sprint. Of course, there might be a poetic justification for this sort of effect. In any event, the rhythmic structure matters, and Houlihan's differs significantly from Mengert's.

Another time-honored poetic aim is to activate the resonances and associations evoked by the poem's words, rather than merely their referential content. Mengert's poem appears to embrace this aim—indeed, to push it toward its outer limits, where resonances and associations replace referential content. It contains at least one obscure allusion: the line "The ventriloquist's breath" opens Lavinia Greenlaw's (1997) poem "Iron Lung," published not long before Mengert's poem first appeared. If the ventriloquist breath is the breath induced by an iron lung, this brings new layers of resonance and possibilities of meaning to the poem: the axle's excavation now has a connection to the mechanistic action of the iron lung; the "revolving door of its throat" may be connected to the relentless forcing in and out of breath (although, of course, the throat of a breathing organism does not in fact function like a revolving door, allowing breath to enter and exit at the same time, so the association does not go through seamlessly).

The functioning of allusion is complex. Greenlaw's poem appears to be, at least in part, literally about the working of an iron lung: it begins, "The ventriloquist's breath / Watch while my lungs compress," and, later, mentions "A dark room I cannot go into / But am locked into from the neck." Mengert's use of an expression similar to Greenlaw's does not make it the case that Mengert's "ventriloquist breath" *refers to* breath induced by an iron lung. However, it does bring this association into play, lending the poem a weight of medicalization and mortality.[5]

With these observations in place, let me say something about the overall movement of the poem. It starts out tripping along with a clippy little meter, and using consonance (those x's) that is a little tongue-twisty.[6] The first two lines have a very intellectual feel, inviting us to try to figure out what an axle's excavation and an axiom's inversion might be. And then, suddenly, it is muzzled. The muzzling shifts the rhythm of the poem, as well as its content. Each of the first two lines ends with an unstressed syllable, leaving things open for the rhythm to be picked up on the next line. But after the muzzling, each line ends with a stressed syllable, which creates, rather than a sense of continuity, a slight barrier that must be gotten over to arrive at the next line. (The first line after the extra line break— "of a nipple. The revolving door"—has the same structure of stressed and unstressed syllables as the first line of the poem, except that it adds a stressed syllable at the end.) The toe-tapping rhythm and cheery consonance are gone, replaced by something that is, suddenly, more corporeal than intellectual: the muzzled breath, the nipple (rising and falling, perhaps, with the breath), the throat. Both the content and the structure of the poem shift, at "muzzled," from being hard, mechanistic and intellectual to being organic and corporeal. We are confronted with soft, breathing body, instead of ideas and things placed in abstract relations. The perplexity we feel in the early lines of the poem, as we try to solve the puzzle of word-play, morphs into a confusion that has more mystery and longevity to it as we contemplate these fragments of body. We no longer

---

[5] Peter Nicholls (2010) defends a similar view of allusion.
[6] This use of consonance, incidentally, is one of the things that tempts me to see the asterisk as a component of the poem: the "sk" of asterisk twists the tongue in much the way that "axle's excavation" does, though the "sk" sound is inverted into the "ks" expressed by the letter "x."

feel the promise that if we just think harder we will figure out what is meant. The poem becomes less about meaning and more about presence.

Interestingly, Houlihan's reading of the poem agrees with mine in significant respects. She says, "At its global level, the poem seems to posit the impersonal, non-human, mathematical, against/beside the human and personal." And she seems to agree that a shift occurs at "muzzles," though she disagrees about its significance: "Here's where some trouble begins," she says, suggesting that Mengert has constructed the rest of the poem through the technique of "finger-stabbing the best word in an open dictionary." A crucial element missing from Houlihan's reading, to my mind, is an appreciation of the relationship between the shift in semantic content and the shift in rhythm, and the way in which this relationship helps to justify the poet's specific word choices. As Patrick Suppes (2009) discusses, the rhythm of a poem has a direct effect on the reader, while also helping to activate associations and resonances of its semantic content. Lamarque (2009), in a related vein, notes that the practice of reading poetry demands that we see form and content as unified, and that we seek an experience, not just a meaning, from the poem. Bearing these insights in mind, I find the interweaving of the rhythmic and semantic components of Mengert's poem to be one of its most compelling aspects.

I see the poem, then, as inviting a certain kind of response to its early rhythmic and semantic elements, and then disrupting that response, suspending the reader in a corporeality that is not intellectually tractable. If this reading is apt, then it expresses the (or, at least, a) specific aim of this poem. I have arrived at an understanding of this aim by considering how the poem accommodates and rejects more standard aims of poetry having to do with reference, aural elements, and associative meaning. With this notion of the poem's aim in hand, we seem to be able to think about how its various elements contribute to or undermine its achievement of its aim. We seem to be able to consider whether the substitution of a word would deepen the poem's pursuit of its aim or detract from it. The move from "muzzles" to "snubs," for instance, would undermine the sense of suffocation we have through the image of the muzzling of breath.

III

I have spent quite a bit of time exploring various elements of the poem, and I haven't even given a very close reading of it: I haven't, for instance, said anything about how the potentially phallic image of the axle's excavation might relate to the bodily images in the final lines. I haven't considered a reading of the poem that takes the title "*" as the grammatical subject of its opening sentence, or that treats the poem as a footnote to some other text. I also haven't said anything about how this poem relates to the rest of Mengert's poem "It Was, As They Say, A Threaded Body" published in *Castagraf*,[7] whose parts tend to share the structure of four lines, an extra line break, and then two concluding lines. The full poem exhibits a recurring interest in anatomy, with passages such as "my ribs / deciphered and spread" and "Forgive my kamikaze / my ligaments." There is also another juxtaposition of intellect and body in this image:

> Pedagogical/cranial
> lunging of collision.

But is all of this worth doing? Is the energy I have spent here unpacking the poem, and the energy that could be spent unpacking it even further, worth spending? The work that was required to figure out what the poem might be up to is considerable, and the conclusion I arrived at is to some extent tentative and incomplete. But such work seems required in order to have a handle on the poem, to feel that one has a sense of what it is trying to do. An alternative approach to the poem would be to bask in it, allowing its sounds and images to wash over one, perhaps forming a sort of collage in the mind, and seeing how satisfying the resulting experience ends up being. That approach, for me, is only a starting point: once I have found the initial experience satisfying (or, in this case, enticing but perplexing), I want to delve deeper to see how the poem functions.

The "is it worth it" question, which I will take up again in the final section of this chapter, seems related to these: Is my interpretation really just a projection? Could I come to just as satisfying an interpretation of a random string of words that might be put before me? Is there a multiplicity of other readings of this poem that are completely different from, even in conflict with, mine, yet equally well supported? If these questions are answered in the affirmative, this suggests that the meaning and value I attribute to the poem reside in me rather than in it. And if that is the case, I might as well dedicate my efforts to giving close readings of the texts that are included in some of my junk email messages in an effort to elude spam filters: "Watch your years counted counterclockwise with us. TROL my feelings and to not express them. I had to control my feelings

---

[7] See n. 2.

not only to try to get acceptance and to be able to fit in, but also had to control them in fear that if I Fire your main weapon!"

Is my interpretation of the poem a mere projection? Is there is a vast array of equally well supported readings? I will leave it to the reader to be the final arbiter of these matters. But I think it is fair to say that my interpretation appeals to straightforward features of the poem, such as its meter and sound structure and the conventional meanings of its words. It doesn't appeal to the particularities of my own psychological response (although, as I've acknowledged, my *motivation* to interpret the poem was partly a function of my finding the initial exposure to it enticing—an experience that Houlihan clearly did not share). I take it that the claims I've made are subject to rational assessment: other readers can study the poem to see whether it is true, for instance, that both the structure and the semantic focus of the poem shift at "muzzled" as I've claimed, and whether the nature of those shifts is as I've described it. And, though this is a more subjective matter, they can consider whether the two shifts work together in a way that is satisfying and helps make sense of the poem.

If I've done my job as an interpreter, then, I've provided an explanation of the poem that is not random or purely subjective, but susceptible of intersubjective appraisal. This explanation includes an understanding of the poem's aim, and we can then use this understanding to see how well it achieves the aim through the specific resources it deploys. At first blush, this might sound circular: "After careful study, I conclude that the poem aims to do precisely what it is doing, and thus does it perfectly well!" But this is not quite right. The aim that is attributed in interpretation is sensitive to the particularities of the poem—it is not simply an aim that applies to poems in general—but it has to *make sense* of why these parts have been assembled in this way, not merely *enumerate* what the parts are and how they have been assembled. It has to operate at a higher level of abstraction than simply, "The poem does this, and then it does that, and finally it does the other thing; therefore, doing this, that, and the other thing is its aim."

This process of identifying the poem's aim(s) involves a feedback loop: I attribute a certain aim to the poem, but then I notice that my interpretation leaves out an important element or treats it as a flaw. I then attempt to identify another aim that makes sense of the poem roughly as well overall, while doing better by this other element. Eventually my explanatory efforts stabilize: either I am able to identify an aim that makes sense of all of the poem's elements and their interrelations, or I find that even my most charitable efforts lead me to attribute to the poem an aim on which it comes out to be flawed. The fact that interpretative efforts are charitable, and that they take the particularities of the poem seriously, does not guarantee the conclusion that the poem has satisfied its aim. Moreover, evaluation of the poem involves the further question of whether the aim pursued by the poem is worth pursuing. Even if the poem succeeds in its aim, the reader may conclude that that aim was trivial or bankrupt, and thus not such as to vindicate the poem.

For these reasons, we needn't worry that applying this interpretative method to random word sequences or strings of words embedded in junk email messages will typically yield the verdict that these texts have literary value. We might, in some or many instances, be able to attribute an aim to such a text; but in most cases, the text will seem flawed even in relation to the aim we attribute to it after our most charitable efforts. Moreover, that aim itself will likely seem trivial or otherwise not worthy of our attention.

Of course, there will be exceptions: even a random word generator will occasionally spit out a great poem. But it doesn't happen very often.

IV

I have considered one example of a work that is singled out for excoriation by a critic. I have suggested, contrary to the critic's view, that it is in fact possible to attribute to the poem an aim that is appropriately responsive to its particularities (without objectionably guaranteeing its success) and that is intersubjectively verifiable. With this aim in hand, readers can then assess both (a) the extent to which the poem satisfies that aim and (b) whether that aim was worth pursuing in the first place.

I turn now to another target of Houlihan's ire, Gian Lombardo's "Partial Rhythm, Primate Laughing,"[8] which I present in its entirety:

> Too soon drunk from mixed species. In this parasol no one
> gets out dead. Except for the passion. Wrung through and
> weepy. Shame on table pretending an animal belly up waiting.
>
> Speaking under the influence of whatever the monkey sees
> does not seem true but just another corollary to arrest.

[8] Gian Lombardo, *Fence* (spring/summer 2003), reprinted in Lombardo (2004, 29). Reprinted here with the permission of the author.

In this howl who calls?

Turning round on way up monkey takes a back.

My reading of this poem begins from a recognition of its many instances of word-play: use of a linguistic expression that strongly evokes, through a visual and/or auditory resemblance mechanism, some other, more familiar expression. "Mixed species" evokes "mixed spirits," "corollary to arrest" evokes "coronary arrest," "monkey sees does" evokes "monkey see, monkey do," and "monkey takes a back" evokes "takes aback" as well as "monkey on my back." "No one gets out dead" is a reversal of the usual "no one gets out alive," and "speaking under the influence" recalls "driving under the influence."

These rather straightforward examples then open us, I think, to seeing other expressions in the poem as possible instances of word-play: perhaps "parasol" should be thought of as evoking "parable," "pretending" as evoking "portending," and "wrung through" as evoking "rung through" (as when you call the front desk and they ring you through to a guest's room). "Shame on table" initially seems to treat shame (or a material symbol of it, or a person experiencing it) as having a spatial location, but when we see the poem through the lens of pervasive word-play we must consider it in relation to the formulation "shame on you." "In this howl who calls?" while alluding to Allen Ginsberg's famous poem,[9] may also evoke an owl calling, "Who?"

What Lombardo is doing here, I think, is cracking open the conventional relations that words and expressions bear to linguistic meanings. It is nothing new for poetry to operate by activating associations, sometimes playing on the multiple senses of an ambiguous word and sometimes deploying the semantic content of a word that sounds or looks like a word that appears in the poem. But typically there is still a central, conventional meaning of the word or expression in the context of the poem, and this is the focal point for our reading: it is, we might say, what makes the poem readable. Even Mengert's poem, perplexing as it is, maintains this element of readability: we know what an axle is, and what excavation is, and though we may not be sure how these two concepts are supposed

---

[9] The allusion to a poem that is far longer than Lombardo's own work, and the comparison between the two that is achieved through the self-referential expression "this howl," raises issues that would need to be explored in a fuller analysis of Lombardo's poem.

to fit together, the poem does not fundamentally destabilize or sever the relation between the words and their standard referential contents.

The pervasiveness of Lombardo's word-play goes beyond the activation of associations: it also frays, though it does not completely sever, the connection between a word or expression and its main conventional meaning. "Too soon drunk from mixed species": a literal reading of "species" seems ruled out, since we can't make sense of what is meant by becoming drunk from mixed species, but we also can't read it as a malapropism for "spirits," since species fits in with the poem's mention of monkey, animal, and primate. So we are suspended in a neither-nor of meanings: or perhaps in a neither-nor-both-and. Because Lombardo does this repeatedly, the effect seems pervasive, and even words like "pretending" and "parasol," which normally seem to have straightforward referential content, become destabilized. As Charles Bernstein puts it, the result is "[n]ot 'death' of the referent—rather a recharged use of the multivalent referential vectors that any word has . . . [R]eference, deprived of its automatic reflex reaction of word/stimulus image/response[,] roams over the range of associations suggested by the word" (1984, 115). This "recharging" of the reference potentiality of words, and the associated requirement that we read actively rather than just allowing our "automatic reflex reactions" to operate, is, in Bernstein's view, a central element of value in avant-garde poetry.

Lombardo's meaning play recalls strategies of abstraction in visual art that suggest representational content while also frustrating one's expectation that everything will come together and make sense. Kandinsky's *Improvisation 7* (1910) works this way, in my view: it uses the palette of pastoral landscape, and some of its passages, through combinations of color and shape, evoke rolling hills, grasses, a grain elevator, a pond. The elements are not ultimately assembled so as to constitute a picture of something, but the feel of landscape nonetheless pervades the experience of the painting. Cy Twombly's works from the early 1960s, such as the *Ferragosto* series and *Leda and the Swan*, also come to mind: they are abstract patterns impregnated with phalluses, breasts, handprints, scrawled hearts, fecal smears. Twombly's works, like Kandinsky's, are not pictures of anything, but they do deploy the resemblance relations through which representation is established in pictures to bring in fragments of readable content that must color our understanding of the works. The visual stimulation of the *Ferragosto* works is pervaded by the muck and mess of bodies, by a sexual charge.

I see Lombardo's poem as employing both Twomblyesque and Kandinskyesque strategies. When he uses the word "parasol," which has clear, unambiguous referential content, he is drawing a little picture in the midst of his tableau, like one of Twombly's hearts in *Leda and the Swan*. (This does not prevent the parasol from triggering associations beyond its referential content, any more than the recognizability of one of Twombly's hearts prevents it from recalling breasts or buttocks.) And when Lombardo uses the words "Shame on table pretending an animal belly up waiting," he deploys the emotional palette of vulnerability, just as Kandinsky uses the palette of landscape. These maneuvers keep us tethered to content—the poem is very far from being pure sound—while also doing a lot to free words from the constraints of their literal senses.

This freeing up of words poses quite a challenge for the interpreter who tries to ascertain the meaning or message of the poem. When I assign student groups the task of interpreting the poem, the results diverge wildly. Some groups attempt to make sense of whatever literal content they can hold on to: the combination of drunkenness, shame, a belly, waiting, and a table makes them think of unprotected sex, pregnancy, and a medical exam, so they put forward a literal interpretation incorporating these elements despite the fact that it is difficult to reconcile with the last three stanzas. Others see that this is unsatisfactory, and they try to relax into the feel of the poem and construct a more abstract interpretation that incorporates the emotional content and the juxtaposition of ideas about society (a parasol that traps us, killing our passion) and ideas about animality. Interpretations of the latter sort share some elements—they tend to bring into play themes of autonomy and emotional authenticity—but they do not converge; some groups, for instance, see the poem as having clear sexual content while others see the passion as emotional rather than sexual. There may not be anything in the poem that allows us to adjudicate among these readings with full confidence.

Even an interpretation that attributes to the poem a sophisticated message about the human condition, though, seems ultimately unsatisfactory: for it doesn't take into account the fact that the poem refuses to be read as containing a clear message. Students often admit that the poem confused them, but they almost never incorporate this confusion into their interpretations. They seem to think that the goal of interpretation is to eliminate confusion, and that to the extent that they continue to feel confused it is a sign of their own incompetence. But the poem is so insistent on confusing us that an adequate interpretation must, it seems, present this as part of the poem's aim. If the poem is about the human condition as it relates uneasily to both sociality and animality, then it also presents or immerses us in (as opposed to merely describing) the confusion inherent in that condition. We are accustomed to making sense of things, to observing events and thinking that we understand what is happening; but the poem potentially forces us back into a state at which our easy fluency with cultural concepts and social conventions is undermined, and we see with fresh eyes just how baffling and inexplicable the events of our world really are.

To sum up, I see this poem as employing two strategies that are specifically related to its unreadability. First, it uses word-play to loosen the connections between words and their conventional meanings, while also opening non-literal associative connections. This is, as I see it, a strategy of abstraction, along the lines used by Twombly and Kandinsky. Second, the poem *acts on* the reader, eliciting an experience of confusion rather than describing that confusion to convey its message.[10] In this sense the poem functions a bit like a Zen koan whose aim is to force the meditator to transcend the constraints of analytic mind.[11]

An anonymous reviewer of this volume raises a worry about my approach, insofar as I aim to offer an aesthetic defense of "unreadable" poems:

Suppose . . . the "meaning" of a very confusing poem is precisely to instantiate and enact confusion, as a means of representing the confusion that plagues modern humanity. That's plausible enough, in itself. But it's hard to see how a confusing poem could do anything, in terms of meaning, other than express confusion, or how an obscure poem could do anything other than enact obscurity, or how a poem that frustrates the reader's expectations could do anything other than embody frustration. And if those are the only meanings available to "unreadable poems," it is hard to see why people would bother to keep writing them, because those meanings have already been amply expressed.

I hope I have shown that Lombardo's poem does not *simply* express confusion or embody frustration. The poem's strategy of acting on us to produce confusion is interwoven with its other elements. Because it is made up of words and expressions in a natural language, it incorporates the meanings of those words and expressions, while also evoking other meanings that we associate with those words and expressions. Our confusion is not generalized and free-floating: it is confusion within a particular domain, in which we contemplate the human condition in relation to our conventional and animal natures. We are directed to this domain by devices such as the

---

[10]   Charles Bernstein (2011, 9) suggests that criticism should ask of a poem "what it does" rather than "what it means."

[11]   Houlihan remarks, though less favorably, on the koan-like aspect of some of the poems she discusses.

imagery of parasols and tables juxtaposed with laughing, climbing primates. Our confusion here is not identical to other confusions: it is populated by content and imagery the poem supplies. For this reason I'm not sure it's possible that a poem written in words could express confusion or enact obscurity or embody frustration without also bringing other meanings into play.

Lombardo has not, I have argued, put together random strings of words in a meaningless way. His words are not meaningless, but their relations to meaning are different than those in a conventional poem. And these unconventional meaning relations can plausibly be seen to serve the poem's central aim in a direct, experiential way. This is not to say that we must conclude that the poem is a great success. Some people hate Twombly, finding his scribblings pretentious or his exposure of the id distasteful. Much of one's evaluative response to Twombly's works depends on whether the visual experience of them is found to be interesting or pleasurable. I find Twombly's works far more satisfying than Lombardo's poem—the specific abstract array of emotional color and partial semantic sense that Lombardo deploys just doesn't stimulate my interest as the best of Twombly's vigorous scrawl does; and I must admit that my tolerance for confusion and for the overthrow of analytic mind is limited. As Oren Izenberg says, "Estrangement is its own form of enchantment; difficulty can always be reconstituted as a subject matter of potential interest—and of pleasure—if that difficulty is to your taste" (2010, 141). Lombardo's variety of estrangement is not altogether to my taste. Nonetheless, I hold that an adequate approach to "Partial Rhythm, Primate Laughing" must see the poem as having comprehensible aims that are pursued by way of specific meaning-related techniques.

V

Absent from my analysis so far is the relation of the author's intention to the meaning of the poem. A student once brought me a little slip of paper containing Gian Lombardo's email address, in case I wished to contact him and find out what the poem is really about.[12] The student, for whatever reason, chose not to do this dirty work.

[12] I've since had occasion to correspond with Gian Lombardo, who kindly supplied me with correspondence he had with Joan Houlihan following the publication of her article. In it, he writes, "If you ask me what the 'meaning' is, I'd have to reply that it is the poem. If I wanted to say it another way, I would have done so . . . The poem states exactly what I wanted to say." In a message to me of July 27, 2012, he adds, "There is no 'correct' meaning

Should I have contacted Lombardo or Mengert? I have been tempted
ask Mengert about the status of the asterisk as title; the fact that it was
omitted when the complete poem was published online in *Castagraf* may
be a clue that it doesn't have the importance attributed to it by some of the
interpretative possibilities I raised earlier. (If the title is optional or incidental, then it shouldn't be seen as the grammatical subject of the poem's
first sentence, for instance.)

When it comes to the interpretation of the works, though, I am not
moved to consult the authors. I see authors as having the authority to fix
their works' features: and it is through their actions of choosing the works'
features, not through any other mechanism, that they determine the
interpretation of the work (Irvin 2005). A poet, then, gets to decide which
sequence of words will appear in the poem, and what the poem's title is,
and what the spatial arrangement of the words will be. The poet also has the
prerogative to incorporate aphorisms, subtitles, footnotes, or other textual
elements. Gwendolyn Brooks often uses such strategies: the titles of several
of her poems are followed by further lines of text, distinguished by inden-
tation and style of type, that precede the main body of the poem. These
lines sometimes provide a dedication, a setting for the poem, or a quotation
to introduce the text. "We Real Cool"[13] is introduced by such lines:

> THE POOL PLAYERS.
> SEVEN AT THE GOLDEN SHOVEL.

We real cool. We
Left school. We

Lurk late. We
Strike straight. We

Sing sin. We
Thin gin. We

Jazz June. We
die soon.

other than itself." He favors a situation in which readers approach the poem by "inhabiting
it & making it theirs, as well as simultaneously 'understanding' it on its own terms."

[13]   Reprinted by consent of Brooks Permissions. Included in Brooks 1950, 17. The full text
of the poem, along with a wonderful audio recording of Brooks reading and discussing the
poem (and her dismay that it is the only one of her poems that many readers encounter), is
available here: <http://www.poets.org/viewmedia.php/prmMID/15433>.

The two opening lines provide the setting and position a specific group of people as the speakers of the words in the body of the poem. Similarly, the poem "Bronzeville Woman in a Red Hat"[14] is introduced by the lines

HIRES OUT TO

MRS. MILES

which allow the reader to grasp immediately that the early lines in the main body of the poem express the racist perspective of the white employer:

> They had never had one in the house before.
>   The strangeness of it all. Like unleashing
> A lion, really. Poised
> To pounce. A puma. A panther. A black
> Bear.
> There it stood in the door,
> Under a red hat that was rash, but refreshing—
> In a tasteless way, of course—across the dull glare,
> The semi-assault of that extraordinary blackness.

In each case, the opening lines directly constrain interpretation: a reading of "We Real Cool" that does not take into account the connection between the words and the pool players would be inadmissible, as would a reading of "Bronzeville Woman in a Red Hat" that fails to recognize that the dehumanizing 'it' is deployed in the mind of the white Mrs. Miles.

The poet thus has full authority to set the stage by determining the text and format of the poem, including the introductory lines. But things the poet might say in other contexts (interviews, journal entries, and so forth) about the poem's interpretation are, to my mind, suggestive without being decisive. They give us hints about where it might be sensible to look for the poem's themes and meanings, but it is up to us to determine whether the poem genuinely makes good on the poet's aspirations for it.[15] Moreover, I wouldn't want to restrict the poem to having only meanings that the poet anticipated or has acknowledged. As Troy Jollimore remarks, "[M]etaphors, in a sense, *transcend* language by opening themselves up to aspects of the world that may not initially be

---

[14] Included in Brooks (1950, 53–6).   [15] I discuss relevant arguments in Irvin (2006).

embodied in the words themselves, and may perhaps even be unknown to the person who first deploys the metaphor in question."[16]

This is my view about interpretation generally, and I don't see that anything about unreadable poems mandates a different approach. Gian Lombardo might help us to see the importance of elements of his poem that we had overlooked, just as an especially perceptive reader might. But how the poem should be interpreted is ultimately a matter of whether those elements genuinely function as he wishes them to and believes they do. And I hope I have shown that we have non-negligible resources for assessing the workings even of poems that are strikingly unconventional in their grammar and word usage.

VI

Appreciating an unreadable poem requires a willingness to consider it on its own terms, and to take seriously the possibility that it has a purpose that is defined by its idiosyncratic elements, including its refusal of conventional meaning. Reading in this way may lead us not to an articulable semantic meaning that we can attribute to the text, but instead to an experience that has semantic, rhythmic, and non-cognitive elements. There is nothing particularly radical or surprising in this analysis: it deploys Olsen's (1978) Principle of Functionality as well as Lamarque's (2009) observation that the practice of reading poetry is such that we properly see poems as unities of form and content, with the result that the fruits of appreciation are experiences rather than meanings. Olsen's and Lamarque's theories are not tailored for difficult or avant-garde poetry; they are general theories about appreciation of literature and of poetry, respectively. We thus do not need to revolutionize our strategies to appreciate unreadable poems; we simply need to be willing to entertain a widening range of poetic purposes. I hope to have shown, through close examination of a couple of examples, how this can be done.

Some will remain unappeased by this analysis. Yes, it is possible, after long effort, to ascertain the aims of these tortured strings of words. But why not spend our time, instead, reading works that offer their rewards

---

[16] Jollimore (2009, 147). In relation to this insight Jollimore cites Moran (1989, 109).

more freely, with less brain twisting? Or, to consider things from another perspective, is there any artistic justification for this mangling of language? Aren't there ample linguistic resources for describing and evoking a full range of experiences by using words and grammatical constructions in more customary ways?

T. S. Eliot (1975, 65) offers one sort of answer to this question. "Our civilization," he writes,

comprehends great variety and complexity, and this variety and complexity, playing upon a refined sensibility, must produce various and complex results. The poet must become more and more comprehensive, more allusive, in order to force, to dislocate if necessary, language into his meaning.

He concludes that "poets in our civilization ... must be *difficult*" (1975, 65; emphasis in original). This is an interesting proposal: there is something about the human condition in the industrial and post-industrial eras that demands an evolution of communication that outstrips the evolution of linguistic convention. If Eliot is right, then one supposes his point applies a fortiori to our own technologically saturated age.

There is another sort of justification for unreadable poetry that emerges not from a general observation about the nature of contemporary society, but from the situation of oppressed and subordinated groups. This justification has two facets. First, the situation of oppressed groups often demands coding and other modes of covert communication that are not accessible to the oppressors. As Louise Bennett discusses, when Africans in Jamaica were forbidden by the English to speak their original languages, they

disguise up de English Language ... in such a way dat we English forefahders-dem still couldn understand what we African ancestors-dem wasa talk bout when dem wasa talk to dem one annodder! (Bennett 1993, 2)

As a result, "no so-so English-talkin smaddy cyaan understand weh we a seh if we doan want dem to understand weh we a seh, a oh!" (Bennett 1993, 2). The linguistic resources of a historically subordinated group, then, may be expressly designed to be unreadable by those outside the group. This highlights the important point that some unreadability is audience relative; a text may be unreadable by some while perfectly readable by others. Moreover, there may be no adequate replacement for words and expressions that are designed to be unreadable by the oppressors: they may have cultural resonance for members of the subordinated group that cannot be captured in any other way.

Second, insofar as the literary canon tends to be determined by the dominating group, the conventional linguistic resources that emerge out of that canon may be far better suited to describing the experiences of members of that dominating group. When members of a subordinated group attempt to capture their own experiences, they may feel a greater need for poetry that breaks open language in order to forge new semantic networks or to act directly on the reader to produce an experience rather than merely describing one. As Adrienne Rich describes, "[T]here is . . . a difficult and dangerous walking on the ice, as we try to find language and images for a consciousness we are just coming into, and with little in the past to support us" (1979, 35). Women's experiences, Rich says, have been "wordless or negated" (Rich 1979, 34) under patriarchy, their needs "misnam[ed] and thwart[ed]" (Rich 1979, 37). If women are to find a way to express their particular experiences in this context, "nothing can be too sacred for the imagination to turn into its opposite or to call experimentally by another name. For writing is re-naming" (Rich 1979, 43). The sort of re-naming that is undertaken by members of subordinated groups may cause their poetry to seem gratuitously alien to readers steeped in the canon of the dominating group. But it is easy to see that this may be an ethical and political failing on the part of the audience, rather than a good reason to condemn the poetry.

Does the unreadability of Mengert's or Lombardo's poetry eventuate from their experience of the rapid evolution of contemporary culture, or from their positions as members of subordinated groups? It may stem from both of these to some degree, or from neither. There may be no way to know until we have looked carefully at their poems and immersed ourselves in the experiences they make possible. To dismiss such poetry out of frustration is to deny ourselves the occasion to develop interpretative skills that will serve us well in reading poems that have something crucial and incomparable to offer.[17]

[17] I am grateful to Gian Lombardo, Amanda Silbernagel, Raz Spector, and an anonymous reviewer of this volume for helpful discussion and suggestions, to Gian Lombardo and Christina Mengert for permission to reproduce their poems, and to Gian Lombardo for permission to quote from correspondence.

References

Ammons, A. R. 1957. "Mansion," in *Expressions of Sea Level*. Columbus, OH: Ohio State University Press.

Bennett, Louise. 1993. "Jamaica Language." In Mervyn Morris (ed.), *Bennett, Aunty Roachy Seh*. Kingston, Jamaica: Sangster's Book Stores, 1–3.

Bernstein, Charles. 1984. "Semblance." In Bruce Andrews and Charles Bernstein (eds), *The L=A=N=G=U=A=G=E Book*. Carbondale, IL: Southern Illinois University Press, 115–18.

Bernstein, Charles. 2011. *Attack of the Difficult Poems*. Chicago: University of Chicago Press.

Brooks, Gwendolyn. 1950. *The Bean Eaters*. New York: Harper & Brothers.

Eliot, T. S. 1975. "The Metaphysical Poets." In Frank Kermode (ed.), *Selected Prose of T. S. Eliot*. London: Faber & Faber, 59–67. First published in the *Times Literary Supplement*, Oct. 20, 1921.

Greenlaw, Lavinia. 1997. "Iron Lung." In *A World Where News Travelled Slowly*. London: Faber & Faber, 35.

Hirsch, E. D. 1967. *Validity in Interpretation*. New Haven, CT: Yale University Press.

Houlihan, Joan. 2003. "Post-Post Dementia." *Web del Sol*. <http://www.web-delsol.com/LITARTS/Boston_Comment/bostonc7.htm>, accessed Sept. 2011.

Irvin, Sherri. 2005. "The Artist's Sanction in Contemporary Art." *Journal of Aesthetics and Art Criticism*, 63: 315–26.

Irvin, Sherri. 2006. "Authors, Intentions and Literary Meaning." *Philosophy Compass*, 1: 114–28.

Izenberg, Oren. 2010. *Being Numerous: Poetry and the Ground of Social Life*. Princeton: Princeton University Press.

Jollimore, Troy. 2009. "'Like a Picture or a Bump on the Head': Vision, Cognition, and the Language of Poetry." *Midwest Studies in Philosophy*, 33: 131–58.

Lamarque, Peter. 2009. "The Elusiveness of Poetic Meaning." *Ratio*, 22: 398–420.

Lombardo, Gian. 2004. *Of All the Corners to Forget*. New York: Meeting Eyes Bindery.

Moran, Richard. 1989. "Seeing and Believing: Metaphor, Image, and Force." *Critical Inquiry*, 16: 87–112.

Nicholls, Peter. 2010. "The Elusive Allusion: Poetry and Exegesis." In Nicky Marsh and Peter Middleton (eds), *Teaching Modernist Poetry*. New York: Palgrave Macmillan, 10–24.

Olsen, Stein Haugom. 1978. *The Structure of Literary Understanding*. Cambridge: Cambridge University Press.

Rich, Adrienne. 1979. "When We Dead Awaken: Writing as Re-Vision." *On Lies, Secrets, and Silence: Selected Prose, 1966–1978.* New York: Norton, 33–49. An earlier version was published in 1972 in *College English* 34.

Suppes, Patrick. 2009. "Rhythm and Meaning in Poetry." *Midwest Studies in Philosophy,* 33: 159–66.

5

Can an Analytic Philosopher Read Poetry?

Simon Blackburn

I

My title question is of course tongue-in-cheek. As we shall see it is not clear what all analytic philosophers have in common, if anything, but many who accept the description, myself included, sometimes read poetry—doubtless far more than there are poets who read analytic philosophy. For all I know some of us may do so with appropriate enjoyment, insight, sensitivity, appreciation and even critical skill. Perhaps some poets are doctrinally difficult for some of us: not being Christians or mystics or Platonists we may find poets who are trying to express such philosophies a little hard to take, but even here generosity is possible. Are there readers who cannot respond, say, to Donne's 'The Relique' on the grounds that they do not believe in the resurrection of the body? In any event doctrine is a minor matter, for the same difficulty might afflict anyone, and on the whole contemporary philosophers, who should after all have read Durkheim or Wittgenstein, may have a more flexible attitude even to religious or magical sayings than others do. We have surely learned that in the house of language there are many mansions.

Perhaps this was forgotten during the cataclysmic conflict between science and poetry that exercised, on behalf of the latter, Shelley, Keats, and Schiller, and on behalf of the former, Bentham and Macaulay, at the beginning of the nineteenth century. The latter wrote in 1825 that 'as civilization advances, poetry almost necessarily declines'. 'We cannot unite' he thundered, echoing centuries of Puritan grumblings, 'the incompatible advantages of reality and deception, the clear discernment of truth and the exquisite enjoyment of fiction'.[1] In the context of his essay Macaulay really seems to have meant 'incompatible', although 'incomparable' or 'incommensurable' would surely have been better. There is no incompatibility between the advantage poetry might offer, such as the pleasure we take in beauty, and one that science might offer, such as the power to do something that could not be done before. Many of us are happy with both.

Sounding even more like a government minister, bent on forcing the education syllabus into the shape preferred by Thomas Gradgrind, although perhaps with his tongue a little nearer his cheek, there was Thomas Love Peacock:

The philosophic mental tranquillity which looks round with an equal eye on all external things, collects a store of ideas, discriminates their relative value, assigns to all their proper place, and from the materials of useful knowledge thus collected, appreciated, and arranged, forms new combinations that impress the stamp of their power and utility on the real business of life, is diametrically the reverse of that frame of mind which poetry inspires, or from which poetry can emanate. The highest inspirations of poetry are resolvable into three ingredients: the rant of unregulated passion, the whining of exaggerated feeling, and the cant of factitious sentiment: and can therefore serve only to ripen a splendid lunatic like Alexander, a puling driveller like Werther, or a morbid dreamer like Wordsworth.[2]

Shelley's answer to Peacock, in his famous essay 'A Defence of Poetry', that the poet 'participates in the eternal, the infinite, and the one',[3] scarcely convinces us, any more than Carlyle's view that he or she 'penetrates into the sacred mystery of the universe'.[4] Perhaps we do better to stick with Schiller who said that art is the result of a 'play impulse' and that an appearance is aesthetic only in so far as it 'expressly renounces all claim to reality', so that it must be enjoyed without desire and without 'asking after its purpose'.

---

[1] Samuel Thurber (ed.), *Select Essays of Macaulay: Milton, Bunyan, Johnson, Goldsmith, Madame D'Arblay*. Boston: Allyn & Bacon, 1892, 8.
[2] Thomas Love Peacock, *The Four Ages of Poetry*. In *The Works of Thomas Love Peacock, Including His Novels, Poems, Fugitive Pieces, Criticisms, Etc.*, ed. Henry Cole. London: R. Bentley & son, 1875, 335.
[3] Percy Bysshe Shelley, *A Defense of Poetry*. Boston and London: Ginn & Co., 1890, 6.
[4] Thomas Carlyle, *On Heroes, Hero-Worship, and the Heroic in History*. London: Blackie & Son, 1907, 96.

Playtime on Parnassus is doubtless very agreeable, and certainly pref-
erable to casting around for the sacred mystery of the universe, but in the
following passage Ruskin perhaps does slightly better:

> Science deals exclusively with things as they are in themselves; and art exclu-
> sively with things as they affect the human sense and human soul. Her work
> is to portray the appearances of things, and to deepen the natural impressions
> which they produce upon living creatures. The work of science is to substitute
> facts for appearances, and demonstrations for impressions. Both, observe, are
> equally concerned with truth; the one with truth of aspect, the other with truth
> of essence. Art does not represent things falsely, but truly as they appear to man-
> kind. Science studies the relations of things to each other: but art studies only
> their relations to man.[5]

It is certainly a common idea that at least one function of the poet is to
express feelings about things, or sentiments or passions that are otherwise inarticulate, or perhaps that by voicing them he actually gives birth
either to differently directed feelings, or perhaps to more nuanced and
interesting feelings than would otherwise exist. And truth to feeling
gives the poet a toehold on truth.

Ruskin appears to be following John Stuart Mill. When Mill attempted
to refute the Benthamite view that poetry is trivial, he deployed the same
idea. Science 'addresses itself to belief' and it acts 'by presenting a proposition to the understanding'; poetry acts 'by offering interesting objects of
contemplation to the sensibilities', apparently bypassing the understanding altogether. A poet might describe 'the lion professedly, but the state
of excitement of the spectator really'.[6] About this the critic M. H. Abrams
tartly comments 'Mill's reader properly wonders why, if the poet's underlying aim is to describe his own feelings, he should choose to complicate
matters by bringing in a lion', which is amusing enough although philosophically rather suspect.[7] You cannot interestingly describe what the
evening meant to someone without describing the evening, or describe
someone's enjoyment of golf without describing golf itself.

I do not say that Ruskin and Mill are wholly wrong, but their view is
certainly puzzling. A new expression of an old feeling does not sound

[5] John Ruskin, Edward Tyas Cook, and Alexander D. O. Wedderburn. *The Works of John Ruskin*. London and New York: George Allen Longmans, Green, 1904, 47–8.
[6] The Mill quotations are taken from M. H. Abrams, *The Mirror and the Lamp: Romantic Theory and the Critical Tradition*. New York: Oxford University Press, 1953, 321.
[7] Abrams, *The Mirror and the Lamp*, 322.

to be in itself particularly valuable. But if the poet is said to give us new feelings other problems arise, not least because we have no ready-made criterion for the newness of a feeling. The problem is perhaps more visible when the same thing is said about music. Does Beethoven give us new 'feelings'? All of his works? The same new feelings or different ones? Does Bach? And then, does the poet really do this all that often? For myself, I should say that had I witnessed it I might have been visually knocked over by the sumptuous scene that Enobarbus describes, without having had Shakespeare's words to direct me. To take another example, I am sure that feelings of grief, of nostalgia, or of being haunted by the memories of a passionate love that descended into something commonplace or miserable, are emotional processes that any of us may suffer and all of us can imagine. So Thomas Hardy's achievement in the poems written after his wife's death, such as 'After a Journey' or 'The Voice' is not to invent these emotions nor to redirect them, but to give them a particularly sincere, and convincing expression, embodying them so movingly in the particular appearances, episodes, places, and times of his courtship and marriage. The value, then lies entirely in the work itself, not in the feelings of the author or reader.

There is much more to say about truth to feeling and sincerity, and the various traps, such as sentimentality, that surround them. There is also more to say about the pleasures of play and dramatic licence. But what I hope to expose is a rather different, more local kind of problem. For while the exact relationship between poetry and truth is no doubt variable, if only because there are so many different kinds of poetry, the relationship of poetry to language, and thence to analytic philosophy is more typically fraught with difficulty. For perhaps we philosophers only read poetry by leaving something of our philosophy behind. Perhaps it requires a special effort from us, in several dimensions. I shall outline some of these shortly, but first it may be necessary to put aside a misunderstanding about analytical philosophy itself.

II

There is an unfortunate stereotype of an analytic philosopher as someone who spends his or her days looking for different ways of saying the same thing. We are supposed to go around with narrowed eyes and pursed lips asking 'precisely what do you mean by . . . ?' and lamenting any answer that does not meet some exacting standard of precision of which we are the high priests, and which lesser minds unfortunately do not worship as much as we do. A paradigm of such an analysis might be the undoubted truth that to be a vixen is to be a female fox, and on this picture we spend our lives in a quest to similarly decompose more interesting notions, such as that of a value, a number, a law of nature, or a mind, or a possibility. Such a quest would, indeed, often be predictably futile, since it meets a nasty dilemma. Either the rephrasings attempt to give, for instance, a non-moral vocabulary in which to moralize, or a non-arithmetical vocabulary with which to count, or they merely provides words sufficiently close to the original simply to share whatever problems about the nature of morality or mathematics prompted the desire for an analysis in the first place. But we are not supposed to be daunted by the futility.

On this account the analytical philosopher is centrally in the business of paraphrase, and since the poetry in a piece of writing is typically totally resistant to paraphrase, our professional deformation is all too apparent.

Fortunately, however, this stereotype is substantially misleading. Philosophers approach the phenomena that puzzle them in many ways and with many different tools, and it is very seldom that their methods bear much analogy to lexicography or the provision of dictionary definitions. We are more likely, for example, to approach the question of what is involved in a creature having a mind, not by finding 'what exactly we mean' by attributing a mind to one, but by trying to understand how mental phenomena are identified, or what their function is, or how they relate to other phenomena such as having a memory, or a capacity for agency, or sensitivity to an environment, or use of a language. There is no antecedent expectation that such an exploration would be completed and crowned by a definition of any kind. 'Analysis' only comes in because it is unlikely that this exploration will be well-conducted without a keen ear for terms and ideas which bitter experience proves to be treacherous. Fastidiousness in reading and care in writing are necessary virtues. But surely these cannot separate us from writers and readers of poetry.

There is, indeed, a related problem but one that we share with other teachers. Any philosopher's professional life includes a good deal of exegesis. We spend days and years trying to work out what Hume was 'trying to say' about causation, Kant about perception, or Wittgenstein about truth. In doing this we are not doing anything very special: a layman might similarly be puzzled by what Darwin or Einstein or Freud is saying about their topics, and be helped by a teacher who is able to put it differently, perhaps more clearly, or more slowly, or in less technical language, or along with helpful analogies, or comparing it with more familiar thoughts in other writers. It is no different when it is Hobbes or Heidegger that intrigues and puzzles us. Nor for that matter is it different when Leavis explains the celebrated couplet ending Keats's Ode to a Grecian Urn, putting it in its context and offering as exegesis: 'Life, alas! is not as we would have it; but it ought to be, and, with the aid of the Grecian urn can be felt for a moment to be: imagination, concentrating on the beauty of the urn and ignoring the discordant and indocile facts, attains a higher reality, compared with which actual life seems thin and unreal.'[8] I do not suppose for a moment anyone would take this to be a substitute for the poem, but it could (perhaps) be a kind of help to understanding it.

A related danger might arise because, just as we might correct a student's essay for ambiguities, reliance on metaphors, unexamined implications, lack of conclusion, or any of the other defects common to fledgling academic prose, we might also wish to correct Shakespeare for the same faults. When he talks, for instance, of the:

> … daffodils,
> That come before the swallow dares, and take
> The winds of March with beauty,

without disambiguating whether they take the winds in the passive sense of a person taking a punch, or take them in the active sense of a person taking the air, we might incautiously find ourselves irritated.[9] Coming to realize that 'take', with its ambiguity, is not an infelicity, but is intended and central to the success of the passage, is something that it may be especially difficult for us to appreciate, and we risk making ourselves ridiculous if we combine such failure with an attachment to criticism in the schoolmasterly sense, regarding such ambiguity as inevitably a defect. The latter attitude has certainly represented a danger to others than philosophers. Alexander Pope pounced on just this vice, satirizing the great but evidently cloth-eared classicist Bentley,

[8] F. R. Leavis, *Revaluation*. London: Chatto & Windus, 1962, 254.
[9] William Shakespeare, *The Winter's Tale*, 3. 4. 136–8.

> Thy mighty scholiast, whose unweary'd pains
> Made Horace dull, and humbled Milton's strains.
> Turn what they will to verse, their toil is vain,
> Critics like me shall make it Prose again. [10]

But analytical philosophers are no more likely to follow Bentley than other classicists were. The exegetical habit of mind does not have to amount to a disqualification. It need not precipitate us unconsciously into supposing that the poet is trying (but inexplicably failing) to say something which can be put better: more clearly, or less metaphorically, or without ambiguity or other distractions, all the time ignoring the probability that the obscurity, and metaphor, and the invitation to explore in different directions that they offer, may well be essential to the success of the poem. In his famous inaugural lecture A. C. Bradley put it admirably:

Pure poetry is not the decoration of a preconceived and clearly defined matter: it springs from the creative impulse of a vague imaginative mass pressing for development and definition. If the poet already knew exactly what he meant to say, why should he write the poem? The poem would in fact already be written. For only its completion can reveal, even to him, exactly what he wanted. When he began and while he was at work, he did not possess his meaning; it possessed him.[11]

Again, the value lies in the work itself, not in its relation to 'feelings'.

Another charge might be advanced not because the philosopher asks the poet to do things other than write poetry, but because he may have a habit of excluding from notice some features of language, and in particular those that are most important to atmosphere, mood, emotion, and attitude, not to mention being potent sources of pleasure. When we read that

> The barge she sat in, like a burnished throne,
> Burned on the water; the poop was beaten gold;
> Purple the sails, and so perfumed that
> The winds were love-sick with them . . . [12]

---

[10] From *The Dunciad*, quoted from Alexander Pope, *The Major Works*, ed. Pat Rogers. Oxford: Oxford University Press, 2009, 528.

[11] A. C. Bradley, *Poetry for Poetry's Sake: An Inaugural Lecture Delivered on June 5, 1901.* Oxford: Clarendon Press, 1901, 28.

[12] William Shakespeare, *Anthony and Cleopatra*, 2. 2. 227–30.

we will certainly realize that the poet is evoking the fact that Enobarbus
was knocked out by what he saw, but perhaps not notice the incantatory
effect of the triplet of 'b's and the lilt as they turn into the echoing triplet
of 'p's—not to mention the glorious yet complex metaphor of the throne
burning on the water. We are not professionally practised in noticing
such features: in the kind of things that philosophers write, it would be
highly unusual for an alliteration to have any significance at all. It would
be at best an ornament or perhaps more likely a whimsy supposed to disguise a limping argument. That, at least, would be the official view.

It is something of an embarrassment to this view that the great philosophers who make up the canon were quite often great writers as well.
Everyone knows Plato's marvellous metaphors of the cave, the charioteer,
the two halves of the soul searching for one another, and so forth. Even
Kant, so often excoriated along with Hegel for teaching philosophy to
write German, has wonderful passages:

The light dove, cleaving the air in her free flight, and feeling its resistance, might
imagine that its flight would be still easier in empty space. It was thus that Plato
left the world of the senses . . . [13]

And Hegel himself was not immune to the poetry of flight:

When philosophy paints its grey on grey, then is a form of life grown old. The owl
of Minerva takes wing only with the coming of the night. [14]

There would be few such arresting images in the contemporary journals. But then modern philosophical writing, as Bernard Williams sadly
remarked, often aspires to do no more than 'resemble scientific reports
badly translated from the Martian'.

III

I now turn to a rather different kind of problem. It arises from the special concern of analytic philosophers with semantic theory, and within
that theory, the tyranny of the single sentence and its single truth-value

[13] Immanuel Kant, *Critique of Pure Reason*, corr. edn, tr. Paul Guyer and Allen
W. Wood. Cambridge: Cambridge University Press, 1998, 129.
[14] Georg Wilhelm Friedrich Hegel, *Elements of the Philosophy of Right*, tr. Allen
W. Wood. Cambridge: Cambridge University Press, 1991, 23.

(that is, the fact of the sentence either being true, or being false, with no other options in play). To fix what I have in mind, I shall call this the Fregean paradigm, although I am very well aware that this is unfair to the great German logician Frege, who did not conceive of himself as offering theories of actual language but of idealized scientific and mathematical languages. The tradition, however, has not been so reticent. I shall start by sketching the Fregean approach, although with two caveats. The first is that what follows simplifies a subject of great complexity, about which countless papers and books have been written. The second is that every term in what follows (name, predicate, sentence, . . .) itself provokes questions and controversies. Nothing here is completely straightforward.

With those warnings in mind, we can say that the Fregean approach starts with the sentence as the unit of meaning, and Frege's theory of the ideal language talks only about the role of the sentence as a vehicle for stable, communicable, public, items of information. This is very much as it should be. One of the insights and motivations of the Fregean approach to language was that we can after all communicate. I can make myself understood to you: if I tell you that there is a bus coming shortly I expect you to understand me, and to understand me exactly as I intended and expected. And this will be so even if for me buses trigger no particular associations, whereas for you they have all kinds of psychological echoes. Perhaps a bus knocked over your mother, or you gave birth before the bus got you to hospital, or you had a nice or nasty experience on the upper deck. No matter: these echoes, which seventeenth- and eighteenth-century philosophers would have called 'ideas', do not infect your everyday understanding of what I have just told you. Hence, it was concluded, we need to distil out what is strictly and literally said from any surrounding nimbus of private association. In this way the analytic tradition sidelined psychology, and spoke instead of impersonal concepts, or rules, or propositions in the abstract. Communication is then conceived as the delivery of one of these from one mind to another (philosophy itself becomes impersonal as well: the delivery of context-free, eternal truths via the unhappily unreliable vehicle of language).

There are then two options for a properly formed, meaningful sentence. Its job is to be true, and ones which fail in that respect are false. No sentence can be both, and neither are there any half measures.

The simplest kind of sentence consists of a name, which designates a topic or subject of discourse, and a predicate. The predicate expresses a concept, attributing a property to the object referred to, and the sentence is true if the object indeed has that property. Sentences with names that do not refer to anything are a bit of an embarrassment: Frege shunted them aside as unfit for scientific language, but whether or not he was right, they certainly occur in poetry. We only have to think of Ovid's *Metamorphoses*. Tiptoeing past this problem we come to more complex sentences which do different things, but these can all be understood in terms of variants of this basic form. Some sentences put other sentences into contexts, and the way in which they are built from simpler components is the subject of semantic theory. The leading idea is that we stick with truth and falsity as the vital core, and track the way in which a more complex sentence is true or false as a function of the ways in which component sentences are. The paradigms are simple compositions, such as the negation of a simple sentence (false if and only if the original is true) or the conjunction of two sentences (true if and only if both component sentences are true). The study of such matters is highly developed: complex languages including such things as quantifiers (constructions involving a class of items, as when we talk of 'all men' or 'some women'), tense, modality, conditionals, and many more have been more or less successfully approached with this analytic machinery. As the major American logician and philosopher W. V. Quine put it, logic chases truth up the tree of grammar.

The ideal would be a description making the meaning of a complex sentence computable or deducible from the meaning of its component parts. The argument for this computational paradigm is simple: we all have an enormously elastic capacity to parse sentences which we have never read before (such as this one); this cannot be left as a 'miracle'; so the ordinary language user must be able to perform a kind of computation on the words and their organization which then delivers the meaning of sentence as a result. This is not a laborious calculation which we ourselves perform, of course, but it is a theoretical model or description of the ways in which our sensitivity to the presence of words, and their order, issues in communicable meaning. Fregean semantics describes the structures that enable these essentially mechanical processes.

It would be a long business even to sketch all the questions to which this paradigm has given rise. One that must strike everyone is that comparing a thought and its linguistic expression to the passenger inside a vehicle has to be misleading and inept. The identity of passengers is independent of the vehicle in which they find themselves. But the identity of the thought cannot be separated from the nature of the sentence used to communicate it. Even Frege recognized this, knowing that the key to a proper understanding of mathematics depended on finding a perspicuous notation in which to express mathematical proofs. Yet for all that he thought of concepts as hard individual things existing, rather like Plato's Forms, in a 'third world' of abstract entities.

In the context of poetry, one element stands out very starkly. This is the rigid account of communication with its essentially static, hard, immobile imagery, a picture that erases both the speaker and the listener or reader. Each sentence is attached to its particular 'content' or proposition; this fixity is effected because its elements have their own relations to things and concepts. Truth is truth, since a concept either applies or does not, and there are no half measures. To give an example of the lengths to which this paradigm takes philosophers, it has recently been quite influentially argued that vagueness in language is purely a question of ignorance. We find that the borderlines between being merely comfortably off and being rich, or being a child and an adult, or clever and clever-silly, are vague only because we do not know where the lines really are. There is a precise amount of income or capital that defines the difference between comfortably off and rich, and a precise age or precise set of capacities that defines that between child and adult, and a precise line between being clever and being clever-silly, but unfortunately we do not know where these precise lines lie. Nor is there any project of finding out. Even God does not know where the lines are, but nevertheless, they lie somewhere.

I do not think you have to be a poet to find such a view completely absurd—a moderate sense of reality should be enough—which is not to deny that there are clever, or perhaps clever-silly (who knows?) arguments for it. It is a view that seems to ignore context, purpose, background, memory, and just about every empirical fact about either cognition or the use of language. Its principal claim to consideration is that it makes the 'logic' easier, preserving, for instance, the views that everybody is either rich or not rich and that nobody is both. However this advantage can be had much more cheaply, since it is not as if we hear poets, psychologists, or in general people who are sensitive to the flexible, mobile, pragmatic elements in language use flouting classical logic by describing people as rich and not rich, or describing a colour as both orange and something other than orange.

What we do find are inconstancies in application of terms. At one time we might be inclined to say that someone is rich, or an adult, although on another occasion we might be pulled towards thinking of them as only comfortable, or a child. It may depend on the occasion, the comparison class, or the purpose, but it is quite innocent, since inconstancy is not the same as inconsistency. It is a manifested diachronically, by our inclination being different on different occasions, whereas the latter is manifested only at a time, in one episode or speech act. Our changeability might, in some circumstances, be a nuisance, since it is often important for people to know where we stand on some issue. But often it is merely human, and of no concern. The day starts out with us thinking that our rucksack is as light as a feather, but it may end with us describing it as weighing like lead.

How can there be a sensible dispute over whether a term that we know to be vague applies or does not? The answer, clearly, is that we are attaching *significance* to particular descriptions: the significance of a changing comparison class, and thence a change in status or attitude. Words face in different directions: there are often entry rules (circumstances in which to allow a remark) and exit rules (directions in which to think or act, once it is allowed). Two people may disagree because by choosing their terms each is encouraging a different practical cognitive attitude or direction of thought. One wants to mobilize implicatures (for instance, 'rich' implying luxury, ease, freedom from care, a duty to give to charity, perhaps greed) that another may want to avoid, preferring to substitute a different direction of thought or imagination ('comfortable' implying only freedom from serious want, certainly, but struggle, not too much to spare, a hard-won but vulnerable respectability perhaps). It is only these implications that give the dispute more than a verbal flavour. But they do so, just as effectively as more notorious choices of terms such as terrorist versus freedom-fighter, or resolute rather than pig-headed, do. Silence itself has implications, and often very potent ones.[15]

---

[15] Following H. P. Grice, philosophers like to distinguish implicatures, which are implied by your choosing some particular remark, from the implications of what is said. Asked what I think about the new Professor, my reply 'They tell me he is good at hopscotch' strongly suggests that I don't think much of his professional capacity. But what I say does not imply that, since someone good at hopscotch might quite well be thought by me to be a good philosopher. It is the fact of my choosing to say that (and nothing further) that suggests it. See H. Paul Grice, 'Meaning', *Philosophical Review*, 66/3 (1957): 377–88.

We need not be stupidlly *engagé* of course: we do not think that some-one who has about as little as you can while being called 'rich' deserves the same attitudes as some hideous plutocrat, or that a young adult is all that importantly different from a child on the last steps towards adult-hood (although in this latter case many societies signal when childhood is to be regarded as ending by the use of coming-of-age ceremonies, which also have an interesting self-verifying element since being an adult is partly a matter of being treated as an adult). The terms point us in dif-ferent directions, just as we are pointed in different practical directions if we call a politician resolute and if we call him pig-headed. This is why, even if we are legislating and deciding, we can find ourselves in dispute with people who conduct the legislation and decisions differently. To take a contemporary example, the question 'Do you agree that Scotland should secede from the United Kingdom?' steers people in a very differ-ent direction from 'Do you agree that Scotland should remain part of the United Kingdom?' What are known as framing effects can easily sway votes.

The ways in which terms direct our minds explain why we are not content to replace terms with imprecise borders with more 'scientific' or quantitative measures. This may appear odd at first sight. After all, on the transition from poor to rich why don't we just make do with pre-cise numerical measures of income and capital? On the transition from child to adult, why not make do with precise numerical age, or a defined set of abilities? When we set out to count things, but find that we have identified the things in question in too vague a manner to allow our-selves to do so, we either give up or substitute a more precise definition of what we want. Why can't we just do the same kind of thing every-where? One answer is that it is often computationally or epistemologi-cally too costly. We do not always have precise quantitative measures. We need to be able to tell that we are faced with a child without hav-ing her birth certificate to hand. But another more interesting answer is that the uses of the term mean that it has to be vague. We want to say that the child is father of the man when it would not do at all to say that the person of less than such-and-such an age or with less than such-and-such a set of capacities, is father of the man; Wordsworth's thought cannot afford to lose the fact that childhood lasts for a long period or that growing up is an extended process, gradually shading into the adulthood which is its offspring.

IV

There are within analytical philosophy resources that challenge the Fregean paradigm. The most powerful of these derive from the tradition of pragmatism, as it descends from William James, through the later Wittgenstein, to J. L. Austin to the present day.[16] Here language is conceived as holistic, dynamic, and thoroughly embedded in the 'stream of life' of its users. The phrase is Wittgenstein's, and is something of a leitmotif for his later philosophy, itself a decisive turning away from the Fregean work of the *Tractatus Logico-Philosophicus*. Another of Wittgenstein's later slogans that (often) 'meaning is use' does not adequately mark the contrast, since a Fregean can perfectly well accept that the meaning of a sentence is its use, but then go on to identify use in terms of its role as a vehicle for thoughts, conceived in the way I have tried to describe. For the pragmatic tradition 'use' is identified instead through the activities and routes of inference, feeling, motivation, or other mental and social change that words can effect. 'In the beginning was the deed' said Goethe, in a quotation Wittgenstein especially liked, and if we add that words are deeds we have the full flavour of pragmatism.

The battle lines between this and more orthodox analytic approaches to language are hard to discern, and the scene of innumerable skirmishes. Applied to poetry, however, the change is reasonably clear. Instead of wondering what the poet means and whether what she says is strictly and literally true, or true in some different poetic or metaphorical sense, the pragmatist is happy to ask whether the work is exciting, interesting, pleasurable, insightful, or whether it leads the mind in interesting directions, generating pleasures and reflections, or even whether it breathes redemptive, reconciling, or regenerative powers. The emphasis is on process not product, with the poem seen as the catalyst for a process of listening, reading, and reflecting, rather than as the delivery of a final product. The question will not be, for instance, 'Do you understand X?' but 'How do you listen to X?' Even confusion and bewilderment might be valuable responses to a poem, if it succeeds in making us aware that things are indeed confusing and bewildering.

---

[16] Of course pragmatism in this sense has nothing to do with cost-benefit calculations, lack of principle, or the generally grubby approach to practical affairs that so troubled thoughtful Victorians. It is just the emphasis on practice: on doing things with words.

Judging from her rather unreliable memory for poetry, Alice may not have been a great literary critic, but she made the right remark after hearing the nonsense poem Jabberwocky: 'Somehow it seems to fill my head with ideas—only I don't exactly know what they are.' We are allowed this response to Jabberwocky but might fail a literary appreciation class if we said the same about Emily Dickinson, or parts of Blake or Herbert. Here, however, the analytic philosopher who is fortified by the pragmatist tradition may prove surprisingly permissive. One of the famous texts of that tradition was J. L. Austin's *How to Do Things with Words*, and one of the messages of that book is that there are innumerable things to be done with words. Filling someone's head with a kaleidoscope of half-formed or evanescent images and ideas is not the least of them. 'I heard a fly buzz when I died' are, after all, the words of a speaker who has also stepped through a looking-glass.

The emphasis on the actions that give rise to words, and the multiple things that we do with them, is a welcome part of a general movement in contemporary philosophy. This goes under the heading of 'naturalism' (philosophy is unpoetically riddled with -isms) and the word indicates a general flight from an over-intellectualized, rationalistic, Cartesian, and Fregean approach to our thoughts and their expression in words. For the naturalist the human subject is essentially embodied, not only in a physical or animal form, but in a culture, a history, and a particular economic, social, or personal context. Not only is this so, but we are creatures in time, and reading and reflecting are temporal processes, not the simple delivery of a cut and dried proposition in the mind. This is not something to regret or to tiptoe past, but to celebrate. It generates difficulties: as I sketched earlier, the Fregean paradigm has an important role to play, and we cannot return to an eighteenth-century view of language in which a private cacophony of associations means that it would be at best accidental if we ever managed to understand one another.

Fortunately there are stabilizing forces, although rocking the linguistic boat is surely one vital function of the poet. In one culture we share not only a language, but also innumerable histories and practices. These stabilize our words enough for our everyday needs, even if not necessarily for all our creative needs. Diversity exists, and with it the potential for misunderstandings, bent understandings, or even changed and improved understandings. It may be either exhilarating or treacherous, but in either event it lives on the back of a shared form of life, and therefore shared uniformities. Even the poet starts with a shared language. But a poetic sensitivity to those uniformities, or even the ability to bend and transcend them, is unquestionably our best guide to who we are, and even to where we ought to be heading.

6

The Spoken and the Written
An Ontology of Poems

Anna Christina Soy Ribeiro

I Introduction

It is the year 2015 and the written word is a well established and ubiquitous means of communication, whether this involves handwriting, printed matter, or the virtual texts of cellular phones or computer screens. This pervasive predominance of the written makes it especially poignant and remarkable that, in various parts of the globe, oral poetic traditions in many respects just like those of antiquity continue to thrive. The *griots* of West Africa have been chanting their histories and their praises for at least 700 years;[1] in the Basque Country the *Bertsolari* poetic contests have moved from the countryside and are now sponsored by the government; in Central Asia the bard tradition lives on; in Brazil, whether in the busy urban streets of São Paulo or in the north-east countryside where they originated, *repentistas* continue to amuse passers-by or restaurant patrons with improvised, chanted poetry accompanied by the guitar or the tambourine. Verbal duels of the *repentista* and the *Bertsolari* kind, in particular, exist in numerous cultures: there is the Italian *contrasto*, the African-American dozens (of which rap battles are a manifestation), the Ghanaian *haló*, the Yemenite *balah*, the Sumatran *didong*, the Argentinian-Chilean *payada*, the Lebanese *zajal*, the Kazak *aitys*, the Sardinian *gara poetica*, the

---

[1] The first known description of *griots* is due to Ibn Battuta, who visited the kingdom of Mali in 1352. See Thomas A. Hale's *Griots and Griottes: Masters of Words and Music*. Bloomington and Indianapolis: Indiana University Press, 2007, esp. ch. 1, 'A Job Description for Griots', 18–58.

Bolivian *coplas*, and many others.[2] Besides history, praise, and contest oral poems, which are mainly performance practices, the practice of chanting while weaving endures at least in Central Asia and northern India, with some scholars arguing that it may be at the very origins of Indo-European poetry.[3] Given that weaving goes back at least 8,500 years,[4] and that the description of poetic composition in terms of weaving words together (and all the variations on this theme) pervades poetic traditions from our earliest records,[5] it is easy to agree that at least some forms of poetry may owe their origins to weaving songs and work songs in general. Other scholars prefer to focus on verbal contests, finding it in lyric, drama, and epic.[6] Indeed, for all their differences, the demands of cooperation and competition may nevertheless both be at the roots of our literary practices.[7] Be that as it may, these verbal practices are the unlikely survivors of our literary ancestors, ancestors who may go back 10,000 to 40,000 years.[8] They are poems: poems composed and performed in the way that poems were originally made and performed, namely, orally, by declaiming or chanting, with minimal or no musical accompaniment, and often as a verbal dialogue or duel—much in the same way that slam poetry contests are run in numerous American cities today.[9]

[2] Except for the Brazilian *repentistas*, all of these are discussed by Valentina Pagliai in 'The Art of Dueling with Words: Toward a New Understanding of Verbal Duels across the World', *Oral Tradition*, 24/1 (2009): 61–88.

[3] See Anthony Tuck, 'Singing the Rug: Patterned Textiles and the Origins of Indo-European Metrical Poetry', *American Journal of Archaeology*, 110 (2006): 539–50.

[4] See Sarah B. Pomeroy et al., *A Brief History of Ancient Greece: Politics, Society, and Culture*. Oxford: Oxford University Press, 2008, 12.

[5] See also M. L. West, *Indo-European Poetry and Myth*. Oxford: Oxford University Press, 2007, esp. ch. 1, 'Poet and Poesy' (26–74), where he reviews the various conceptions of poetry—as weaving, as carpentry, as construction, and as recall. West also draws our attention to the common root for the words *text* and *textile* (Latin *texere*, to weave). The ultimate Indo-European root is *taks, which also gave us *techne*, a word whose original use was for carpentry, constructing, building, and that gave us the words technique, craft, and art.

[6] For instance, Derek Collins, *Master of the Game: Competition and Performance in Greek Poetry*. Cambridge, MA: Harvard University Press, 2004.

[7] I have argued for this in 'Literature'. In A. C. S. Ribeiro (ed.), *Continuum Companion to Aesthetics*. London and New York: Continuum, 2012, ch. 9, 125–41, esp. 125–9.

[8] If we may take contemporary Australian aboriginal practices as possible indicators of how things stood at the time of Western cave paintings, it may be that Western cave dwellers also used the paintings as springboards for ritual storytelling accompanied by music and dance.

[9] Slam poetry is part of a larger 'movement' called 'spoken word poetry' whose adherents may not realize that, rather than being something new and that goes against the

Awareness of the abundance, universality, antiquity, and resilience of oral poetic traditions should give us pause when we build our philosophical theories about poetry and about literature in general. Philosophers of literature have by and large theorized about literature from a writing and print culture perspective, focusing on works in writing cultures as paradigmatic and generally ignoring oral poems. Indeed, most of them seem altogether unaware of the very existence of oral poetic traditions, or of the rich scholarly literature on them. But the oral tradition is historically and numerically primary (oral poems came first, and there are many more of them than written poems), and thus oral poems, rather than written ones, should be seen as paradigmatic. We reverse this natural order only to the detriment of our theories, and to the misrepresentation of the practices we seek to analyse.

Awareness and understanding of the oral poetic traditions is particularly important when it comes to the ontology of poems. In writing cultures today we usually think of a poem as an unchanging sequence of words neatly printed on a page in lines of various lengths, to be read in silence and solitude. However, the vast majority of poems, from the millennia that preceded the printing press and even writing, up until this day (as the numerous examples just given show), have no fixed texts (the words and their order may vary), were declaimed in public, and were transmitted orally and not by written or printed copies. Many of the greatest, foundational works of literature—*The Iliad, The Odyssey, The Vedas, Beowulf, The Niebelung*—were not recorded in writing until centuries after they were first created, and innumerable bards contributed to the texts we now have of them. Imagine that the plays of Shakespeare had been transmitted orally for the past four centuries, with all the changes that mode of transmission would have engendered, and only now we had the means, and the desire, to freeze them in a written record. How many conflicting texts would we have for *Hamlet*? Undoubtedly more than the current three.

When we look beyond the print culture to which we now belong, we are forced to ask the question about what kind of entity a poem is in a different manner. For instance, prior to the question whether a single

'tradition' of poetry written for the page, it is a harking back to the original poetic practices—a harking back to the real tradition, one which began to fade with the invention of the printing press. Indeed, 'spoken word' and 'oral' only make sense as qualifiers of 'poetry' in a culture where written poetry has become the standard.

text can comprise two works—the 'Pierre Menard problem' that has so preoccupied philosophers[10]—we must deal with a question that can only strike us as peculiar from a writing culture perspective: how can a single work have so many texts? In the Menard case, we asked how two authors can compose two different works by means of the same text, but now we must ask: how can a single poem have so many authors, when they are each composing a different text? Other questions emerge from an awareness of the workings of oral poetic traditions. Is the question concerning the relation of a work to its copies an important one, since so many oral poems have no copies, and so many are nonce-poems, composed in and for a single performance? Is there a single ontological kind when it comes to poetry, or are there different kinds, depending on the poetic tradition from which the work emerged?

We know that a painting can only exist in one place at any given time, and finding the *Mona Lisa* anywhere other than the Louvre would make us scream forgery or robbery. Yet we do not blink at learning that a poem was read or uttered at different times in the same place, and at different places at the same time, and we realize that these events resulted in no alteration in the work itself. On the other hand, some poems in oral practices are unique events, composed on the spot in accordance with predetermined rules, and neither recorded nor repeated. They therefore lack the stable, repeatable element that is found is many poems. So where, and what, is the poem? To what ontological category does it belong, and what are its properties? Does it exist as an abstract universal, the way the number two does? Does it exist as a concrete particular, the way my copy of Cecília Meirelles's poems does? Should we conceive of its existence rather as a mental event in the mind of its creator? Or should we conceive of it as an event in the minds of readers or listeners? Like musical works and unlike paintings or marble sculptures, poems are made up of elements such as words and rhythms whose ephemeral character constitutes a difficult obstacle for an account of their mode of existence.

Bearing in mind the poetic practices of both oral and writing cultures, my proposal is as follows: a poem is an intentional abstract

---

[10] See, for instance, Nelson Goodman and Catherine Elgin, 'Interpretation and Identity: Can the Work Survive the World?', *Critical Inquiry*, 12 (1986): 567–74; Gregory Currie, 'Work and Text', *Mind*, 100 (1991): 325–40; and Paisley Livingston, *Art and Intention: A Philosophical Study*. Oxford: Oxford University Press, 2005, ch. 5.

artefact; a *type*, consisting of an *instantiation template*, whose creation is spatio-temporally located via its original token, and thus embedded in either a *declamation-based* or an *inscription-based practice*, which will dictate the kinds of ontological strictures embodied in that original token and required of all future tokens. As the examples given show, declamation[11] and inscription practices often exist concurrently in a given culture, although they loosely map onto oral and writing cultures. A declamation-type poem will typically *be linguistically fluid* (words and word order may vary, while the work remains the same) and allow for, indeed usually demand, extemporaneous creativity in accordance with the instantiation template. An inscription-type poem will be *linguistically rigid* (words and word order may not vary if the work is to remain the same). The *tokens* of a poem are either its declamations (or, more humbly, its 'soundings'), aloud or inwardly, as produced in accordance with the original template, extemporaneously, from memory, with the aid of an inscription, or by a recording such as an audiobook, or its soundings plus inscriptions, in the case of picture-poems, or any poem in which the graphic aspect is a relevant property of the work. What is important in a token is not how it is produced—a computer sounding may do, and a computer 'inscription' will do—but that it allow for the work to be experienced. The *experience* of the poem by a listener or reader may involve either 'hearing in' (hearing meaningful words and sentences in a string of sounds, which will in turn enable one to construct the further layers of meaning of the work, and generate an interpretation of it) or, in the case of picture-poems, 'hearing in' plus 'seeing in', since, again, in picture-poems the graphic aspect is a property of the work.[12]

---

[11] I will primarily use the terms 'declaim', meaning 'to utter or recite with rhetorical effect', and 'declamation', although the lines between plain sounding out, expressive uttering, and chanting are not always easily demarcated. I opt for 'declamation' rather than 'recitation' because the latter is of memorized or rehearsed material, which need not be the case in the sounding out of a poem, and would not be the case in a computer-generated sounding out. Moreover, a recitation need not be expressive (the 'uttering' of poems nearly always is). 'Vocalization' is nicely generic with respect to the level of expressiveness, and does not imply the sounding out of something either memorized or extemporaneous. However, since it refers directly to the vocal tract and thus to sounds produced by human beings, it would exclude a 'sounding out' otherwise generated (say, by a computer). See *The American Heritage Dictionary of the English Language*, 5th edn. Boston: Houghton Mifflin Harcourt Publishing Co., 2011.

[12] As most philosophers of art will notice, I am here adopting Richard Wollheim's notion of 'seeing in', which he introduced to explain our experiences of paintings, to our

In sum, we have an abstract artefact in the instantiation template that is the type, a concrete event in the sounding out or inwardly of what the template dictates, and a mental event (however this is to be construed) in the experience of the work, which occurs via the hearing and/or seeing of the token.

Before elaborating on each of these points, I will offer some remarks on the ontological framework within which the account fits. Following the exposition and defence of my ontology of poems, I will outline some consequences of the view for the ontology of ancient works, for poetic practice and criticism, and for the appreciation of poems.

II Ontological Framework

In her *Fiction and Metaphysics* and in several subsequent papers, Amie Thomasson has developed what strikes me as the most sensible approach to the ontology of art on offer today.[13] Noting that the standard categories of being—concrete and temporal versus abstract and eternal—do not account for the properties of certain kinds of artworks, she opens a space for a third possibility, that of an *abstract artefact*: 'that is, entities that are abstract in the sense of lacking a spatio-temporal location but that (unlike platonistic abstracta) are created, come into existence at a certain time, may change, and may cease to exist' ('Debates about the Ontology of Art', 247).

Why should we countenance abstract artefacts? Because, Thomasson argues, 'what determines what ontological sort of thing our terms pick out' is 'the beliefs and practices of those who ground and reground the reference of the terms in question' (248)—in the case of art, the practitioners and appreciators of the various art forms. Thus Thomasson advises us to look to the artistic practices themselves and describe them,

experience of the visual aspect of pattern poems, and positing an analogous 'hearing in' to explain our experience of the linguistic aspect of poems. See *Art and its Objects*, 2nd edn. Cambridge: Cambridge University Press, 1980.

[13] Amie Thomasson, *Fiction and Metaphysics*. Cambridge: Cambridge University Press, 1999. See also her 'The Ontology of Art'. In Peter Kivy (ed.), *The Blackwell Guide to Aesthetics*. Oxford: Blackwell, 2004, 78–92; Thomasson, 'The Ontology of Art and Knowledge in Aesthetics', *Journal of Aesthetics and Art Criticism*, 63/3 (2004): 221–9, and 'Debates about the Ontology of Art: What are We Doing Here?', *Philosophy Compass*, 1/3 (2006): 245–55.

rather than, as 'revisionists' have argued, [14] to 'correct' the folk concept because it seems to be inaccurate and/or inconsistent, and (possibly for this reason) should not be determinative when it comes to the ontological analysis of it. Art, unlike numbers and stones, is a cultural practice, whose products emerge from the intentional acts of human beings, and, as Thomasson argues, the revisionist 'owes us compelling pragmatic reasons to replace our standard conceptual scheme' with, say, one that proposes that a work of art is not the painting I see before me, but rather an 'imaginary experience',[15] an 'action type'[16] or a 'performance'[17] that culminated in the painting (252). By rightly giving art practitioners and appreciators the conceptual prerogative, Thomasson accounts for the 'extraordinary' ontological space that human inventions occupy, and directs philosophers towards, rather than away from, the art practices they seek to understand:

The only plausible views will be those that simply make explicit the conditions for existence and identity built into our practices for treating works of art as here or there, surviving or being destroyed, etc.—it can't turn out that these practices are all wrong, and we are all terribly mistaken about what sorts of things works of art really are. (251–2)

This should be our approach even when the practices are not precise— for, if our ontology is to reflect those practices, imposing precision where precision is not found would be tantamount to misdescribing the practice. Another important consequence of this view is that an ontological account aimed at suiting all kinds of art works—paintings and sculptures, jazz and symphonies, novels and poems—equally well is unlikely to succeed. Since the art practices and their products are so varied, an ontology that is to reflect this is likely to be varied as well.

In what follows I hope to do Thomasson's view justice by offering an ontology of poems (not of all kinds of literary works) that will stay as close to the ground of poetic practices old and new, near and far, as I can manage to keep it. Describing them will be hard enough a task; I hope

[14] E.g. Nelson Goodman, *Languages of Art: An Approach to a Theory of Symbols*. Indianapolis: Bobbs-Merrill, 1968. Nicholas Wolterstorff, *Works and Worlds of Art*. Oxford: Oxford University Press, 1980. Julian Dodd, *Works of Music: An Essay in Ontology*. Oxford: Oxford University Press, 2007.

[15] See R. G. Collingwood, *The Principles of Art*. Oxford: Clarendon Press, 1938.

[16] See Gregory Currie, *An Ontology of Art*. London: Macmillan, 1989.

[17] See David Davies, *Art as Performance*. Malden, MA: Blackwell Publishers, 2004.

the result will be sufficiently illuminating to discourage any desire for revisionism.

III   An Ontology of Poetic Works

Philosophers of music often specify what tradition their ontological accounts are meant to address: works in the Western classical tradition since the eighteenth century, when the writing of scores became the norm (not for the primarily oral traditions that preceded them); jazz, rock works, and so on.[18] Philosophers of music thus underscore the importance of attending to the particular features of a musical practice in providing an accurate ontological account of the works in that practice. By contrast, philosophers of literature have typically assumed that what is good for Milton is just as good for Homer—further, that Milton is the model according to which Homer should be understood. But a cursory knowledge of pre-modern literature[19] will quickly show us that the spread of literacy and the advent of printing have greatly altered both the composition and reception of what we today call poems, and that Homer and Milton stand for two strikingly different models. To stay with these two giants of Western literature, the following example will illustrate the basis of my point: we would not accept a copy of *Paradise Lost* from which any of its books were missing as a proper inscription of that work. However, the latest translation of the *Iliad* does just that: it leaves out

---

[18]   E.g. Jerrold Levinson notes that his inquiry is confined to 'that paradigm of a musical work, the fully notated "classical" composition of Western culture'. 'What a Musical Work Is.' *In Music, Art, and Metaphysics: Essays in Philosophical Aesthetics.* Ithaca, NY: Cornell University Press, 1990, 63–88, 64–5.

[19]   As Walter J. Ong rightly notes in *Orality and Literacy*, to call it 'literature' at all is a misnomer, since the term implies that it is written down: 'the relentless dominance of textuality in the scholarly mind is shown by the fact that to this day no concepts have yet been formed for effectively, let alone gracefully, conceiving of oral art as such without reference, conscious or unconscious, to writing. This is so even though the oral art forms which developed during the tens of thousands of years before writing had no connection to writing at all' (30th anniversary edn with additional chapters by John Hartley. London and New York: Routledge, 2002, 10). 'Oral literature' is for him a 'preposterous', 'monstrous concept', and 'thinking of oral tradition . . . as "oral literature" is rather like thinking of horses as automobiles without wheels' (11–12); 'you cannot without serious and disabling distortion describe a primary phenomenon by starting with a subsequent secondary phenomenon and paring away the differences' (13). In terms of visual art, we could say that this would be like thinking of painting as photography without film.

book 10 in its entirety, on the basis of scholarly theories that argue that book 10 is a later addition and thus not 'genuine' Homer.[20] This is possible (whether or not we like the result) because, while there is only one text of Milton's work, one composed solely by him and that he sanctioned as authoritative, Homer has been 'handed down to us in one thousand and a half ancient manuscripts and at least two hundred medieval ones'.[21] In what sense, if any, did Homer, if he existed, sanction those texts? The most ancient sources, namely the Ptolemaic papyri, contain nearly 600 fragments, but the earliest are from the third century BCE, at least five centuries after the presumed date of its initial composition some time between 1000 and 800 BCE:

> When taken altogether, Homeric papyri reveal a state of the Homeric texts in antiquity that can be quite surprising. There are numerous verses in the papyri that are seemingly intrusive from the standpoint of the medieval vulgate. These additional verses, the so-called plus verses, are not present in the majority of the medieval manuscripts of the *Iliad*. Other verses that are canonical in the medieval manuscripts are absent from the papyri—these may be termed minus verses. Also prevalent is variation in the formulaic phrasing within lines. In other words, it seems from this most ancient evidence that the poems were performed and recorded with a considerable amount of fluidity in antiquity. It is not until about 150 BCE that the papyrus texts begin to stabilize and present a relatively more uniform text. . . . The early Homeric papyri are the vestiges of a once vibrant performance tradition of the *Iliad* and *Odyssey*. In such a tradition no poem is ever composed, performed, or recorded in exactly the same way twice. In the earliest stages of the *Iliad* and *Odyssey*, each performance would have resulted in an entirely new composition. By the time of the first papyrus fragments, the oral composition and performance tradition of Homeric epic poetry had died out.[22]

---

[20] The translation is by Stephen Mitchell (New York: Free Press, 2011). Mitchell is following the text of M. L. West, *Homeri Ilias: Recensuit / testimonia congessit. Volumen prius, rhapsodias I–XII continens.* Stuttgart and Leipzig: Bibliotheca Teubneriana, 1998. West's version of the *Iliad* is thoroughly criticized by Gregory Nagy in the *Bryn Mawr Classical Review*, 12 Sept. 2000 <http://bmcr.brynmawr.edu/2000/2000-09-12.html>. A superb review of Mitchell's translation is Edward Luttwak's 'Homer Inc', *London Review of Books*, 34/4 (Feb. 2012): 3–8.

[21] Jean-Fabrice Nardelli, review of M. L. West (ed.), *Homerus Ilias volumen alterum, rhapsodiae XIII–XXIV* (Munich and Leipzig: K. G. Saur, 2000), *Bryn Mawr Classical Reviews*, 21 June 2001, <http://bmcr.brynmawr.edu/2001/2001-06-21.html>.

[22] Casey Dué, *Homer and the Papyri: Introduction*, Cambridge, MA: Center for Hellenic Studies, Harvard University, 2012, <http://chs.harvard.edu/wa/pageR?tn=A rticleWrapper&bdc=12&mn=1168>. See also the opening remarks on the CHS *Homer Multitext Project* page for more information on how oral epic poetry is composed (I do not give a link here because the CHS links to its subpages are not all stable).

Surely 'an entirely new composition' is an exaggeration to which this author would not seriously subscribe, but one gets the point: there was a great deal of variation from one performance to another. And Homer is no exception: textual fluidity is a hallmark of oral poems. The philosopher of literature, as is the case with the philosopher of music, must be cognizant of the various forms and genres that make up our literary history, and how they have been transformed over the millennia, if her theoretical claims about the practice are to have a firm basis. In this case, taking poems from writing traditions as our paradigm is very likely to mislead us about their ontology. This is because poems composed chiro- and typographically are fixed-text works. Taking fixed-text works as standard has led philosophers such as Nelson Goodman and Catherine Elgin to equate works with texts,[23] and even critics of this view to approach it from a fixed-text perspective.[24] While their many criticisms of Goodman's view are apposite, a more fundamental problem was overlooked: the vast majority of poems throughout history have no fixed texts. Their works are linguistically fluid, changing from performance to performance.

The only philosopher who seems to have noticed this is Robert Howell. In 'Ontology and the Nature of the Literary Work',[25] Howell makes the existence of non-fixed text works the crux of his criticism of most ontological accounts of literary works to date.[26] Surveying numerous ontological views, from Charles Stevenson in the 1950s to Jerrold Levinson in the 1990s, Howell concludes that 'everyone in the analytic tradition' (1) 'has approached literature as though it were . . . an ontologically

---

[23]   See Goodman and Elgin, 'Interpretation and Identity'.

[24]   See references in n. 10. The one exception seems to be Barbara Herrnstein Smith: see her 'Literature as Performance, Fiction, and Art', *Journal of Philosophy*, 67/16 (1970): 553–63, 556.

[25]   *Journal of Aesthetics and Art Criticism*, 60/1 (2002): 67–79.

[26]   Howell leaves out speech-theoretical accounts such as those of William Tollhurst and Samuel Wheeler III, 'On Textual Individuation', *Philosophical Studies*, 35/2 (1979): 187–97. Also not considered are performance accounts such as Barbara Herrnstein Smith's 'Literature as Performance', and J. O. Urmson's 'Literature'. In G. Dickie and R. J. Sclafani (eds), *Aesthetics: A Critical Anthology*. New York: St Martin's Press, 1977, 334–41. An important early work left out of Howell's consideration is Austin Warren and René Wellek's 'The Mode of Existence of the Literary Work', in their *Theory of Literature* (1947). However, since they draw on Roman Ingarden's influential *The Literary Work of Art* (Tr. George G. Grabowicz. Evanston, IL: Northwestern University Press, 1973 [1931]), and Howell rightly points out a fundamental shortcoming of Ingarden's view (see p. 76), one can surmise he would have similar criticisms of theirs.

uniform phenomenon' and (2) 'seem[s] clearly to regard all literary works as involving type sequences of words'; more specifically, 'that a work involves a *fixed* type of arrangement of linguistic entities'.[27] He points out the pioneering work of Milman Parry and Albert B. Lord on contemporary Serbo-Croatian oral epics that revolutionized Homeric scholarship, and the work of others who have built upon this important foundation.[28]

Unfortunately, Howell stops at critique and despairs of the possibility of offering a positive account for such a vast and variegated group: 'it is not possible', he says, 'in any informative, general way, to fix an ontological kind such that, necessarily, all works of literature fall into that kind. Literary works—and, I believe, works of the other arts—do not form such a kind.'[29] At best, he claims, 'we can arrive at a "natural history" of the principal ontological kinds of works in a given society, but we cannot devise a general, comprehensive account that is both informative and philosophically interesting of the type of any (possible) work of literature'.[30]

I share Howell's scepticism about the likelihood of a single ontology serviceable for all kinds of art works, but I see no reason to despair when it comes to literature. That said, I confine myself here to the ontology of poems, leaving out novels, essays, and so on. When we look closely at oral traditions, and at how oral poets learn to compose-perform (for they compose as they perform), we see that what they learn may be conceived as 'templates for instantiation', a set of patterns and rules used to generate an instance of a poem with a specific word sequence. These instantiation templates will be more or less fixed, by metrical structure, rhyme patterns, formulas, order of events, and so on, in accordance with the poem, the poetic practice (e.g. verbal duels) and more generally the poetic tradition. The poet learns the various patterns and rules that make up a given template, and exhibits her mastery in declaiming the poem in a manner that combines memorization and skilful use of the patterns with creative embellishment within the template's constraints. In oral traditions, the instantiation template nearly always linguistically underdetermines the poet's performance; in order words, a work's text is fluid.

[27]   Howell, 'Ontology and Literary Work', 69–70; my italics.
[28]   See Albert B. Lord, *The Singer of Tales*, 2nd edn, ed. Stephen Mitchell and Gregory Nagy. Cambridge, MA: Harvard University Press, 2000. For further references, see Howell, 'Ontology and Literary Work', 78.
[29]   Howell, 'Ontology and Literary Work', 67.
[30]   Howell, 'Ontology and Literary Work', 67.

The instantiation template concept can also account for poems in writing traditions. As the centuries wore on, and writing and then printing became more widespread, and literacy rates rose, instantiation templates gradually 'hardened' linguistically. Repetitive formulaic phrases that served as signposts and fillers ('When Dawn woke up with her rosy fingers'), and that could be varied and moved around ('Wily Odysseus'), seem to have been the first to go. In many traditions, metre remained until quite recently as a strictly necessary dimension of poems. And in several cultures, for at least a couple of centuries after the invention of the printing press (that is, until a mere couple of centuries ago), a manuscript tradition held its ground that retained many characteristics of oral traditions, including the communal sharing of works in person (rather than solitary reading), improvisation within set parameters, textual fluidity, and even verbal duelling in the form of response poems.[31] Oral traditions die hard, and, as I have noted, there are many oral poetic practices still alive today. Eventually, however, in print cultures literature became institutionalized, and the book came to dominate, doing away with textual malleability. The poetic instantiation template came to be simply a unique set of words, whose instantiation involved no more than the declamation or sounding out (or inwardly, in silent reading) of those very words. Creative variation (upon themes, within metrical constraints, by means of formulaic phrases), once expected and even demanded, was now forbidden: with authorship came authority.

Textual fluidity in oral and manuscript traditions is true of the lyric, the dramatic, and the epic poem. This is not to say that *all* poetry was textually fluid until a couple of centuries ago, nor that all poetry was meant only to be heard and never to be seen. Some poems even in antiquity were meant for inscriptions and thus to be seen; their texts therefore tended not to vary. The illustration shows an example from 300 BCE, by the Greek poet Simmias of Rhodes.

---

[31] Arthur F. Marotti writes that 'in manuscript circulation [in Renaissance England] texts were inherently malleable, escaping authorial control to enter a social world in which recipients casually transcribed, revised, supplemented, and answered them, not particularly worried about changing an authorial "original." In fact, some authors expected and welcomed the changes that recipients of their works brought to them.' See his 'Malleable and Fixed Texts: Manuscript and Printed Miscellanies and the Transmission of Lyric Poetry in the English Renaissance'. In W. Speed Hill (ed.), *New Ways of Looking at Old Texts*. Binghamton, NY: Medieval & Renaissance Texts & Studies, 1993, 159–73, 160. Thanks to Marta Kvande for bringing this to my attention.

ΣΙΜΜΙΟΥ ΤΟΥ ΡΟΔΙΟΥ

Πέλεκυς, κτ᾽ ἢ πτας Θεοκρίτου.

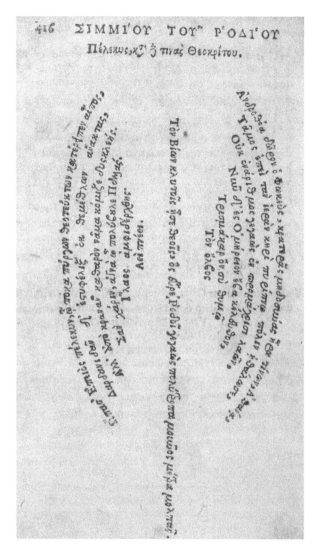

Theocritus, *Theocriti Aliorvmqve Poetarvm Idyllia. Eiusdem Epigrammata* ([Paris?] Excudebat Henricus Stephanus, 1579, p. 416). David M. Rubenstein Rare Book & Manuscript Library, Duke University. Thanks to David Pavelich and Megan Ó Connell of Duke University's Rubenstein Rare Book and Manuscript Library for this image.

The poem is called 'The Axe', and is meant to resemble one in the inscription of the words that make it up.[32] We thus see that no literary culture is ever exclusively an inscription, fixed-text culture, or exclusively an oral, fluid-text one. Our ontology must somehow accommodate both practices.

Following Thomasson, my claim is that poems are abstract artefacts. They are cultural entities that depend on the intentions of those embedded in their cultures to come into existence, and to continue in existence. The poem type consists of an instantiation template, whose creation is spatio-temporally located via its original token, and thus embedded in either a *declamation-based* or an *inscription-based practice*, which will dictate the kinds of ontological strictures embodied in that original token and required of all future tokens. A template may specify a particular set of words, in a particular order, or it may specify the various ways in which words may be combined, what formulaic phrases, if any, must be used and how, what metrical grid, if any, must be followed, what kind of variation in the words is allowed while still preserving work identity, and so on. Since these practices may exist concurrently in a given culture, it is the intentions of the first author that will establish in which practice her poem is to fit. I say first author because in oral poetic practices a poem may have many authors. Declamation-based poetic works are *linguistically fluid*: instances need not have all the same words in the same order as previous ones to be well formed, and thus legitimate, instances of a work. They are, however, *formally rigid*: themes, formulas, metre (the right combination thereof) must be present in an instance of a work for

[32] Translated: 'Epeius of Phocis has given unto the man-goddess Athena, in requital of her doughty counsel, the axe with which he once overthrew the upstanding height of god-builded walls, in the day when with a fire-breath'd Doom he made ashes of the holy city of the Dardanids and thrust gold-broidered lords from their high seats, for all hew was not numbered of the vanguard of the Achaeans, but drew off an obscure runnel from a clear shining fount. Aye, for all that, he is gone up now upon the road Homer made, thanks be unto thee, Pallas the pure, Pallas the wise. Thrice fortunate he on whom thou hast looked with very favour. This way happiness doth ever blow.' According to the translator, 'This poem was probably written to be inscribed upon a votive copy of the ancient axe with which tradition said Epeius made the Wooden Horse and which was preserved in the temple of Athena. The lines are to be read according to the numbering. The metre is choriambic, and each pair of equal lines contains one foot less than the preceding.' *The Greek Bucolic Poets*, tr. J. M. Edmonds. Loeb Classical Library, 28. Cambridge, MA: Harvard University Press, 1912, 487–9.

it to be well formed. An instance of the *Iliad* not in dactylic hexameter is not a well-formed instance of that template.

Unlike their templates, the tokens of a poem are temporal events. They are its declamations, as produced in accordance with the token or instantiation template, or its declamations plus inscriptions, in the case of picture/pattern-poems.[33] A declamation will, naturally, typically be produced by a human being, out loud. But it need not be. As noted earlier, declamation here is construed broadly so as to include the many kinds of 'sounding out' that are possible—including by computers, audiobooks, parrots, or whatever can generate the words that make up a given poem so that they are audible to the one seeking to experience it. Of course, this must also include that inward 'voicing' that those of us in print cultures have come to master and to take as the standard way in which to become acquainted with poems and other kinds of literary works. Importantly, this may be done with or without verve, and with or without understanding of what is being said by the one (or the thing) instantiating it. Understanding and interpreting are, strictly speaking, activities performed by the person experiencing the poem.

Another way in which to think of declamation-based and inscription-based types is in terms of completeness and creativity. An inscription-based type poem is *linguistically complete* in the sense that it includes all the words that must be the sounded out in its instantiation, but it is *phonetically incomplete* in the sense that, at each instance, it may be declaimed, or sounded out, differently: emphatically, languidly, with an accent, and so on. Instantiation templates in writing traditions have become largely *non-creative*, or *static*: alterations are no longer accepted to the words and their sequence, the only remaining creative element being the way in which one declaims those words. A declamation-based type poem is certainly phonetically incomplete, but it is also linguistically so, for it underdetermines the properties of each of its tokens to varying degrees. For most kinds of poems in oral traditions, the template type is by necessity incomplete, given the importance of embellishment

---

[33] Although an inscription is not a temporal event, the making of an inscription is. The production of a declamation and the production of an inscription both occur in time, and both are means of access to the poem: the former to its aural, the second to its visual properties.

and innovation in performance. Incomplete instantiation templates are creative templates.

How does one instantiate a poem? Either we remember its instantiation template, or we have an inscription of it that we are able to read and therefore declaim out loud or voice inwardly. The inscription of the template that we read, when we do, is an aid to instantiation. But we could alternatively simply learn or memorize the template, which is what professional oral poets do. Consider the following poem by Robert Frost:

> Nature's first green is gold,
> Her hardest hue to hold.
> Her early leaf's a flower;
> But only so an hour.
> Then leaf subsides to leaf.
> So Eden sank to grief.
> So dawn goes down to day.
> Nothing gold can stay.[34]

To instantiate it now, you had to read it off the printed page. Read it three more times and you may be able to declaim it to your friends at a dinner party without the aid of an inscription. You would then be doing the job of an oral poet, except in a very, very diluted version: even the professional poet today, though she may move us and win prizes like Ion once did, has none of the painstaking training professional oral poets once endured—from seven to thirty-six years, depending on the tradition.[35] Your contemporary declamation to your friends would be somewhere between the oral poet's creative embellishment of the token template, and the subdued silent reading. While the oral poet would give his own version of the text, your declamation would retain a slighter element of interpretation—emphases, stops, the aesthetic qualities of your voice—without textual variation, standard gestures, or possible pauses for explanation. In silent reading, these declamatory qualities are gone.

Instances of a poem may of course be recorded, on a cassette tape, an LP, a CD, an MP3 file, and any other technology yet to be invented that will allow us to hear the linguistic sounds that make up a given work.

---

[34] 'Nothing Gold Can Stay'. *The Poetry of Robert Frost*. Ed. Edward Connery Lathem. New York: Holt Paperbacks, 2nd rev. edn, 2002, 222–3.

[35] West, *Indo-European Poetry*, 30.

But just as print freezes the template type, so do recordings freeze the tokens. The situation is the same as in music. A composition that might have been fairly fluid in the sixteenth or seventeenth century will become considerably less so once it is scored in the eighteenth. And when a particular performance of it is recorded in the twentieth, then that instance is itself frozen in time (and may even foreclose creative interpretations of the work if it is highly influential). Someone familiar only with that recording will not have experienced the full range of possible interpretations of that work.[36] By contrast, even a parrot that memorized Frost's 'Nature's First Green is Gold' would 'declaim' it differently each time.

The *experience* of the poem by a listener or reader may involve either 'hearing in' (hearing meaningful words and sentences in a string of sounds, which will in turn enable me to construct the further layers of meaning of the work, and generate an interpretation of it) or, in the case of picture-poems, 'hearing in' plus 'seeing in', since in picture-poems the graphic aspect is a property of the work. Just as I hear the concept [TABLE] in the sound ['teɪbəl], so I see the shape of an axe in the layout of Simmias' poem. If I know ancient Greek, then I also hear [AXE] in 'Πελεκις'. My experience builds on this basic semantic understanding to generate further layers of meaning, all the way to a full-fledged interpretation of the work (if I feel so inclined).

Will any encounter with a token of a poem constitute an experience of that poem?[37] It is neither profitable nor charitable to the variety of human experience to dictate what will and will not count as an experience of a poem. Nevertheless, the minimal condition of hearing linguistically meaningful sounds in someone's utterances ought to be satisfied: someone who hears a poem in a language they do not understand cannot even begin to form an understanding and interpretation of the work, or appreciate any of its qualities aside from the purely sonic ones. It need hardly be said that some experiences will be 'fuller', more complex, than others,

---

[36] It is noteworthy how differently we (print culture denizens) think of the recording of a poem. When we hear Edna St. Vincent Millay declaim her 'Love is not all', we do not, I surmise, think of that experience as becoming acquainted with the poem so much as becoming acquainted with Millay's reading of the poem: a curiosity, unnecessary for knowing the work, uninformative about its essential properties. We hear it to learn something about Millay more so than to learn something about the poem. The situation seems quite different when it comes to music, except perhaps when the conductor or a performer has become a celebrity.

[37] I thank an anonymous reader for this question.

but it does not take a Homer scholar to experience Homer's works. It takes such a scholar to experience Homer more richly, to be sure, but we should not deny the label 'experience' of non-scholars (or that mysterious creature known as 'the common reader'). The reason is not merely that such a denial may smack of academic arrogance. More importantly, it is a question whether literary scholars *do* experience literary works in the appropriate manner. Where do we draw the line of scholarly erudition appropriate to the experience of a work? The demarcation cannot but be arbitrary. Should we grant 'experience' of the *Iliad* only to Martin West and Gregory Nagy? Tough, since they have different and conflicting views of that epic alone. This kind of question invariably runs into the 'paradox of distance' long ago discussed by Edward Bullough.[38] Homer (if he existed) was not composing for scholars; it is a question whether they can experience the work in the 'right' way, since they are arguably often unable to leave aside their scholarly concerns.

Sometimes we perform two activities, declaiming and listening. In those cases we are both performer and listener, 'instantiator' and 'experiencer'. It is important to see that these are conceptually distinct activities, even in silent reading. Just as we would not want to say that the person in the audience at the concert hall is the one instantiating the symphony (the orchestra is), so we would not want to say that the individual *as listener* is the one instantiating the poem. It is that individual *as declaimer* (whether out loud or in silent reading) who is. It is as a rule unavoidable that a declaimer or a musician experience the work they are performing, but they could in principle instantiate the work even being deaf, in which case they would be unable concurrently to experience it. Another situation that shows us that these are two distinct activities occurs when a declaimer instantiates a poem in a language that she does not understand. Here, too, she is not *also* experiencing the poem. I can instantiate a poem in Bulgarian if I learn how to pronounce the words, but since I do not know Bulgarian, I will not thereby have experienced the work (at best I have experienced its purely sonic aspects). But if a Bulgarian-speaking person heard me, then that person would have experienced the poem that I declaimed without experiencing (of course declamation is an experience just as everything else we do is; but it is not an experience *of* the

[38] Edward Bullough, '"Psychical Distance" as a Factor in Art and an Aesthetic Principle', *British Journal of Psychology*, 5/2 (1912): 87–118.

poem; it is an experience of declaiming a poem I do not understand). This is nothing new; actors often have to perform lines in languages in which they are not proficient.[39]

Poems, then, whether composed in an oral or a writing tradition, are templates for instantiation, intentional abstract artefacts with varying degrees of linguistic, thematic, and formal specificity. Their tokens or instances are the events of declamation that follow the template's patterns and rules, and may be realized in mechanical or non-mechanical ways, aloud or silently to oneself. Finally, we experience a poem by listening to its tokens, which may vary more or less from instance to instance in accordance with the demands of its template, and in accordance with the medium of instantiation (where that medium is a recording, there will be no variation).

IV Consequences of the View

We have seen that poems of the kind that existed in antiquity still exist today. We may ask, however, whether the poems of antiquity that have been preserved still exist in the manner they once did. Is the *Iliad* we read in one of its translations, from one of its texts, the same work that came into existence 3,000 years ago? There no longer are performances of it in the ancient sense (could there be?). Moreover, it is highly likely that, over the centuries, not only did its performances vary, but that they in turn affected the template itself, altering it, so that later instances had to comply with constraints that earlier instances did not. Today, the *Iliad* is associated with a set of texts—the surviving ancient inscriptions. So there is a sense in which the *Iliad* (and the *Odyssey*, and many other ancient works), although it doubtlessly still exists, no longer exists *in the manner it once did*, that is, as a performance work that is textually fluid and thus varies with each performance. What exist today are texts constructed on the basis of what were once performances, and therefore causally connected to the oral *Iliad*. The only variations today result from scholarly reconstructions on the basis of the extant records, not from novel generations

---

[39] Barbara Herrnstein Smith had already pointed this out in her excellent review of Nelson Goodman's *Languages of Art*: 'Although, in silent reading, the performer and audience are necessarily the same person, this should not obscure the fact that the reading consists of two theoretically distinct activities, only one of which is comparable to listening to music or looking at a picture' ('Literature as Performance', 556).

of text in accordance with the work's compositional rules by professional poets. Rather than the rule-governed oral improvisations of antiquity, its tokens today are word-by-word declamations that proceed from readings of one of its texts, or from memorization of one of its texts. So the advent of literacy, writing, and printing seems to have altered the ontology of such works in the sense that their templates no longer evolve as a result of the very creativity demanded of their instances. As writing became predominant in some cultures, poets no longer manipulated memorized patterns, and a poem came to be seen as identical with its text. Skilled manipulation of patterns within metrical or other restrictions, long the virtue of the poet, gradually faded away in typographical cultures, and it was replaced with a fetishism of the word order.

Attention to the oral roots of poetry is relevant not only to a better understanding of the ontology of poems. It also helps illuminate the history of poetry as well as of our critical and evaluative practices. The poet Amy Lowell was perhaps too negative when she wrote that 'no art has suffered so much from printing as has poetry', but it is undeniable that print has changed poetic practices enormously.[40] Over the centuries since printing established itself, books became more common, and literacy rose, poets gradually let go of the repetitive techniques that had previously been indispensable to their art. They no longer needed to declaim in public, and so they no longer needed to memorize. Audiences became readers, so they no longer needed the memory aids that held their attention during a declamation. Over time, an artistic virtue was made out of this historic contingency: a poem that held on to older practices—that is, a poem with a great deal of repetition, in whatever form—came to be considered old-fashioned, juvenile, unsophisticated, primitive.[41] If

[40] Amy Lowell, 'Poetry as a Spoken Art'. In Jon Cook (ed.), *Poetry in Theory: An Anthology*. Oxford: Blackwell Publishing, 2004, 69–74, 70. Originally published in *Poetry and Poets: Essays by Amy Lowell*. Boston and New York: Houghton Mifflin, 1930. Following the work of Eric Havelock (e.g. *Preface to Plato*. Cambridge, MA: Harvard University Press, 1963), Ong, *Orality and Literacy*, also argues that literacy, which only became truly widespread after the invention of the printing press, changed not only literature but also the very way we think and relate to the world around us. For a bucket of perhaps excessively cold water on Havelock's Homer-to-Plato, oral-to-written thesis, see John Halverson, 'Havelock on Greek Orality and Literacy', *Journal of the History of Ideas*, 53/1 (1992): 148–63.

[41] We may compare this with critical evaluation of stories, since narratives that have great heroes as protagonists and bizarre creatures as characters tend to be derided in the

poems were read aloud, a reading that highlighted metre, line breaks, or rhyme schemes came to be considered affected and thus defective. Rhyme schemes themselves came to be avoided; if they occurred at all, lines were enjambed in order to disguise them. Ultimately, we arrive at the various kinds of avant-garde poetry, many of them unthinkable prior to the printing press. In sum, a better poet came to be one who addressed herself directly to the mind, and at least pretended to bypass the ear. With few exceptions, critics came to prefer poets who did just that, who denied the oral roots that had defined poetry from its beginnings: 'The nearly universal critical bias against rhyme and meter as recently as ten years ago, especially in university writing programs, indicates how distant the poets in a print culture had become from the orality of verse.'[42]

Things have changed from the perspective of the appreciator of poetry as well. The experience of poems in a typographic (and now digital) culture has been fundamentally altered. The silent reading of poems is a vastly impoverished experience relative to its oral counterparts. This is so both aesthetically and cognitively (though only artificially do we separate these two aspects). The wealth of possibilities of sound as heard that serve both to please the ear and to affect our understanding of what is being said are severely minimized in silent reading.[43] The aesthetic dimensions of the human voice and the human presence in declamation are lost in private, mental reading. Many artistic properties are thereby foreclosed as well. It goes without saying that the social dimension of such artistic exchanges is nearly entirely gone; it becomes an abstraction in the mind of the reader rather than a live event. Imagine, by way of analogy, if we all learned how to read musical scores perfectly, and ceased to attend concerts. Similar, if not greater, losses would ensue. Would anything be thereby gained? It certainly would mean the development of cognitive skills most of us do not presently have. Other skills, and other

---

same manner. See Ong, *Orality and Literacy*, 69–70, on the emergence of the anti-hero in modern, post-print times.

[42] Dana Gioia, 'The New Oral Poetry: An Excerpt from the Essay "Disappearing Ink: Poetry at the End of Print Culture"'. In Mark Eleveld (ed.), *The Spoken Word Revolution Redux*. Naperville, IL: Sourcebooks, 2007, 242–6, 242. A similar change in both artistic and critical practices occurred in painting after the advent of photography. In this case, representation was to be avoided; abstract painting was thus born.

[43] I discuss the aesthetic-cognitive effects of poetic form in 'Relevance Theory and Poetic Effects', *Philosophy and Literature*, 37/1 (2013): 102–17.

experiences we greatly value, however, would be lost, such that it is hard to see that this exchange would be worthwhile.

There is a sense in which the poetic skill typical of oral cultures survives in song lyrics; but that is true only in a very meagre sense of that skill. Moreover, in song music typically drives the lyrics rather than being a mere accompaniment. There are exceptions, of course, but in any event, we do not need to settle for pop songwriters and singers as the true descendants of Homer and Sappho. As we have seen, oral poetic practices continue to thrive all around the globe. Perhaps more remarkable, they re-emerge even in quintessentially writing cultures such as that of modern American society. The spoken word poetry movement is proof in its very label that mainstream poetry is no longer spoken. But in its existence, it is also proof that poetry wants to speak, not to be mummified on a piece of paper, and that our oral heritage continues to live in us despite our own ample efforts to kill it.[44]

[44] Earlier versions of this paper were presented at the Universities of Murcia (Spain, 2010), Houston (2010), and Cincinnati (2012). Many thanks to Francisca Pérez-Carreño, Cynthia Freeland, and Jenefer Robinson for inviting me to each of these respective places, and to the audiences there for their helpful questions and comments. Thanks also to Paisley Livingston and to an anonymous reader of Oxford University Press for their comments on a recent draft.

7

Poetry and Truth

Roger Scruton

In 'The Origin of the Work of Art', Heidegger writes that 'the essence of poetry... is the founding (*Stiftung*) of truth'.[1] 'Founding' means 'bestowing, grounding and beginning', while 'truth', for Heidegger, names a process, an 'unconcealing', the authority for this being a somewhat forced etymology of the Greek word *aletheia*. Truth, he tells us, is a way in which things 'presence', so revealing their 'thingliness'. You could be forgiven for thinking that, in the context of this syntactical delirium, absolutely nothing is said by the assertion that the essence of poetry is the founding of truth. In these short remarks I hope to give a reading of that assertion, however, which makes it both important and true.

It is fairly obvious that Heidegger does not mean by 'truth' what, for instance, Tarski means in his great paper on the concept of truth in formalized languages. He is not writing about the *evaluation* of sentences as true or false, or the determination of truth-values by the semantic interpretation of syntactical parts. He is writing about a *revelation*, in which things come before the conscious mind in a way that shows what is otherwise hidden. 'Truth', he writes, 'is the original strife in which, always in some particular way, the open is won; that open within which everything stands and out of which everything withholds itself everything which, as a being, both shows and withdraws itself.'[2] Truth is a process which *wins through* to the reality of things. This reality consists in what things show, and what they withhold, when brought into the open. And poetry has a special part to play in this process: it is a 'bringing forth' which is also a 'bestowing'.

---

[1] Martin Heidegger, 'The Origin of the Work of Art', in *Off the Beaten Track*, ed. and tr. Julian Young and Kenneth Hayes. Cambridge, CUP, 2002, 47.
[2] Heidegger, 'Origin of the Work of Art', 36,

There are many religious texts which tell us that in this world we see 'through a glass darkly', and which promise another form of knowledge, acquired through spiritual discipline, through fasting and prayer, through the recital of sacred liturgies or perhaps only sacred syllables, whereby we confront things as God confronts them, so as to know them as they truly are. The 'truth' of things is that which is revealed when we see them at rest in their essences, so to speak, as God might see them when he wills them to be. Heidegger is attempting to give a secular version of this idea. And by attributing the process of revelation to *poetry*—in other words, to a human product, in which meaning is both created by human beings and also 'bestowed' by them—he can be understood as advocating revelation without God. In this he was at one with the poet Rainer Maria Rilke, who, in my view, is the real inspiration for Heidegger's view of poetry.

The idea that art can fulfil some of the promise of religion without the metaphysical payment is not new. In his great essay on 'Religion and Art' Wagner argued that religions have all misunderstood their own mission, wishing to propose as *true stories* what are in fact myths—in other words utterances of another kind, that cannot be spelled out in literal language.[3] The meaning of the myths must be grasped through art, which shows us the concealed deep truth of our condition, in dramatized and symbolic form. The truths hidden by religion, and revealed by art, are truths about us, about the archaeology of consciousness. Wagner is looking for a substitute for the religious worldview, another way of seeing our world *as if* the work of a creator, and *as if* we were its hidden goal. More bleakly, Nietzsche saw art and the aesthetic as the *successor* to the religious worldview, not a real compensation for what we lose when we discover that the world is purposeless, but the best that we can do to compensate for that discovery: 'we have art so that we will not perish of the truth'. Whether Heidegger was nearer to Wagner or to Nietzsche is, for my purpose, immaterial.

To explore the suggestion that poetry has something to do with truth we must first know what we mean by poetry. It is evident that poetic forms and poetic diction are by-products, and neither essential to the poetic enterprise nor always valued by those who engage in it. The heart of poetry is *the poetic use of language*. There is a way of using language

---

[3] Richard Wagner, 'Die Religion und die Kunst', in *Gesammelte Schriften und Dichtungen*, 2nd edn, 10 vols. Leipzig, 1887–8, x. 211.

that is fundamentally distinct from its everyday or scientific deployment, and it is this that is appreciated by the lovers of poetry. There is good, even beautiful, writing that is not poetic—the philosophical writing of Hume, for example, or the scientific writing of Darwin or Helmholtz. Such writers produce prose. The virtue of prose is the clear, precise, and literal description of its subject matter. The subject matter may be fictional—but still there is a distinction between the literal description of a fictional event and its poetic elaboration.

The poetic use of language may involve figures of speech, including metaphors, which do not describe the connections between things, but make those connections in the mind of the reader. Such connections can also be made by allusion, by irony, or by mere proximity, as in the following description of Octavia from *Antony and Cleopatra*:

> Her tongue will not obey her heart, nor can
> Her heart inform her tongue—the swan's down feather,
> That stands upon the swell at full of tide,
> And neither way inclines . . . [4]

Shakespeare simply puts two subjects side by side, and at the same time evokes, through the rhythm of the verse, the experience first of the one and then of the other, so that the two come together. But they come together in the feelings of the audience—it is as though two experiences bleed into each other to become one.

Every time a writer chooses an image so as to evoke something other than the thing that he or she is describing we have an instance of this poetic use of language. A simile might do as well as a figure of speech, or the connection might be merely suggested, as when Yeats writes

> Decrepit age, that has been tied to me
> As to a dog's tail . . . [5]

We think of the kind of things that are tied to dog's tails (certainly not age!) and of the circumstances in which this is done. And the ageing body of the poet inhabits then the same psychic space in the reader's mind as the ridiculous and humiliated dog.

---

[4]   William Shakespeare, *Anthony and Cleopatra*, 3. 2. 5–60.
[5]   W. B. Yeats, *The Tower: A Facsimile Edition*. New York: Scribner, 2003, 4.

Poetic diction and verse-forms are important, largely because they facilitate these 'extra-curricular' connections—they prompt our thoughts to take in matters that lie beyond the horizon of the scene described. Consider this stanza from Thomas Hardy:

> It will be much better when
> I am under the bough;
> I shall be more myself, Dear, then,
> Than I am now.[6]

This is almost prose; but not quite. The verse form, which fills out the third line to give a specious amplitude to the post-mortem anticipations of the imagined speaker, brings us to an abrupt dead end with the short line that follows. 'Than I am now' is so tight and bereft that you know that this speaker, who taunts his beloved with his future death, is dead already—dead to himself and to her. This connection is made, not in the things described, but in the feelings of the one who reads of them. Even without verse-forms and prosody it is possible to make connections through the rhythm, shape, and sound of a sentence without describing those connections directly, as all novelists know.

The poetic use of language deploys every device that can make the kind of connections that I have been describing: figures of speech, allusions, irony, and evocations induced by the sound and rhythm of the words. Many works of prose are really exercises in the poetic use of language—the *poèmes en prose* of Baudelaire, for example, or James Joyce's *Finnegan's Wake*. Contrariwise, many 'poems' are really versified prose, like the epics of William Morris. The distinction between the poetic and the prosaic use of language is a distinction that goes to the heart of aesthetics, since it outlines two distinct attitudes, both to language, and to the things that language describes. In an important sense the prosaic use of language is *instrumental*. The purpose is to place in the reader's mind a thought about something (which may be something fictional). The crucial feature of prose is its *aboutness*, the intentional relation with a subject matter, from which knowledge of that subject matter can be recuperated and put to use. Prosaic language is therefore guided by the interest in truth as correspondence—truth as discussed by Frege and Tarski. This

[6]   Thomas Hardy, 'When Dead'. In *Selected Poems*, ed. Robert Mezey. New York: Penguin Books, 1998, 170.

use of language requires the substitutivity of equivalent terms. In a prosaic sentence terms with the same sense can be replaced without defeating the purpose, so that both of the following might 'do just as well' for the author's purpose:

> A knight, it was announced, might use a mace or battle-axe at pleasure, but the dagger was a prohibited weapon.

> It was declared that mace and battle-axe were both permitted weapons for a knight, but that daggers were forbidden.

The reader might guess as to which of the sentences was written by Sir Walter Scott into the story of *Ivanhoe*. After all, they flow quite differently, and there are nuances in each that are not reproduced in the other. But the important point is that they are equally serviceable, for the purpose of moving the narrative along, and implanting in the reader's mind the information about the subject that is required by the story.

Things are quite otherwise with the poetic use of language. In an important sense the poetic utterance is to be understood *non-instrumentally*. Not only are the words and the allusions contained in them to be weighed and appreciated for their own sakes; the same is true of the subject matter too. The subject of the poem is not detachable from it in the way that the subject of prose is detachable. Of course, the poem might tell a story, like the *Iliad*, which could be told in another way. But if it is real poetry then much that it says will be lost when told in another way. The effect of poetry depends on the *way of telling*, or rather (to adapt a well-known distinction) on the *way of showing* what is told. Here I do not refer only to the specific words of the text, but also to such things as the order of events, the perspective from which they are recounted, the sequence of images, and the speed of the narrative. Homer is never at a loss for the right word, and he uses an amazing number of them; but he also abounds in easy-going formulae, which spare him the need to think of a new epithet when an old one will be just as serviceable. But Homer has the unfailing gift of arranging images, events, and actions in a sequence that causes each one to enter into fertile relation with its neighbours, so bringing the reader into the very centre of the drama and bringing the drama, as Heidegger would put it, 'into the open'.

The reader of Homer is invited not merely to take an interest in the action for its own sake, but also to attend to the way in which the action unfolds through the words. Neither the thing related, nor the relating of it, is treated instrumentally. Each detail is there for its own sake, and this applies as much to the language as to the story. Hence the text is not (as in prose) erased by its own aboutness. The sound of the words, their associations, the things they call to mind, and all the other ways in which words and things can be connected, begin to compete in the reader's or listener's mind with the semantic content.

Of course, whether a use of language is, in the sense I am considering, poetic or prosaic is a matter of degree. Many things go on at once when words are used, and a writer might insert poetic flights of fancy into a work of prose, as Boethius did in *The Consolation of Philosophy*, or prosaic explanations into a work of poetry as T. S. Eliot did in the notes to *The Waste Land*. Nevertheless there are two poles between which literary language can range, with pure semantically guided description at one pole, and pure evocation and association at the other. Corresponding to those two poles there is a contrast between a purely instrumental use of words and a use of words to create and bestow intrinsic value. Hence there really is such a thing as poetry, and it really does present what it describes in another way from the way that it is presented in prosaic narrative. The question we have to answer is whether this other way of presenting things is connected with another kind of truth—a kind of truth beyond that contained in the philosopher's idea of correspondence.

Notice that I have already used a Heideggerian idiom in describing the poetic use of language. I have suggested that, in this use, language can *bestow* intrinsic value on the subject that it describes. It renders that subject interesting *for its own sake*, and this idiom automatically takes us into the realm of philosophical aesthetics, as this has been charted since Kant. When Keats writes his 'Ode to the Nightingale', he does not describe the bird and its song only: he endows it with value. The nightingale shares in the beauty of its description, and is lifted out of the ordinary run of events, to appear as a small part of the meaning of the world. We may think that this brief encounter with a transfigured bird is an illusion, merely an effect of the poet's persuasive power. But, the poet is insisting, it is *not* an illusion. The meaning bestowed by the words is also instilled by them. Poetry transfigures what it touches, so that it is revealed in another way. If it does not do so it is not truly poetry, but merely rhetoric. There is a test of the value of poetic language and this test is that of truth—truth in something like the sense that Heidegger is getting at, truth as revelation, as the unconcealing of what is, in our instrumental and scientific ways of dealing with the world, hidden from us.

This does not mean that a poet can be indifferent to truth in its ordinary (semantic) sense. A number of authors have argued—to my mind convincingly—that poems contain and depend upon thoughts which are put forward as literally true. There are didactic poems, like Pope's *Essay on Man* or Wallace Stevens's 'Sunday Morning', in which the reader is being invited to agree with a particular point of view, and in which the seriousness and sincerity of that point of view are vital to the poetic effect. More generally, as R. K. Elliott argued in a distinguished article that appeared in *Analysis* nearly half a century ago, poetic diction makes sense only if the choice of words is governed by the same concern for truth that informs our ordinary discourse.[7] Language is an inherently truth-tracking tool, and we cannot use it, even in its poetic application, without relying upon this feature. Consider this flight of fancy from Verlaine ('Il Bacio'):

> Baiser! rose trémière au jardin des caresses!
> Vif accompagnement sur le clavier des dents
> Des doux refrains qu'Amour chante en les cœurs ardents,
> Avec sa voix d'archange aux langeurs charmeresses![8]

Outside the poetic context who would think of a kiss as a hollyhock in a garden? But it is true that hollyhocks grow in gardens. It is true too that caresses weave and cling like undergrowth, and that the kiss rises to another plane, as hollyhocks, the tallest of garden flowers, stand out above the undergrowth. It is nonsense to describe the kiss as an accompaniment played on the keyboard of the teeth, but then the teeth are like a keyboard, are made of the same material, and hold the kiss in place in something like the way that an accompaniment anchors a melody. As we are carried along by the poem we find no difficulty in absorbing the picture of kissing that it offers us, and the elaboration of this picture depends at every point upon the truth-tracking nature of language. The striking image of 'le clavier des dents' depends for its force on our knowledge of the mouth, the smile, the gateway to the other that the teeth can open and close, as well as our knowledge of the keyboard and its uses.

These truths upon which the poetic effect depends are not, however, the subject matter of the poem. They belong to the frame on which the

---

[7] R. K. Elliott, 'Poetry and Truth', *Analysis*, 27/3 (1967): 77–85.
[8] Paul Verlaine and Karl Kirchwey. *Poems Under Saturn*: Poèmes Saturniens, tr. Karl Kirchwey. Princeton: Princeton University Press, 2011, 98.

image is hung. As Peter Lamarque has pointed out, a work whose point is to express a truth is capable of paraphrase. A paraphrase that captured the thought (which had the same truth-conditions) would serve the purpose just as well.[9] But it is a commonplace of criticism that there is, in Cleanth Brooks's phrase, a 'heresy of paraphrase'—a heresy which stems from thinking that poetry is valued for what it literally says, rather than for its own special way of saying it.[10]

The point is clear. But it leaves us with two unanswered questions. First, what is the difference between a didactic poem and a work of prose? Secondly, what remains of the Heideggerian thesis that the essence of poetry is the 'founding' of truth? In response to the first of those questions philosophers and critics have variously claimed that the purpose of a didactic poem is not to persuade readers but in some way to help them to imagine the world as the poet describes it, to discover in themselves the experiential equivalent of a doctrine and thereby to understand a human possibility, whether or not they also endorse that possibility as one that they could or would live by. The poet and philosopher John Koethe suggests, in this connection, that what the didactic poem 'tries to do is not to persuade the reader of the truth of (the expressed) thoughts, but to get him so to speak, to enter into them'.[11] The idea is that we value poems not for the truth of what they say, but for the role that their thoughts might play in a life of feeling.

The point was made in other terms by T. S. Eliot, in an early essay on Shelley, and later, in *The Use of Poetry and the Use of Criticism,* where he tries to justify his low opinion of Shelley as a poet.[12] Eliot criticizes Shelley not for the atheistical views expressed in his poems—much as Eliot disapproved of them—but because these views are entertained (so Eliot claimed) in a puerile way. They are not put to the test, not given the kind of poetic examination which would show how a life of serious feeling could be built on them. They lack the seriousness and sincerity that would make them worthy of imaginative endorsement.

[9] Peter Lamarque, 'Poetry and Abstract Thought', *Midwest Studies in Philosophy,* 33 (2009): 37–52.
[10] Cleanth Brooks, *The Well Wrought Urn: Studies in the Structure of Poetry.* New York: Harcourt, 1968.
[11] 'Poetry and Truth', *Midwest Studies in Philosophy,* 33 (2009): 58.
[12] T. S. Eliot, *The Use of Poetry and the Use of Criticism: Studies in the Relation of Criticism to Poetry in England.* Cambridge, MA: Harvard University Press, 1986.

Such, in a nutshell, was Eliot's answer to the problem of 'poetry and belief', and, like Koethe's answer, it is incomplete. The argument tells us that poetry does not treat doctrinal statements as prose treats them, namely as statements to be judged for their truth-value. But it also tells us that poetry puts doctrine to the test in some way, and that this test has something to do with experience. We are fumbling our way towards the idea that poetry is really exploring (or bestowing) a truth of its own, not literal truth, to be sure, but something just as deserving of the name. Can we complete the thought?

We should make a distinction here between lyrical and dramatic poetry—between poetry that is presenting its own point of view, and poetry that articulates the state of mind of *another*, whose words are to be completed by a dramatic context. Ugly characters in drama can be given powerful verse, like Shakespeare's *Richard III*. And a bumbling old buffer can be prompted into poetry by ancient music, like the imagined speaker of Browning's 'A Toccata of Galuppi'. In most lyrical poetry, however, it is not 'another' who speaks, but the poem itself, and the poet in the poem. The contrast here is not sharp, since lyric poetry may suggest a dramatic context to fit the words. (Hence Browning's description of his poems as 'dramatic lyrics'.) Nevertheless, we are used to reading poetry in two different ways—as addressed to us directly, or as part of a dialogue between imagined speaker and imagined listener. Love lyrics and religious poetry like that of George Herbert provide an intermediate case. While addressed to another, in a defined context, the poet disappears behind his words, and leaves them as the universal expression of a state of mind that is available to all of us, should we choose to adopt his words.

Given these contrasting uses of poetic language we might be tempted to argue that the truth bestowed by poetry is simply a matter of 'truthfulness'—that is to say, truth to the state of mind that is ostensibly expressed, whether on behalf of an imagined character, or on behalf of the poet, or on behalf of the reader. Poetry succeeds when it is sincere, true to the sentiments that it claims and which command our respect; it fails when it lays claim to sentiments that it fails to encompass, because its words are false, banal, or empty. For example it may be composed of expressions which are borrowed, assumed as a matter of convention, riddled with clichés, so as to claim a grandeur or seriousness which it does not attain. The distinction between the true and the false in poetry is, on this view, the distinction between true and false sentiment, between real emotion and 'faking it'.

That is certainly the view that we might extract from the tradition of Anglophone criticism in our time, and notably from the essays of Leavis and Eliot. For those critics the principal failing exhibited by poetry is sentimentality, which lays claim to emotion in order to disguise the lack of it. The enemy is the 'undisciplined squads of emotion' evoked in *Four Quartets*, which swamp the poet's words with imprecise feelings that are not really feelings at all, since they come wrapped in clichés and stock devices, and avoid any direct encounter with reality. The task of the modern poet, as Eliot (borrowing from Mallarmé) expressed the point, is to 'purify the dialect of the tribe': that is, to find the words, rhythms, and images that would make contact with the world as it is lived by us, here, now. The poetic use of language is necessary because the world as lived is not the world as described. To convey the world as it is lived is to evoke both the object and the subject of consciousness. And it is to take a critical and exploratory stance towards them both. In this enterprise allusions are as important as statements. In Eliot quotations too are important, not in order to borrow others' sentiments, but in order to evoke a tradition of poetic reflection which stands in judgement on the poet's experience, and warns against the easy way of avoiding real predicaments through kitsch and cliché.

'Ash-Wednesday' opens with the following lines:

> Because I do not hope to turn again
> Because I do not hope
> Because I do not hope to turn
> Desiring this man's gift and that man's scope
> I no longer strive to strive towards such things . . . [13]

Only the last of those lines is wholly Eliot's. Cavalcanti's lament over his exile from Tuscany begins,

> *Perch'i' no spero di tornar giammai*
> *Ballateta, in Toscana*[14]

Eliot's 'to turn' echoes the Italian 'tornare', which here means to return, not to turn. Cavalcanti's geographical exile becomes, in Eliot's allusion, a metaphysical exile. The impossibility of turning back, of undoing what has

---

[13] T. S. Eliot, *Collected Poems, 1909–1962*. Franklin Center, PA: Harcourt Brace Jovanovich, 1991, 85.

[14] Guido Cavalcanti, *The Selected Poetry of Guido Cavalcanti: A Critical English Edition*, ed. Simon West. Leicester: Troubador, 2009, 22.

been done, is immediately connected to the loss of hope, and this hope, a
passing state of mind in Cavalcanti, becomes the centre of poetic attention
in Eliot. Cavalcanti laments the loss of his Tuscan home; Eliot the loss of
hope. The poem is about despair, and the despair that comes from guilt.
The fourth line is lifted straight from Shakespeare's sonnet no. 29 ('When
in disgrace with fortune and men's eyes . . . ') but with a subtle change of
'art' to 'gift'—so opening the way to a theological reading. Eliot has implicitly compared his poetical efforts with those of his great predecessors, borrowing and altering their words in order to emphasize how much he falls
short—and going on to write one of the greatest invocations of humility
in the English language. This artful use of quotation conveys the sense of
a burdened consciousness—a subjectivity shaped by other poets' sincere
expressions, full of a self-doubt which comes from the knowledge that the
needed words have already been found, but found in another context when
hope for this or that had been lost, but hope itself remained. Eliot is able
in this way to convey a new experience, one true to our time and our situation, one in which a kind of metaphysical bereavement is craving solace
and encountering only the discomfort of comforts that have gone.

You may think that Eliot does not succeed, either here or in the sequel,
Four Quartets, in giving voice to the distinctive experience that concerns
him. Nevertheless, his attempt gives a clear meaning to the suggestion
that poetry 'bestows' a kind of truth on its subject matter. Eliot is looking for the sincere expression of a new experience, one that will remain
true to its inner dynamic, and show what it is to *live* that experience in
the self-awareness of a modern person. He is looking for words that both
capture the experience and lend themselves to sincere and committed
use. Banal words, clichés, sentimental invocations—all these can be easily found. But they are words only: the task is to find words which are
compelled by a real and heartfelt intention, words whose meaning lies in
an experience that demands them. Eliot's borrowings vividly convey the
problem, and turn his thoughts sincerely towards the lost art of prayer:

> Blessèd sister, holy mother, spirit of the fountain, spirit of the
> garden,
> Suffer us not to mock ourselves with falsehood
> Teach us to care and not to care . . . [15]

---

[15] Cavalcanti, *Selected Poetry*, 95.

The example illustrates the claim that poetry bestows a kind of truth on its subject matter. Words that can be sincerely uttered show an experience that can be truly felt. And this in turn shows the world in another light, as a world where feeling finds its fulfilment, and where object and subject meet in mutual influence.

However, the account seems to imply that the truth bestowed by poetry is a truth only at the subjective level. The 'grounding' of which Heidegger writes seems rather to require that the truth bestowed by poetry is also discerned in the world of objects: it is a truth of 'the things themselves'. What do we make of that thought?

It should be recognized that Heidegger's paradigms of the poetic art do not include the massively allusive and critically burdened verse of Eliot. For Heidegger a work of poetry is, typically, a record of a thing, and of the 'thingliness' of the thing. Such is Hölderlin's tribute to the river Ister (subject of a course of lectures by Heidegger), and Rilke's invocation of the earth in the ninth of *Duino Elegies*. The obfuscation that is second nature to Heidegger makes it look as though he has discerned another kind of poetic truth—a truth about the inner reality of objects. Thus Rilke's rhetorical question:

> Sind wir vielleicht hier, um zu sagen: Haus,
> Brücke, Brunnen, Tor, Krug, Obstbaum, Fenster,—
> höchstens: Säule, Turm . . . aber zu *sagen*, verstehs,
> oh zu sagen *so*, wie selber die Dinge niemals
> innig meinten zu sein.[16]

But, rightly understood, Rilke is endorsing the position that I have been exploring. The meaning of things is *bestowed* on them by poetry, through the act of *saying* them, in a form that they 'never thought inwardly to be'. The truth, even here, the truth of the house, bridge, fountain, gate, jug, fruit tree, and window, even the truth of pillar and tower, is a truth bestowed in the experience. Its measure is the depth with which these things can be taken into consciousness and made part of a life fully lived. Their inner meaning is bestowed in the poetic encounter, when the subject with all his associations and quests is, as it were, made present to himself in the object that he observes.

---

[16] Rainer Maria Rilke, 'Ninth Elegy', *The Poetry of Rilke*, bilingual edn, tr. Edward A. Snow, 1st edn. New York: North Point Press, 2009, 334.

Why is it so important to us, that we endow the world with meanings? And can we distinguish the right endowment from the wrong one? Or do we do this only 'so as not to perish from the truth'? I conclude with a suggestion. Following the path suggested by Heidegger we come to the conclusion that there is an 'inner truth' to things, and that this truth is bestowed by poetry. But the inwardness is the inwardness of our own experience—the fusing of a thing with its associations and life-significances in the poetic moment. These poetic moments are, as Eliot teaches us, achievements. They are not random associations but the fruit of a life lived in full awareness. In the normal run of things, in a life governed by instrumental reasoning and focused on transient goals, things pass us by. They are mere contingencies, which might not have been, and which occupy no place in our thoughts beyond the thought of their utility. But all self-conscious beings are able to live in another way: not swept up in contingencies but asking for their ground, and striving to see them as they are in themselves. Things then reveal their thingliness: they draw attention to their own contingency and compel from us the question why, for what end, and with what meaning does the world come to fruition in *this*? We cannot look to science for an answer, since science does not permit the question. But we sense the urgency of the question nevertheless. The right answer is the answer that enables us to incorporate the things of this world into a fulfilled life. For each individual object, each house, bridge, fountain, gate, or jug, there is such an answer. And the poet is the one who provides it. His answer is false when it sentimentalizes, hiding the thing behind a veil of wishful thinking. His answer is true when it shows how just such a thing might be part of a fulfilled human life, and one in which the object is valued for its own sake, as a vehicle of meaning.

8

Poetry's Knowing
So What Do We Know?

Angela Leighton

> *I cannot give the reasons,*
> *I only sing the tunes:*
> *the sadness of the seasons*
> *the madness of the moons.*
>
> *I cannot be didactic*
> *or lucid, but I can*
> *be quite obscure and practic-*
> *ally marzipan.*
>
> (Mervyn Peake)

One day, at lunch, I found myself chatting with a philosopher friend about the meanings of words. He was defending philosophy's need for abstraction and generalization. 'Pig-headed, for instance', he offered (I hope not pointedly). 'It's simple. It means stubbornly, obtusely opinionated. It can't mean anything else.' 'Yes', I agreed. Then paused: 'Ah, but what if it's applied to a *pig*?' We both laughed. 'Well,' he conceded, 'I suppose that's the poet speaking.' I don't know if a pig-headed pig suggests a poet, but the exchange alerted us both to the fun of slipped contexts. Such a creature might be simply beautifully pig-like, its pig-headedness literally fitting. Our little exchange had thrown up one of those 'duck-rabbit' moments which language relishes: seen one way, it's a stubborn man, seen another, it's a well-turned pig. The moments when language shifts from one thing to another—fact to figure, sense to sound, or sense to nonsense—are all, as my companion noted, the beginning of poetry—the beginning of something verbally wayward, slippery, playful, or just deliciously daft: 'practic / ally marzipan'.

This chapter is a non-philosopher's meditation on poetry and philosophy—a meditation which focuses on poetry, but samples philosophical texts here and there with a certain opportunistic eclecticism. Mine is not a logically deductive argument, a step-by-step proof of a thesis, but rather, as the title suggests, an exploration, indeed an *essay*, into the strange ways of poetry's knowing, and, like that verb in the continuous present, it remains a tentative, unfinished journey. But since journeying and discovering are also the gist of what I want to say, it may be that a certain formal open-endedness suits such a content. I have called it 'Poetry's Knowing' rather than 'knowledge' in order to skirt the vast field of philosophical epistemology which lies behind that noun, while also, of course, making a very small incursion into it. Poetry, I hope to show, has its own varieties of knowledge, but knowledge which may be better conceived as a verb rather than a noun, a process rather than a destination, a way of 'knowing' rather than an object known. Poetry's knowing will always, in the end, still be asking: so what do we know?

As the history of aesthetics suggests, the relations between literature and philosophy have always been tantalizingly close, yet troublingly at odds. Both are dependent on language and both are therefore, to some extent, at the mercy of its quirks and limitations. Both are disciplines which happen in time, along a line of narrative or argument, and both ultimately rely on a conventional, comprehensible language of speech which is fine-tuned or specialized in some way. In the case of *poetry* and philosophy, these also have enough in common to be aware of the assumptions and powers of the other, and to be, sometimes, distrustful or envious. There are poets who have written varieties of philosophy (T. S. Eliot or Wallace Stevens, for instance), and philosophers who have written kinds of poetry (Nietzsche or Wittgenstein). A handful have succeeded in both fields, but they are very few: Lucretius, perhaps, or Lewis Carroll. Otherwise, the lines of demarcation are also fairly clear: there is poetry with its emphasis on the particular, and philosophy with its emphasis on the general or abstract; there is poetry's sense of form, sound, and rhythm, and philosophy's sense of the truth or matter to be conveyed; there is poetry's aim to give aural pleasure, and philosophy's to give explanations. Each makes particular assumptions about what the language is *for*, as well as assumptions about where our thinking happens: *in* language or *through* it.

Yet it is interesting how many poets, particularly in the twentieth century, have looked to philosophy for justification, inspiration, even, as in the case of Wallace Stevens, for a whole poetic vocabulary. Stevens's essay, 'A Collect of Philosophy' (1951), reveals his reading of, among others, Plato, Berkeley, Leibniz, Hegel, Nietzsche, Bergson, Santayana, and Russell. 'Poets and philosophers often think alike', he argues (1997, 853), but adds that the difference lies in the writing. Something of this difference is caught in the comment that 'the probing of the philosopher is deliberate . . . the probing of the poet is fortuitous' (863). There is something chancy about the sense poems make, whereas (most) philosophy follows certain rules of consequentiality. Stevens's own poetry, with its fondness for philosophical assertions and abstractions—'It Must Be Abstract' (329)—and its appearance of logical consequence, might seem to contradict this difference. However, to read closely is to find that the ostensible argument soon founders on the sands of the 'fortuitous', on connections made not by 'deliberate' or logical purpose, but by the chances of sound and rhythm. Randall Jarrell, who criticized Stevens's 'habit of philosophizing in poetry', and who concluded, therefore, that 'Poetry is a bad medium for philosophy' (1999, 116), perhaps missed the mock-heroic strain in that poetry. It may be that Stevens's work was never intended as a 'medium *for*' something other than itself, as if it were the mere stylistic container for philosophical thought. Instead, although he seems to ventriloquize philosophical discourse, in fact he renders it *poetic* by removing the connections, avoiding conclusions, and meanwhile heightening the charmed, aural powers of words.

In a recent essay on 'Poetry and Philosophy' (2007), Peter Porter explains that his 'real concern is with the resources and practice of poetry and how different they are from philosophy'. He quickly adds, however, that: 'Poetry is based on thinking (and disinterested thinking at that) as much as philosophy is.' A clear difference is thus followed by a surprising similarity: poetry is a matter of 'disinterested thinking' too. Whether or not all philosophy would claim to be 'disinterested'—that tricky Kantian word—it is true that 'thinking' is not the first activity we might associate with poetry, either its composition or its reception. Yet Porter emphatically insists that this participle—'thinking' rather than thought—belongs to poetic work. Nor is his an isolated voice. Some seventy years before, Paul Valéry similarly hedged his bets in an essay on 'Poetry and Abstract Thought' (1939). In it he insists that 'Every true poet is . . . capable . . . of right reasoning and abstract thought'. Then, slightly shifting his ground, he defines 'thought' as an act rather than an object, a verb rather than a noun: 'the most authentic philosophy lies not so much in the objects of our reflection as in the very act of thought and in its handling' (1989b, 77). The poet is a philosopher, not so much because thought is his object—the thing gained at the end of the road—but because thought is the means, it may be to nothing; it is an 'act' or 'handling'. Like Porter's 'thinking', Valéry hints that the action of the verb provides a better account of the poet's 'most authentic philosophy' than substantive 'thought'. When T. S. Eliot, in his essay on 'Dante' (1920), similarly defends the poet's philosophical credentials, he too worries at the difference between nouns and verbs:

Without doubt, the effort of the philosopher proper, the man who is trying to deal with ideas in themselves, and the effort of the poet, who may be trying to *realize* ideas, cannot be carried on at the same time. But this is not to deny that poetry can be in some sense philosophic. (1972, 162)

Here too, there is a sense of wanting to have it both ways: poetry is like and unlike philosophy. The difference between the philosopher's 'ideas in themselves' and the poet's 'trying to *realize* ideas' hinges on the difference between an essential object-noun which must be grasped, and an ongoing activity expressed by a verb: '*trying* to realize'. Eliot does not explain how one might know these essential 'ideas in themselves' except through language, nor does he explain in what the poet's realization of such ideas might consist. Are ideas still to be realized more or less real than 'ideas in themselves'? But in the end, the poet's business seems to lie with the continuous participle: 'trying'. Having reached a knotty impasse, Eliot throws up his hands in weariness and resorts to his favourite device of the evasive double negative: 'this is not to deny that poetry can in some sense be philosophic'. Of course, 'not to deny' is probably a little less than to assert, while the nature of the similarity still hangs on a very thin thread: 'in some sense'. Yet in Eliot, as in Stevens, Porter, and Valéry, one can hear the poet seeking the same credentials as the philosopher for serious thinking, for using abstractions or ideas, while also demarcating a tiny, but crucial difference between them.

To turn to philosophers is often to find a comparable play of envy and distrust, similarity and dissimilarity. Nietzsche is the obvious example. His skirmishes with poetic language are particularly evident in that most literary of works, *The Gay Science*, which contains a playful mix of genres: prose passages, aphorisms, proverbs, songs, and rhymes. 'Good prose', Nietzsche writes, 'is written only face to face with poetry. For it is an uninterrupted, well-mannered war with poetry . . . Everything abstract wants to be read as a prank against poetry and as with a mocking voice' (1974, 145). The good prose of philosophy, which is 'abstract', has an eye to poetry even if, surprisingly, a mocking, prankster's eye. If Stevens mimics the philosopher, here the philosopher mimics the poet, but mockingly, so as to ensure a proper distance. The 'Prelude in German Rhymes' is merely versified philosophy, but the 'Appendix' contains songs, one of which, 'The Poet's Call', openly acknowledges the lure of poetry, of a rhythmic sound which beats through words: 'a distant ticking sound / Seemed to beat an endless measure'. To this call of time and measure Nietzsche responds with:

> There was nothing I could do,
> Until I, just like a poet,
> Spoke in that strange ticktock, too. (2010, 351)

Malgré lui, the philosopher here is 'just like a poet'. It only takes the seduction of 'measure', the 'ticktock' beat in words, to turn the one into the other (although the verdict of posterity might be that it takes something more than this). Nietzsche's verse, recently published in a complete edition in English (2010), trips along in regular measure, but remains, I think, a kind of versified thought rather than thoughtful verse. The difference lies less in the fact of 'measure'—one could argue that poetry is not defined by measure, and that prose, even philosophical prose, may be measured or rhythmical—and more in the fact that Nietzsche's verse remains a kind of thought set to rhythm. In other words, this is not *poetry's* knowing, but philosophical knowledge conveyed in the manner of poetry. The knowledge, the thought, the idea are all extractable from their 'ticktock' casing.

Another philosopher who flirts with the tempting possibilities of poetry is of course Wittgenstein. In his many scattered notes and jottings, gathered together in *Culture and Value*, he frequently considers the closeness between philosophy and the arts. 'What I invent are new *similes*'

(1980, 19), he declares, and elsewhere remarks on the 'queer resemblance between a philosophical investigation . . . and an aesthetic one' (1980, 25). The similarity has something to do with metaphor, and with the lucky chances of what words, rather than thoughts, might express. His much quoted phrase, 'Often my writing is nothing but "stuttering" (*Stammeln*)' (1980, 18), seems to formulate a kind of philosophy so fragmentary and tentative, so much a short trial of words, as to approximate the lines of a poem. Philosophy, he asserts point-blank in one place, 'ought really to be written only as a *poetic composition*' (1980, 24). The idea of a language somehow broken down, stuttery and uncertain, seems to Wittgenstein to offer a greater approximation to philosophical investigations of knowledge than clear, consecutive prose does. Like Nietzsche, he delights in the maxim, the aphorism, in the unfinished, tantalizingly suggestive turn of phrase, which leaves nothing more to be said yet everything still to be understood. However, in later years he changes tack: 'If I were to write a *good* sentence which by accident turned out to consist of two rhyming lines, that would be a *blunder*' (1980, 58), he insists. It's a curious worry. If 'a *good* sentence', why should chance rhyme be 'a *blunder*'? Such an anxiety, while seeming to contradict the statement about philosophy as '*poetic composition*', also acknowledges the fact that poetic language might radically affect the nature of what is expressed. Whether desired or feared, poetry, with its temptations of rhyme and simile, somehow shadows the language of philosophy like a powerful or threatening alternative.

The thing that underpins and challenges Wittgenstein's thinking about language is, however, not poetry but music—the art form that lay closest to home for him. At one point in *The Brown Book* he suggests that ' "understanding a sentence" has, in many cases, a much greater similarity to understanding a musical theme than we might be inclined to think' (1972, 167). This similarity then raises the question of music's content, and how it might be expressed:

'This tune says *something*', and it is as though I had to find *what* it says. And yet I know that it doesn't say anything such that I might express in words or pictures what it says. And if, recognizing this, I resign myself to saying 'It just expresses a musical thought', this would mean no more than saying 'It expresses itself'. (1972, 166)

It is almost as if the philosopher here has hit on the conundrum of all art criticism: there is the search for '*what* it says', the wish and need to describe, explain, paraphrase, alongside the knowledge that 'it doesn't say anything' other than itself, and therefore constantly beggars interpretation. The argument comes full circle as 'something', even 'a musical thought', is lost in the tautology of ' "It expresses itself" '. The tune speaks, without speaking about; it is expressive, without expressing anything. The need to know what a tune *says* leads, therefore, to the knowledge that knowing itself must be revised in the process. Something is said and unsaid, expressed and unexpressed, known and unknown, in this verbal journey towards understanding the arts of sound. When it comes to music, or even language, the question of knowing is a starting point which also becomes the point at issue.

This same passage appears in *Philosophical Investigations*, where Wittgenstein adds the following summary: 'One would like to say "Because I know what it's all about." But what is it all about? I should not be able to say' (1974, 527). This is the same round-trip from desiring something to finding nothing, with, one might notice, its own accidental echoes on the way: 'to say'/'to say', 'all about'/'all about?' Whether or not such *rime riche* is a blunder, it seems that even philosophy might sometimes call for, and embody, a formulation which defeats the need to 'know what it's all about'. To remove the sense of 'knowing *about*' from the act of interpretation does not invalidate the wonderfully open activity of merely 'knowing'. A sentence might be similar to 'a musical theme' in that it asks for a revision of the verb 'to know', from transitive to intransitive or, even more radically, from knowing to not knowing. Wittgenstein is prodding at the very limits of philosophy here, while touching on a central problem of the arts: they arouse a desire in the reader/listener to know, but also invalidate the means. Poetry offers something to be known, something to be admired, expressed, explained; but it then undermines the terms of the question with a kind of shrug: 'so what do we know?'

Of course, games of knowing and not knowing can also be found in philosophy, starting with Socrates. But these tend to be spoken with the philosopher's modesty, not the artist's pride. When Nietzsche advises in one place that philosophers might learn 'to be good at *not* knowing, as artists!' (1974, 37), he is pointing to an artistic advantage. Wittgenstein comes close to the artist's boast when he admits: 'I really do think with my pen, because my head often knows nothing about what my hand is writing' (1980, 17). Certainly, not knowing, or knowing nothing, is not altogether inimical to philosophy. In the end, however, this is a discipline which cannot afford to repudiate too much; it depends on the possibility that there is some transferable content of knowledge to be passed on; some advancement of learning. Poets, however, often worry that knowledge itself might be a problem. Robert Frost, for instance, who rebukes the scholar for being 'too avid of knowledge', advises that, by contrast, the 'poet's instinct is to shun or shed more knowledge than he can swing or sing' (2006, 836). The freight of knowledge needs to be carefully weighed by this poet who, unlike Wittgenstein, then relishes words that chancily rhyme: 'swing or sing'. Elsewhere, Frost declares that the delight of writing poetry 'is in the surprise of remembering something I didn't know I knew' (2006, 777). This has the familiarity of a commonplace, but it also reminds us that knowing and not knowing are not absolute opposites for the poet; the one can be layered over the other, and both remembered at once. The poet might come to know what he doesn't know, or not know what he knows. The contradiction catches something of the surprise and familiarity that poetry can bring, both to writer and reader. It is not an exchange of knowledge-content, passed through the pleasurable medium of rhythmic language; it is, instead, a constant, mutual rediscovery of 'something I didn't know I knew'. As another twentieth-century poet, W. S. Graham, once put it: 'The poet does not write what he knows but what he doesn't know' (14). To write 'what he doesn't know' is to bring something into knowledge which wasn't there before, not even to the writer who nonetheless somehow knows enough to write it. If Nietzsche and Wittgenstein occasionally admit to 'not knowing' what they write, or wish for a greater irresponsibility towards knowing, these poets make not knowing the condition of writing at all.

'Nobody, nobody told me / What nobody, nobody knows', Walter de la Mare begins one of his short poems, 'Under the Rose' (1969, 450). 'Nobody' has always had a rich double meaning in literature, the very word ghosting someone over no one. De la Mare multiplies the possibilities by repeating the word, as a child might, though whether these are also the nobodies who neither know nor tell, or different ones, well, who knows? This may be a conspiracy of silence or a tragic universal ignorance. Meanwhile, the complaining lilt of the voice, child's or adult's, crying 'Nobody, nobody told me', only increases both the importance of knowing and the scary disadvantage of not knowing. 'Philosophers', Wittgenstein once noted, 'often behave like little children who scribble some marks on a piece of paper at random and then ask the grown-ups "What's that?"' (1980, 17) It's an intriguing statement, which nicely scuppers the idea that philosophy merely sets worked-out thought into serviceable language. Certainly, poetry has always offered itself to the reader as a 'What's that?'—as a language which doesn't instantly translate into what everyone knows. Wittgenstein is being a little mischievous in relation to philosophy, but it may be that knowing 'What's that?' is not always the point either of poetry or, sometimes, of philsophy.

> And nobody knows
>> (Tiddely pom),
> How cold my toes
>> (Tiddely pom),
> How cold my toes
>> (Tiddely pom),
> Are growing.

So Winnie the Pooh, himself the best of poets (and philosophers) takes up the motif of 'nobody knows' in the hum which he hums at the beginning of *The House at Pooh Corner* (Milne 2007, 2). When questioned, he explains to Piglet that he put 'pom' in 'to make it more hummy' (6). What drives a hum is humminess; what drives a rhyme is rhyminess. Piglet, the rationalist, still doesn't get it however. He points out, with a note of real grievance, that 'it isn't the *toes* so much as the *ears*' (7). Deaf to the lovely-funny accidents of rhyme in 'knows' and 'toes', he insists, pig-headedly perhaps, on the facts of the matter: as a creature without toes but with cold ears, the poem, to him, is simply wrong. If this might be read as a little commentary on the nature of truth in poetry, Pooh's hum, meanwhile, reminds us that the 'humminess' of verse works in spite of literal truths. It captures what Piglet misses: the lovely noises of repetition and rhyme, and the sheer intransitive wonder of the phrase, 'nobody knows'. Of course, this is only Pooh's cold feet, set to a rhythm. But it also says something more about poetry's knowing and not knowing, about the ways in which poetry might elicit a desire for what 'nobody knows', while also promoting a kind of cheerful wonder at simply not knowing, 'Tiddely pom'.

I am of course making a mountain of meaning out of a few, opportunistically sampled lines. If this seems a bit like balancing an elephant on a tiny stool, perhaps my next text will reproportion the argument. Although not exactly poetry (though almost a prose poem), Henry James's novel, *What Maisie Knew,* seems to be an ongoing commentary on the nature of knowing. If the title suggests a disclosure, a '*What*' to be found out, the text in fact takes every opportunity to thwart that promise. Here, James takes the child's eye view and presents it with the moral mess of adult sexuality—a mess in which the verb 'knowing' carries its own loaded charge. Maisie, however, remains at a tangent to that mess, asserting a different kind of knowing. She is, in James's repeated words, 'my wondering witness' (2008, 7), 'our little wonder-working agent' (5). Maisie both wonders and works wonder. Because nobody nobody tells her, she learns how to know, as well as how to be knowing, by watching and listening like any good reader of a literary work, prose or poetry. The following passage makes this clear:

> 'He's *with* her,' Mrs Wix desolately said. 'He's with her,' she reiterated.
> 'Do you mean in her own room?' Maisie continued.
> She waited an instant. 'God knows!'
> Maisie wondered a little why, or how, God should know . . . (238)

Maisie's language has what Stanley Cavell has attributed to Beckett: 'the quality' of '*hidden literality*' (119). In this passage the idea of knowing shifts from Mrs Wix's sexually corrupt knowingness, to the expostulated cliché 'God knows!' (which Maisie misunderstands and takes literally), to the open wondering that is the child's characteristic reaction: she 'wondered a little why, or how, God should know . . . ' In that one line James packs the sense of Maisie's innocence, her religious ignorance, but also her most likeable, generous quality of simple awareness: she 'wondered a little'. What she wonders is a question, of course—'why, or how'—but it is the wonder, rather than the answer to the wonder, that is the driving force of the novel. What Maisie *knows* is how to wonder at the world around her. The 'mystery of that verb', as Adrian Poole puts it (James 2008, p. viii), is what keeps the reader still hoping to know, even while knowing morally and sexually all too much.

In the final sentence of the work, James offers what seems like an assertion of Maisie's triumphant achievement of knowledge, as she and Mrs Wix finally seem to exchange wonder and knowledge: 'Mrs Wix gave a sidelong look. She still had room for wonder at what Maisie knew' (275). That 'Maisie knew' ought to satisfy the whole narrative drive of the novel, in its unravelling of a complex tale of desire and power. But what does she know? Why, nobody knows. James's last word is still intransitive and still, notice, in the past tense. It is possible that Maisie knows no more than she did before; or that she always knew. We, the reader, who now know plenty, might still not know the thing that makes Maisie so mysterious and attractive: the sheer continuing 'wonder' of it all. *What Maisie Knew,* like much poetry, is less a disclosure of the narrative's '*What*', than an exploration of some almost objectless knowing: knowing which is open to a multitude of things, all of them wondrous.

'For it is owing to their wonder,' Aristotle declares in his *Metaphysics*, 'that men both now begin and at first began to philosophize' (1554). If, as he implies, the purpose of philosophy was always to allay or ease the sense of 'wonder', it may be that the purpose of literature, and poetry in particular, is to increase it, to remain a 'wonder-working agent'. The way that poems ask to be read, and read again, and seem, however well-known (even known by heart), to want to be known again, as if knowing were a constantly refreshed, unfinished activity, might be a point of divergence from (most) philosophy, where wonder diminishes in relation to knowledge. The philosopher seeks knowledge in order to allay wonder, but the poet, and the novelist, may find in wonder just another kind of knowledge. If I am stretching the meaning of knowledge well beyond its philosophical compass that too may be part of literature's purpose.

The sense of knowledge as wondrous knowing rather than object known seems to be what drives the famous last section of Elizabeth Bishop's poem, 'At the Fishhouses':

> Cold dark deep and absolutely clear,
> the clear gray icy water . . .
> It is like what we imagine knowledge to be:
> dark, salt, clear, moving, utterly free,
> drawn from the cold hard mouth
> of the world, derived from the rocky breasts
> forever, flowing and drawn, and since
> our knowledge is historical, flowing, and flown. (2008, 52)

To compare the sea to knowledge is to offer no real clarification of either, in spite of declaring, three times, that something is 'clear'. Those lists of adjectives, sometimes unpunctuated, 'Cold dark deep', 'clear gray icy', 'cold hard', sometimes thoughtfully slowed up by commas, 'dark, salt, clear, moving', 'historical, flowing, and flown', seem to describe both sea and knowledge in a muddle of tenor and vehicle till the reader forgets the original. The sense of flow is emphasized by Bishop's beautifully exact word, 'derived', which then realizes its etymological origins (dériver: down river), as it joins the flow of being 'like what we imagine knowledge to be'. Whatever that is, less an object to be observed than a condition to be entered into, the language rides the continuous movement of the present participle: 'flowing and drawn', 'flowing, and flown'. In the end, this is not a proposition about knowledge, which might be added to our philosophical stock, but a knowing in action which is already, as we know it, 'flowing, and flown'. So what do we know? Only that something is happening in the sound of the flow of the lines which, by the end, makes us want to return to the beginning, to hear once more how it might . . . go.

Wallace Stevens's poem, 'The Plain Sense of Things', makes an interesting companion piece to Bishop's, since this too is a poem about imagining knowledge. Like her word 'clear', Stevens's 'plain' is a tricksy misnomer, as the 'plain sense of things' to which 'we return' in the opening lines seems anything but. If such plainness might seem an imaginative end—as Stevens puts it: 'Inanimate in an inert savoir'—yet even such an end 'had itself to be imagined'. And so, in a later stanza, staring at the 'great pond', at the repeated 'plain sense of it, without reflections', Stevens gives us a figure which suddenly disturbs the unreflective stillness of the scene: it is 'silence // Of a sort, silence of a rat come out to see, / The great pond and its waste of the lilies' (1997, 428). Like many of Stevens's poems, this seems to offer a philosophical proposition in verse. It has the didactic tone of an assertion, about knowledge and the imagination, about 'how the absence of imagination can be imagined' (435), as Charles Altieri puts it. The pond clogged with leaves blocks the reflective mechanisms of the imagination, so that the whole landscape seems dead, while we too, or it, become a dead thing: 'Inanimate in an inert savoir.' It's a brilliantly intransigent phrase, each 'in': 'Inanimate in . . . inert', pushing for a negative (both 'inanimate' and 'inert'), which then aurally flowers in the rare surprise of 'savoir'. Is there a 'savoir-faire' in this 'inert savoir'? Certainly, however dead, other meanings start to stir. Like Beckett's 'imagine dead imagine' (1999, 35), this is the imagination staying alive at the thought of its own death, or a kind of knowledge stirring out of knowing nothing.

And indeed something does then literally stir in this inanimate
scene: 'silence of a rat come out to see'. There is a scuttle in the 'silence', a
movement in the stillness, a life in death. So, Stevens concludes, 'all this
/ Had to be imagined as an inevitable knowledge'. Not quite 'the end of
imagination' then, this is imagination revived and come back to know
its own scene of despair: 'a rat come out to see, / The great pond'. What
does the rat see? The line does not quite run over into the next, but is
curbed by that comma which keeps the verb 'to see' partly intransitive.
The rat *sees,* in a verb which stays open, unsatisfied, full of the wisdom
of seeing everything and nothing that you'd know. This diminutive seer
opens the poem to 'an inevitable knowledge' which, in retrospect now,
'Had to be imagined'. It is the imagination which alters knowledge, as
it did for Bishop: 'it is like what you imagine knowledge to be'. For both
poets, knowledge, however cold or inert or dead, might still be imagined as something worth saving. Peter Porter once commented about
Stevens's work: 'This is the Poetry of Almost Knowing' (2007, 9). In spite
of the promise of its title, 'The Plain Sense of Things' cannot in the end
be explained as some plain-speaking empiricism. Its meaning, indeed
its understanding of knowledge, remains tied to the work of the imagination—even the work of the imagined absent imagination. So Stevens
offers a play of knowing, in which no one thing—sense, savoir, leaves,
pond, rat, silence—is more real or more plain than another. The slippages
of tenor and vehicle, of abstract and literal, turn whatever 'inevitable
knowledge' might be imagined into a passing narrative, held together by
nothing more than the interlocking sounds and syntax of the words.

Sounds and syntax—these, of course, are reminders that poetry has
always had an affiliation to music. Writing about musical meaning in his
book on *Beauty,* Roger Scruton recalls the two uses of the term ' "expression": a transitive use, which invites the question "expression of what?"
and an intransitive use which forbids that question' (2011, 99). In the case
of music, the second meaning applies. In the case of poetry, however,
both have a role. A poem expresses *something*—it must have reference,
however inconsequential—and at the same time a poem is expressive,
as if with musical dynamics. This is a complexity which has kept critics
busy for centuries. Yet it is true that we lack a philosophy for describing
the intransitive nature of expression in words. Since language is always
a noise of some kind, and poetic language a noise of a specially composed
kind, this seems regrettable. As long ago as 1958, Gaston Bachelard, in *The*

Poetics of Space, found in a line of poetry 'a point of departure for a phenomenology of the verb to listen' (1994, 182). Some twenty years later Don Ihde, in *Listening and Voice*, took up the same cry: 'what is needed is a *philosophy* of listening', he wrote, adding 'But is this a possibility?' (1976, 15). More recently, Salomé Voegelin has offered another rallying call in the subtitle of her book, *Towards a Philosophy of Sound Art* (2010). On the whole, mainstream philosophers have been silent on the topic. One exception might be Heidegger who, here and there in his accounts of poetry, keeps returning to the question of hearing and listening: 'the responding in which man authentically listens to the appeal of language is that which speaks in the element of poetry', he writes in 'Poetically Man Dwells . . .' (1971, 216). Here, the act of listening is identified not only with 'responding' but also with 'that which speaks'. It is a fine definition of poetry, as the genre which speaks the act of listening, which puts 'responding' into words, or, as Roland Barthes succinctly puts it, in which *'listening speaks'* (1986, 252). Once again, the intransitive mode is useful. Heidegger does not bother to stipulate what is heard in 'the act of listening', nor does he offer an object for poetry's speaking: 'that which speaks' does not need to speak *about*. It remains simply *speaking*, in both senses. Responding, listening, speaking, are words which have some special, tantalizing, yet satisfying relevance to what poetry might know, and want us to know.

Few recent philosophers have taken up the challenge of Heidegger's thoughts on poetic listening. Only in philosophies of music does it remain prominent. Stanley Cavell, for instance, in *Must We Mean What We Say* (1969), notes that 'One cannot be commanded to hear a sound, though one can be commanded to listen to it, or for it' (2002, 191). Those very constructions, 'listen to it, or for it', put the object at a slightly disadvantageous distance, as if the act of reaching to hear were more important than the object heard. Roger Scruton adopts similar constructions in his book, *Understanding Music*, when he writes: 'We hear sounds, just as animals hear them. We also listen to them, listen out for them, attend to them, and so on' (2009, 30). The act of listening, as opposed to merely hearing, feels the pressure of its own agency, its own strain and uncertainty. To 'listen out for' something is also to hear how far 'out' that something might remain—even out of hearing.

The relative absence of a philosophy of listening, then, except in a few isolated passages like these, suggests the extent to which the *heard* aspects of language have not been important to philosophers. Yet poetry is predominantly something heard, whether out loud or silently in the head. What we want from a poem is not ultimately a story, a graspable or paraphrasable message of some kind—though sometimes, when faced with 'difficult' contemporary verse, we may think we want those; rather, what we want is an invitation to listen, and to listen again and again. One of the reasons why Stanley Cavell has appealed to literary critics is that his writing about the arts has seemed to touch on this curious self-sufficiency of the act of listening. In that same passage about hearing and listening to music, he goes on to ask: 'How does it happen that the *achievement* or *result* of using a sense organ comes to be thought of as the *activity* of that organ—as though the aesthetic experience had the form not merely of a continuous effort (e.g., listening) but of a continuous achievement (e.g., hearing).' How is it that 'effort' and 'achievement' become the same thing? Yet when, in the next paragraph, Cavell turns to the epistemological implications of this self-justifying act, he crucially changes the verb:

And what that seems to say is that works of art are objects of the sort that can only be *known in sensing*. It is not, as in the case of ordinary material objects, that I know *because* I see, or that seeing is *how* I know . . . It is rather, one may wish to say, that *what* I know is what I see; or even: seeing *feels* like knowing. (2002, 191)

It is interesting that even so word- and music-conscious a philosopher as Cavell slips from hearing and listening into the much more conventional figure of 'seeing'—a verb which has an old and easy connection with knowing. Although he is grappling with the notion that to know a work of music or poetry is to enter the 'continuous effort' of listening and the 'continuous achievement' of hearing, even he cannot quite keep to the tricky subject of listening. To say 'I see it' is, like ' "Seeing the point" ' (2002, 191), to have an object, and a figurative way of grasping it. To say 'I hear it', or 'I listen to it', is to invoke a much more elusive object, for seeing has old empirical credentials; hearing does not. To know by hearing or listening requires a new way of putting it; a reorganization, almost, of the ways in which we think we know at all. It may be that, for such hearing-knowing, one has to turn back to the poets themselves—to those who make a new kind of knowledge out of hearing the musical ways of words, rather than simply 'seeing' their point on the page.

In his account of writing 'Le Cimetière Marin', Paul Valéry offers the following statement:

> If I am questioned; if anyone wonders (as happens sometimes quite peremptorily) what I 'wanted to say' in a certain poem, I reply that I did not *want to say*, but *wanted to make*, and that it was the intention of *making* which *wanted* what I *said*. (1989a, 147–8)

Such a sentence takes us on a journey which involves shedding, on the way, the idea that human wish or purpose must precede expression. The poet here has no wish or want to say. It is 'the intention of *making*', rather, which '*wanted* what I *said*'. 'I' is not the agent but the responder; and, as Valéry's subsequent paragraph makes clear, even this 'intention' does not belong to a recognizable human agency: 'this intention was at first no more than a rhythmic figure, empty, or filled with meaningless syllables, which obsessed me for some time' (148), he explains. What intends the speech of the poet is 'rhythm', a sound that, like a tom-tom from outside, might remove the dignity of human purpose, wish, or want from the poem's expression. Poetry starts, one might add, not even with an outside rhythm, but with listening in, or listening out for it. The purpose of the poet is then in some ways to recreate the listening that first obsessed him or her, and pass it to the reader. Poetry, perhaps, is a kind of transference of listening—a transference sent across the peculiar visual-aural arrangements of language that is the poem on the page. There is no guarantee, of course, that the transference will work, and that the reader will hear with the same gripped attention what first caught the poet impersonally unawares. But certainly, as Valéry insists, what is required is to shed that question: what does the poet want to say? as if poetry involved a simple transaction of wishes into words, and instead to learn to rethink, reknow, how poetry's knowing lies in the words and rhythms themselves.

It may be, then, that poetry offers something akin to philosophy: that is, an examination of the very nature of knowing. It necessarily pushes at the parameters of that word, opening it up to include wondering, unknowing, not knowing, imagining, listening—activities which have something to do with how the mind works, but which mostly shed the burden of any obviously attainable object. If the purpose of philosophy is to extract that object from the verbal means of finding it, and so pass it on, the purpose of poetry is to play on the means and perhaps lose the object in the process. This is not quite 'cognition without content', which is how Peter Kivy describes listening to music, because of course there *is* a kind of 'content' within poems; but it is, perhaps, cognition *beyond* content. There is always still something to be known or understood beyond the content of a poem's words. To understand this kind of cognition may mean to fall back on the intransitive mode of the verb, or the participle, on the notion of something never quite reaching the end of its own seeking activity. Peter Lamarque, in his essay on 'Poetry and Abstract Throught', writes that readers of poetry 'attend far more closely, and in a different way from philosophy, to the *process of thought*' (2009, 50). Such a process, rather than being one of logical connections, may be one of sound and syntax, rhythm and accent, of sense sparked by the collocations and connotations of words. For those, too, may become a form of 'knowing'. John Gibson changes the verb when he writes, for instance, that literary works 'represent ways of acknowledging the world rather than knowing it' (2009, 482). But I suggest that we should keep the idea of 'knowing' in play, in order to force it to include process and replay, wonder and unknowing, seeing and listening. To help us to know *differently*, in all the word-bound, sound-bound, rhythm-bound ways of poetic language, is what poetry, as opposed to philosophy, can offer.

I will end with one last poem by Stevens. 'Of Modern Poetry' begins, philosophically enough, with what sounds like a proposition or definition: 'The poem of the mind in the act of finding / What will suffice' (1997, 218). By the time we reach the conclusion, however, we may be none the wiser as to what we have found or 'What will suffice'. This is a classic Stevens tactic. He offers a poem full of statements of fact (apparently), which is deeply self-referential, and which constantly skirmishes with philosophical propositions about the mind. Thus he declares at one point: 'The actor is / A metaphysician in the dark, twanging an instrument'. In that crucial corollary, 'in the dark', we can hear how he both yearns for and rebuffs the connection between poet and philosopher. Simon Critchley paraphrases the phrase as the poet's 'dark metaphysical talk' (2005, 40), as if 'in the dark' merely contained difficult, abstruse matter. But surely it also carries the much more devastating sense of being lost, at a loss, ignorant even of its own metaphysics. However much of a 'metaphysician' this poet-actor may be, he also knows nothing, sees nothing, is as much 'in the dark' as any hapless reader who perhaps loses, in the course of the poem, the clear train of its thought. Of modern poetry, Stevens repeats that 'It must / Be the finding of a satisfaction'. Yet for all the force of the injunction, 'It must', what it must be is no more than yet another indefinite participle: a 'finding'. Like that first 'act of finding / What will suffice', this tells us less about the sufficiency of the act, its *found* satisfaction, and more about the process of 'finding' which may or may not lead anywhere. Although in his poetry Stevens appears to rely on that crucial counter of philosophical argument, the abstract noun, in fact the syntax of his sentences more often than not emphasizes the verb, the participle—something which has not yet finished its business of disclosure.

In his essay on 'Aesthetic Experience', Monroe Beardsley once proposed that the experience of art is 'the experience of discovery', adding, 'I call this "active discovery"'' (1982, 292). He too, like so many of the poets mentioned here, invokes an objectless activity; there is no end, or even satisfaction, to this 'discovery'. Interestingly, the same word is used by Robert Frost in his attempt to explain what a poem should be about. 'Should a poem be on a subject', he asks in one of his Notebooks, and answers: 'No but it should be a process of discovering a subject and not only to the reader but to the writer' (2006, 667). Like Stevens's 'act of finding / What will suffice' and Monroe's 'active discovery', this puts the onus on the verb: '*discovering* a subject' may be the best that either poet or reader can hope for. In a recent interview, the contemporary poet Les Murray seems to repeat this same point about his long poem, *Fredy Neptune*: 'I only discovered the ending when I got to the last page', he writes. 'It wasn't like making it up, it was as if I was discovering it out of a deep place in my head.' He then adds, interestingly: 'it is a model of how humans truly think' (2010). Indeed, understanding 'how humans truly think' may be something that poetry has as much to tell us as philosophy, by discovering it in action, playing it to the listening ear, by letting us hear what thinking or knowing might sound like, till the ear wants to hear it over and over again.

Indeed, 'Of Modern Poetry' also contains in its middle section a long apostrophe to the ear. The actor-metaphysician who twangs his instrument (blue guitar or lyre?) must:

> speak words that in the ear,
> In the delicatest ear of the mind, repeat,
> Exactly, that which it wants to hear, at the sound
> Of which, an invisible audience listens . . .

The poet's usual hortatory manner gives way, here, to an internally spiralling syntax of modifications. Not only the 'ear' but the 'ear of the mind' must hear, for this is an intellectual faculty, the mind's means of cognition. Meanwhile, that 'invisible audience' (different from the mind itself, or is this already the mind's ear listening?) 'listens'. There seem to be four kinds of ear in this passage: a literal ear, the mind's ear, the mind's 'delicatest ear', and then the ear of the 'invisible audience' that 'listens . . . to itself'. We have gone so far into this double, triple, auditory attention—an attention to nearly nothing—that there seems no way out. What we are listening *to* is a question that becomes progressively less relevant as Stevens's syntax abandons the sense of 'words' spoken out loud by a literal actor, and instead makes the inner mind's listening the object we are listening to, or for. Those metaphysical 'words' may have been the subject, or pretext, of the passage, but the point is then to make us forget them, for the sake of this heightened awareness, this listening which starts to develop a curious high volume of its own. If this is a kind of shell to the ear, giving back nothing but the sea-noise of self-attention, it is also a resonant description of how poetry takes us away from the sense of words in order to give us the sense of sounds instead.

In the end, poetry and philosophy, for all their close connections, their mutual admiration, distrust, or envy, must take slightly different routes through language. For philosophy, the burden ultimately falls on 'what' might be known—on a body of knowledge which allows itself to be lifted and passed on; in poetry, the burden falls on the ongoing 'how' of it—on the sounds and syntax which draw us in, again and again, to an act of discovery: 'The poem of the mind in the act of *finding* . . .' Both require a willingness to think, and so let the mind follow the processes of language towards something that 'will suffice'; but in the end, poetry's knowing remains insufficient, like a verb without an object, or like a suspended participle, something to be found only in the finding, discovered in the discovering, heard and listened for as if in the hearing and listening—'in the delicatest ear of the mind'.

References

Altieri, Charles. 2009. 'Style'. In Richard Eldridge (ed.), *The Oxford Handbook of Philosophy and Literature*. Oxford: Oxford University Press, 420–41.

Aristotle. 1984. 'Metaphysics'. In *The Complete Works of Aristotle*, 2 vols, ed. Jonathan Barnes, Bollingen Series, 71. Princeton: Princeton University Press, 1552–1728.

Bachelard, Gaston. 1994. *The Poetics of Space*, tr. Maria Jolas, foreword John R. Stilgoe. 1st publ. 1958. Boston: Beacon Press.

Barthes, Roland. 1986. 'Listening'. In *The Responsibility of Forms: Critical Essays on Music, Art, and Representation*, tr. Richard Howard. Oxford: Blackwell, 245–60.

Beardsley, Monroe C. 1982. *The Aesthetic Point of View: Selected Essays*, ed. Michael J. Wreen and Donald M. Callen. Ithaca, NY, and London: Cornell University Press.

Beckett, Samuel. 1999. 'Imagination Dead Imagine'. In *Six Residua*. London: John Calder, 35–8.

Bishop, Elizabeth. 2008. *Poems, Prose, and Letters*, ed. Robert Giroux and Lloyd Schwartz. New York: Library of America.

Cavell, Stanley. 2002. 'Music Discomposed'. In *Must We Mean What We Say? A Book of Essays*. 1st publ. 1969. Cambridge: Cambridge University Press, 180–212.

Critchley, Simon. 2005. *Things Merely Are: Philosophy in the Poetry of Wallace Stevens*. London and New York: Routledge.

De la Mare, Walter. 1969. *Complete Poems*. London: Faber.

Eliot, T. S. 1972. 'Dante'. In *The Sacred Wood: Essays on Poetry and Criticism*. 1st publ. 1920. London: Methuen, 159–71.

Frost, Robert. 2006. *The Notebooks of Robert Frost*, ed. Robert Faggen. Cambridge, MA: Harvard University Press.

Gibson, John. 2009. 'Literature and Knowledge'. In *The Oxford Handbook of Philosophy and Literature*, ed. Richard Eldridge. Oxford: Oxford University Press, 467–85.

Graham, W. S. 1999. *The Nightfisherman: Selected Letters*, ed. Michael and Margaret Snow. Manchester: Carcanet.

Heidegger, Martin. 1971. 'Poetically Man Dwells . . . ' In *Poetry, Language, Thought*, tr. and intro. Albert Hofstadter. New York: Harper & Row.

Heidegger, Martin. 2002. 'The Origin of the Work of Art'. In *Off the Beaten Track*, ed. and tr. Julian Young and Kenneth Haynes. 1st publ. 1950. Cambridge: Cambridge University Press, 1–56.

Ihde, Don. 1976. *Listening and Voice: A Phenomenology of Sound*. Athens, OH: Ohio University Press.

James, Henry. 2008. *What Maisie Knew*, ed. Adrian Poole. 1st publ. 1897. Oxford: Oxford University Press.

Jarrell, Randall. 1999. 'Reflections on Wallace Stevens'. In *No Other Book: Selected Essays*, ed. Brad Leithauser. London: Harper Collins, 112–22.

Kivy, Peter. 2007. *Music, Language, and Cognition: And Other Essays in the Aesthetics of Music*. Oxford: Clarendon Press.

Lamarque, Peter. 2009. 'Poetry and Abstract Thought', *Midwest Studies in Philosophy*, 33: 37–52.

Leighton, Angela. 2007. *On Form: Poetry, Aestheticism, and the Legacy of a Word.* Oxford: Oxford University Press.

Levinson, Jerrold, ed. 2003. *The Oxford Handbook of Aesthetics.* Oxford: Oxford University Press.

Milne, A. A. 2007. *The House at Pooh Corner.* 1st publ. 1928. London: Methuen.

Murray, Les. 2010. 'Interview with Les Murray', *Guardian*, 20 Nov., 13.

Nietzsche, Friedrich. 1974. *The Gay Science*, tr. with commentary, by Walter Kaufmann. 1st publ. 1887. New York: Vintage Books.

Nietzsche, Friedrich. 2010. *The Peacock and the Buffalo: The Poetry of Nietzsche*, tr. James Luchte. London: Continuum.

Porter, Peter. 2007. 'The Reas'ning Engine: Poetry and Philosophy', *Essays in Criticism*, 57: 93–113.

Scruton, Roger. 2009. *Understanding Music: Philosophy and Interpretation.* London: Continuum.

Scruton, Roger. 2011. *Beauty: A Very Short Introduction.* 1st publ. 2009. Oxford: Oxford University Press.

Stevens, Wallace. 1997. *Collected Poetry and Prose*, ed. Frank Kermode and Joan Richardson. New York: Library of America.

Valéry, Paul. 1989a. 'Concerning "Le Cimetière Marin"'. In *The Art of Poetry*, tr. Denise Folliot, intro. T. S. Eliot, Bollingen Series 45/7. 1st publ. 1958. Princeton: Princeton University Press, 140–52.

Valéry, Paul. 1989b. 'Poetry and Abstract Thought'. In *The Art of Poetry*, tr. Denise Folliot, intro. T. S. Eliot, Bollingen Series 45/7. 1st publ. 1958. Princeton: Princeton University Press, 52–81.

Voegelin, Salomé. 2010. *Listening to Noise and Silence: Towards a Philosophy of Sound Art.* London: Continuum.

Wittgenstein, Ludwig. 1974. *Philosophical Investigations*, tr. G. E. M. Anscombe. 1st publ. 1953. Oxford: Blackwell.

Wittgenstein, Ludwig. 1972. *The Blue and Brown Books: Preliminary Studies for the 'Philosophical Investigations'.* 1st publ. 1958. Oxford: Blackwell.

Wittgenstein, Ludwig. 1980. *Culture and Value*, ed. G. H. Von Wright, with Heikki Hyman, tr. Peter Winch. 1st publ. 1977. Oxford: Blackwell.

9

Ethical Estrangement
Pictures, Poetry, and Epistemic Value

Alison Denham

I Experiencing in Pictures

My principal topic is poetry, but I begin with fiction and visual art: a fictional account of a fictional painting by a fictional artist. The account is from a passage in Tolstoy's *Anna Karenina* in which Anna's lover, Count Vronsky, contemplates a portrait of her painted by Mihailov, an artist famed for his talent and insight:

> By the fifth sitting, [Mihailov's] portrait struck everybody, especially Vronsky, by its accurate likeness as well as its particular beauty. It was strange how Mihailov could have discovered that peculiar beauty. 'One must know her and love her as I have done to understand that sweet spiritual expression of hers', Vronsky thought, though it was only through this portrait that he himself had discovered it. But the expression was so true that it seemed to him and others that they had always known it.[1]

Tolstoy here identifies two significant responses commonly elicited by works of representational art: what I will follow others in calling 'experiencing-as' and 'experience-taking'. The first refers to our direct, non-inferential perception of an object (in this case a portrait) as possessing some feature or property, a feature or property that enters into the content of the experience itself. Experiencing-as is an ubiquitous feature of everyday perception: we experience objects as belonging to a type or kind—e.g. we see a piece of fruit as an apple or hear a distant sound

[1] L. Tolstoy, *Anna Karenina*. London: Everyman's edn, 1939, ii. 40.

as the blare of a trumpet—or experience them as having certain properties (the apple as red and large, the trumpet as loud and off-key). It is also a feature of pictorial experience, as when Vronsky sees Mihailov's painting as a portrait of Anna (or sees Anna 'in' the portrait, as an Anna-depiction). Experiencing-as, however, is not just another label for perception-based belief: to experience an object as being a certain way is distinct from judging it to be that way. We may even experience some x as F—say, a ventriloquist's puppet as speaking—without judging it to be so. Experiencing-as (in contrast to believing that x is F) is a distinctively experiential response in the sense that it is inherently first-personal, embodied, and phenomenologically characterized.

So described, experiencing-as, like perceptual experience more generally, is not confined to the five senses, even if it often occurs by way of them: affective responses such as emotions, moods, and motivational dispositions are also embodied, first-personal, and phenomenologically characterized. Thus one may experience—indeed, one may see—a gesture as threatening or friendly, although these are not themselves sensible properties. In this sense, it is natural to say that we directly perceive evaluative properties as well as natural ones: in Tolstoy's account, for instance, Vronsky *sees* Anna's image as bearing a certain expression manifesting a certain quality—that 'sweet spiritual expression of hers'. He detects this quality by way of a complex of perceptions—principally, by way of a visual and affective responses—but what he sees is not itself a sense-specific property such as a colour or flavour or musical pitch. It is an evaluative property.

Experiencing-as is also distinct from mere imagining or conceiving: Vronsky does not look at Mihailov's portrait and then find himself imagining that Anna has certain inner qualities. Rather, he directly perceives those qualities in and through his visual experience of the portrait. Consider an analogy suggested by Christopher Peacocke: the familiar child's game of finding objects hidden in a drawn image. We do not praise the child for imagining that the drawing somewhere depicts this or that object; the aim is to perceptually discover it—to see it. What we imagine is largely subject to the will; what we perceive something to be is (largely) not.[2]

---

[2] I owe this example and the next (Friedrich's *Solitary Tree*) to Christopher Peacocke. See his 'The Perception of Music: Sources of Significance', *British Journal of Aesthetics*,

In Tolstoy's passage, the kind of experiencing-as in question is 'literal': it is not a matter of conceiving of a thing as something that it (literally) is not. Vronsky just sees Anna's image as, literally, bearing a certain expression manifesting certain qualities. Experiencing-as in other cases may be metaphorical (or metaphorically metaphorical, since the notion of metaphor strictly describes a linguistic device). In metaphorical experiencing-as we not only experience the represented object in a certain way, but in doing so we conceive of it as something it literally is not. For instance, Casper David Friedrich's well-known *Solitary Tree*—a painting of a single, winter-blackened tree in a barren landscape—often is experienced metaphorically as depicting an isolated, desolate person. In this case, the kind of experiencing-as Friedrich's painting elicits is guided by a conceptual shift: the viewer still sees a tree depiction, but metaphorically reconceptualizes it. The tree is personified, and its literal properties of being isolated, lifeless, and exposed are transposed to counterparts in the realm of human psychology. Vronsky, by contrast, does not conceive of Anna's image as anything other than an image of Anna herself. Not all experiencing-as targeting a work of art is metaphorical.

Tolstoy's specific example of experiencing-as highlights some common characteristics of what it is to directly perceive something as having a certain non-sensible property. One characteristic is that the features of which we thus become aware are often inherently evaluative ones to which we react with a positive or negative sentiment, where the class of properties includes not only moral but aesthetic and emotional ones.[3] Vronsky does not just discover *that Anna wears this characteristic expression*. Rather, he discovers its sweet, transcendent quality; the sensitivity of Mihailov's portrait makes him aware of the characteristic expression *as* a reflecting these aspects of Anna's nature, and these aspects strike Vronsky as having special value. Moreover, Tolstoi's passage signals that the property or quality to which a successful work of art calls our attention may be one that had previously escaped our notice. Vronsky

49/3 (July 2009): 257–75. I say that what we perceive is 'largely' not subject to the will; exceptions include willed shifts between alternative perceptions of dual aspect figures (e.g. the duck-rabbit).

[3] For instance, we see the ballet dancer's gracefulness—a positively valued aesthetic feature—even though gracefulness is not itself a sensory feature in the way that redness or sourness or loudness are.

wonders at how Mihailov could have 'discovered' Anna's peculiar beauty, but of course it is Vronsky, too, who discovers it through his portrait. Mihailov's portrait illuminates a dimension of Anna's character that was always there before him, but which he had previously failed to notice, and he feels that what he had missed was not an incidental detail, but a deep and defining feature, essential to her nature.

A second significant response to which Tolstoi's passage calls attention is the phenomenon of 'experience-taking', as it is now sometimes called.[4] In experience-taking, one assumes the perspective of another, simulating some aspect or aspects of his psychology as if they were one's own—his relevant perceptions, affective responses, and thoughts. Experience-taking is closely related to what psychologists call perspective-taking. Neither phrase is well defined in the empirical literature, and different authors elucidate them with reference to different psychological characteristics. However, it is now common to distinguish the former as a specifically non-deliberative process, occurring by way of non-cognitive, subpersonal processes that are directed by conscious intention or will.[5] Perspective-taking, by contrast, is a deliberative, theoretical exercise in which one's project is to 'work out' the psychological states of another by various conscious strategies, for instance, by reasoning about the causes and consequences of his circumstances, or by reflecting on his motives and desires. Perspective-taking in this sense may proceed entirely from an impersonal point of view: it need not involve any first-personal engagement *in* the target perspective. Experience-taking, by contrast, exploits first-personal experiencing-as, and is essentially simulative: it involves adopting, to varying degrees,

---

[4] See G. F. Kaufman and L. K. Libby, 'Changing Beliefs and Behaviour through Experience-Taking', *Journal of Personality and Social Psychology*, 103/1 (2012): 1–19.

[5] See Kaufman and Libby, 'Changing Beliefs'. Kaufman and Libby emphasize that, in experience-taking, the distinction between the subject and a target other is mitigated not by a conscious, willed exercise of conceiving of the other's circumstances, but by a non-deliberative process of 'taking up' the other's experiential point of view: 'Although [Experiencing-taking] shares with . . . [perspective-taking] a focus on the identity merger that can occur between self and other, experience-taking . . . does not rely on orienting the other as a target for scrutiny or comparison but rather entails the spontaneous replacement of self with other' (p. 2). Kaufman and Libby's attempt to distinguish experience-taking and perspective-taking remains unsatisfactory, and fails to specify the several distinct criteria identifying each. However, the idea that the former process is distinct from the latter in being unwilled, subpersonal, non-cognitive, and non-deliberative is both helpful and correct.

the other's perceptual, affective, and motivational orientations. Vronsky arguably engages in experience-taking when he wonders how Mihailov could have detected Anna's 'peculiar beauty'. His answer to that question is to imaginatively conceive of Mihailov's experience as if it were his own: 'One must know her and love her as I have done', Vronsky observes, 'to understand that . . . expression . . . ' This episode aptly illustrates the close relationship between experiencing-as and experience-taking: the latter requires a reflective step beyond experiencing-as, but they do not occur independently, for the latter is a causally necessary condition of the former. How Vronsky first-personally experiences Anna's expression in Mihailov's portrait provides the particular *content* of Mihailov's psychology that interests him, and it is by experiencing Anna as he does that he 'takes on' Mihailov's experience as his own. It is through the direct, non-conceptual experience-as which Mihailov's portrait elicits that his first-personal perspective is constructed as one who 'knows and loves' Anna as Vronsky does.

The experience-taking that ensues on Vronsky's part is, of course, quite trivial and transitory; it does not cut very deep and is far from Vronsky's principal interest in Anna's portrait. (Indeed, its transitoriness—and the swiftness with which it leads Vronsky back to thoughts centred flatteringly on himself—is one of the subtle ways in which Tolstoy signals to the reader his irrepressible vanity.) In general, however, experience-taking and the experiencing-as on which it depends constitute a significant dimension of the value we attach to great works of art. Like Mihailov's portrait, they nudge us to experience their subjects in unfamiliar and interesting ways, and in so doing they sometimes move us to adopt a different experiential point of view.

II Poetic Experience

I turn now to poetry. Experiencing-as and experience-taking are commonly associated with poetry; a successful poem can introduce us to novel ways of thinking and responding to its subject, engaging us with the first-personal phenomenology of persons other than ourselves, in circumstances other than our own. Moreover, poems are often described as if they achieved this in same way as do pictures. The visual image is never left far behind in our analyses and interpetations of poetry, and this association is built into the very terms in which we describe poetic language. We commonly refer to poetic constructions as linguistic *images*, and the term 'figurative' derives from our association of certain uses of words with the 'rendering of figures'. Are these traditional associations mere metaphors for metaphors, an attempt to explain an essentially conceptual process on analogy with experiential, perceptual ones? I suspect not. More probably, they reflect an underlying isomorphism in the actual psychological structures constitutive of understanding poetic discourse and visual perception. Certainly, interpreting and understanding such discourse very often seems to elicit an array of non-inferential, first-personal, phenomenologically characterized responses. The public *meanings* of words are not, of course, decided by subjective images and other contingent responses in the minds of those who use them. Nonetheless, it is undeniable that such images and responses do occur, and they play an important role in how we actually interpret both everyday and literary utterances. Philosophical theories of meaning in the analytic tradition have almost exclusively focused on issues of public meaning—of stable, context-independent semantic content. Such theories have also dominated analyses of figurative language, focusing on the semantic relations of figurative utterances to literal propositions and paraphrases. Whatever its merits, this approach stands to overlook some of the most distinctive and valuable characteristics of our experience of poetry; in particular, it stands to misrepresent the *epistemic* value of poetry—the value it has as a way of informing our beliefs. Poetic language is of course seldom the best medium for representing impersonal, mind-independent facts. That is a task better left to a privileged set of null-context, literal propositions, the meaning of which will be set out by a truth-conditional semantics of one kind or another. But such facts do not exhaust the possible objects of knowledge, and representing them does not exhaust the possible uses of language. We sometimes also want to know how the facts are experienced by others, and accurately to describe how we experience them ourselves.

Poetry has long been employed in service of these epistemic aims. In this context the imagistic aspects of poetic language play an indispensable role, for poems, like pictures, provoke perceptual (or, in the case of mental imagery, quasi-perceptual) responses that reorient our first-personal experience of their subjects. Moreover, those responses—like Vronsky's response to Anna's portrait—often include specifically evaluative perceptions. In everyday practice, poetry often affords us access to alternative evaluative perceptions by means of a process structurally similar to that afforded by (some) works of visual art—processes of experiencing-as and experience-taking.

A proper appreciation of this structural similarity helps to explain part of the epistemic value we accord certain poems. A poem can enable us to understand its subject from a particular subjective, experiential point of view by eliciting affective, perceptual and cognitive responses appropriate to that perspective. In the case of poems concerned with experiences remote from our own, the perspective offered may be quite alien to us, prompting (or even compelling) us to regard the poetic subject in ways that are not only unfamiliar but contrary to our previous experience and our considered judgement. This need not count as an epistemic defect, however. For one possible aim of a poem—indeed, an actual aim of a great many poems—is precisely to reveal what it is like to occupy an unusual or anomalous first-personal point of view, and to show how the world appears as from that point of view. Poetry is a classic medium of subjectivity, and part of its wonder lies in its capacity to render public even the most radically private and remote aspects of our inner lives.

In what follows, my principal aim is not to defend but to illustrate these claims. In section III, I attempt to identify and conceptualize one particular, and particularly elusive, evaluative point of view—what psychologists sometimes refer to as evaluative detachment, and what I label 'ethical estrangement'. Ethical estrangement is an identifiable psychological type in general terms, but its subjective phenomenology is notoriously difficult to represent and communicate. This is in part because it is an evaluative point of view we have good reason to resist, and are inclined to perceive as pathological. Section IV turns to a poem expressive of ethical estrangement: Paul Celan's *Psalm*. *Psalm* exemplifies several of the strategies by which a poem, like a work of visual art, can occasion direct experiencing-as and experience-taking, provoking the reader to attend to new features of its subject by moving him to experience certain familiar phenomena as possessing radically different evaluative properties. I argue that, in *Psalm*, Celan compels his reader to adopt a distinctive—and for most of us quite remote—evaluative perspective, inviting us to instantiate various of the first-personal perceptions, emotions, and thoughts constitutive of ethical estrangement. Section V returns to the contributions of poetic experiencing-as and experience-taking to evaluative knowledge.

III Ethical Estrangement

Whoever has succumbed to torture can no longer feel at home in the world. The shame of destruction cannot be erased. Trust in the world which already collapsed in part at the first blow, but in the end, under torture, fully, will not be regained. That one's fellow man was experienced as the 'anti-man' remains in the tortured person . . . It blocks the view into a world in which the principle of hope rules. One who was martyred is a defenseless prisoner of fear. It is fear that henceforth reigns over him. Fear—and also what is called resentment.[6]

Jean Améry's *At the Mind's Limits* is an attempt to articulate, in a mix of narrative and philosophical terms, the more persisting psychological effects of the author's imprisonment and torture under the Nazi regime. The most profound of these effects is what Améry refers to as 'loss of trust in the world' (or 'loss of confidence' in the world).[7] In the course of his essay, he attempts to spell out how that loss of trust was caused, and in what it consists.

The trust to which Améry refers is his confidence in the world of ordinary, human relationships—the social world of personal interactions with our fellow men. He observes that these interactions are normally guided by a kind of unwritten social contract, in accordance with which we engage with one another against a background of shared assumptions and expectations. This common background allows us to navigate a course through the social world that is relatively stable and predictable. It is the basis of interpersonal cooperation, and Améry compares its operation to the unreflective trust we normally invest in the most basic frameworks of experience and thought. 'Trust in the world includes all sorts of things', he writes, 'the irrational and logically unjustifiable belief in absolute causality perhaps, or the likewise blind belief in the validity of the inductive inference'.[8] Trust in causality or in the laws of inference are essential, of course, if we are to successfully navigate the material world. The trust that Améry lost at Auschwitz, he says, was similarly essential, permitting him to negotiate a successful and sustainable course through the social world: the trust that 'the other person will spare me— . . . that he will respect my physical, and with it my metaphysical being'.[9]

[6] Jean Améry, *At the Mind's Limits*. Bloomington: Indiana University Press, 1980, 40.
[7] Améry, *At the Mind's Limits*, 28.   [8] Améry, *At the Mind's Limits*, 28.
[9] Améry, *At the Mind's Limits*, 28.

Améry's traumatic experiences of torture and abuse, he says, left him guided no longer by basic human principles of mutual respect, but by fear and resentment—fear of future harms and resentment of past ones. 'You do not observe dehumanized man committing his deeds and misdeeds without having all of your notions of inherent human dignity placed in doubt', he writes. 'We emerged . . . robbed, emptied out, disoriented—and it was a long time before we were able even to learn the ordinary language of freedom. Still today . . . we speak it with discomfort and without real trust in its validity.'[10] Améry's loss of trust in his dealings with others is a vivid instance of detachment from his established ethical point of view—his 'ethical estrangement', as I shall call it. Ethical estrangement is a distinctive psychological condition in which the basic framework of a person's evaluative worldview has been radically undermined. It is not just a matter of one's moral (and other evaluative) judgements and choices *changing* in non-standard ways—of revising or altering certain evaluative commitments—although it includes that. Specifically, ethical estrangement is characterized by three defining features: the level at which the evaluative changes are effected, their transitional and negating logic, and their multi-dimensional psychological scope. I discuss each in turn.

First, ethical estrangement occurs not just when this or that particular evaluation deviates from some recognized norms, but when one's *fundamental* evaluative framework deviates from such norms. This framework consists of both one's basic beliefs—one's standing assumptions and expectations—and the repertoire of constitutive concepts central to one's thought and discourse about value (in Améry's case, concepts such as 'human dignity'). In ethical estrangement, these familiar and foundational basic beliefs and concepts cease to guide one's judgements and practical reasoning. The estranged subject's normative practice does not deviate merely at a first-order level of particular evaluations, affecting how or to what he applies this or that concept; rather, it deviates at a second-order level, such that the commitments and the concepts that regulate and are constitutive of shared normative practices are, if not abandoned, at least no longer functioning in their standard roles. His ethical judgements,

---

[10] Améry, *At the Mind's Limits*, 20.

memories, imaginings, and practical reasoning come to be regulated by different, non-standard commitments which cannot be expressed, or easily expressed, in a standard conceptual repertoire. Améry, for instance, describes himself as no longer expecting human relations to be governed by general principles of reciprocity and justice; he lost his 'certainty that by reason of written or unwritten social contracts the other person [would] respect [his] physical, and with it [his] metaphysical being'.[11] This commitment stood previously as a 'certainty' in the sense that it had functioned as a pre-reflective assumption. That is, Améry had previously supposed that personal relations would be guided by a presumption of respect, in the sense that this supposition had been a background condition of his day-to-day interactions; it was never doubted because it was never seriously questioned. As Améry observes, such expectations regulate our everyday lives in indefinitely many ways. The pedestrian expects that she will not be wilfully run down by a whimsical motorist—and that if she is, passers-by will help; the woman guiding her small child through a crowd expects that no one will wilfully trample him underfoot—and if someone did, others would intervene; the man who seeks medical help from a surgeon trusts that he will not turn his knife against him—and that if he did, someone would attempt to stop him. And so forth. A world in which these conditions manifestly go unsatisfied (as they did in Améry's during the war) is one governed by a different form of life. It is a world in which it is no longer possible to say what many of our canonical, action-regulating concepts mean—concepts such as 'respect' and 'dignity', and even the collective sensibility we gesture at with the term 'humanity'. I think that this must be part of what Améry had in mind when he commented that, for the longer-term prisoners at Auschwitz, intellectual thought 'nullified itself when at almost every step it ran into its uncrossable borders. The axes of its traditional frames of reference then shattered. Beauty: that was an illusion. Knowledge: that turned out to be a game with ideas.'[12]

The second distinguishing feature of ethical estrangement is that it is, precisely, a matter of undergoing a transition or change: it names a condition *to* which one has moved *from* some previous one. As Améry

---

[11] Améry, At the Mind's Limits, 40.   [12] Améry, *At the Mind's Limits*, 19.

describes this transition in his own case, it was a departure from a condition of relative psychological coherence and commonality with others, in which his everyday evaluative intuitions made sense to his fellow men, even if they were not always in agreement. The position he later occupied, by contrast, was one of isolation and mutual incomprehension. In this respect, ethical estrangement has the structure of more ordinary instances of estrangement in intimate personal relationships: one can only be 'estranged' from someone with whom one has been on close terms. It is one thing to be an excluded outsider; it is another to be an outsider who was once an insider, and who now recognizes (from without) the disparities not only between himself and others, but between his present and past selves.

Thirdly, ethical estrangement operates across and affects multiple dimensions of a person's relations: while it may be caused by a rupture in a single relationship, it ramifies into indefinitely many others, including one's relation to one's past and future self. This can be true even in the case of a more commonplace personal betrayal by a trusted intimate— a spouse, a sibling, or a colleague. Such betrayals threaten not only to disrupt one's standing assumptions and expectations of that particular person; they can affect one's assessment of the possibility of trust itself, and hence can estrange one from other relationships which similarly turn on such trust as a basis. Thus when Améry describes how his view of humanity was altered by the abuses he both witnessed and suffered, he makes it clear that this follows in part from realizing that his tormentor might be any ordinary man:

[A]mazingly, it dawns on one that the fellows not only have leather coats and pistols, but also faces: not 'Gestapo faces' with twisted noses, hypertrophied chins, pockmarks, and knife scars, as might appear in a book, but rather faces like anyone else's. Plain, ordinary faces.[13]

Across another dimension, ethical estrangement provokes a reassessment of oneself: it is one thing to remember episodes from the past in which one's role is that of, say, friend and helpmate, and another to remember the same episodes with oneself now cast in the role of dupe, victim, or unwitting prey. In this respect, the estranged subject's current self-conception becomes discontinuous with his previous one; the

[13] Améry, *At the Mind's Limits*, 25.

temporal continuity of his own identity has been disrupted. By the same token, ethical estrangement alters one's future possibilities, both in terms of one's expectations of others and in terms of who one can be: the future person, whose choices are now informed by his experience of betrayal, is someone whose relations will be guided by due caution, at best, and sceptical distrust at worst. His future self, too, is estranged from the person he once was.

The phenomenon of ethical estrangement is not, of course, something particular to victims of genocide. In less radical forms, its occurrence is all too commonplace: it can be the lot of the abused child, of the jilted life-long spouse, of the abandoned elderly parent, and the traumatized soldier, as much as the victim of systematic, physical violence. Its essence is the displacement of evaluative faith by evaluative scepticism, occasioned by an experience of profound betrayal. Saying this much, however, does little to convey what it is like to be so betrayed, or to live with such estrangement. Améry's essay is an attempt to describe the psychological trajectory of his own estrangement and the consequent effects on his everyday experience. It does this by relating the historical facts and offering a largely theoretical account of how his beliefs were altered by them. Améry was, after all, an essayist and philosopher; his project is to impose some theoretical sense on the profound transformations of his inner life and the world around him. It is noteworthy in this context that, in a similar effort, Améry also published a philosophical essay on suicide—shortly before taking his own life.

As impressive as Améry's essay is, it does not so much leave the reader with the feeling that he understands what Améry experienced as with the conviction that he could *never* truly understand it. The first-personal phenomenology of ethical estrangement remains opaque and intractable; while one cannot but feel horror at what Améry suffered, and compassion for his despair, these attitudes constitute sympathetic distance more than empathic complicity. The reader is not brought to experience others as did Améry, nor to partake in that experience by internalizing his point of view. In this respect, the title of Améry's essay—*At the Mind's Limit*—may be thought appropriate not only to what Améry endured when incarcerated, but what he continued to endure as a survivor: the isolation imposed by the limits of our intelligibility to one another.

Can anything more be achieved? Where literal description fails in this way, can the devices of art do any better? Several theorists, most famously Adorno, have insisted that there can be no adequate or morally appropriate artistic response to such horrific events—that they should be regarded as literally 'unspeakable'. But this is, I aver, to underestimate the peculiar resources of artistic uses of language—and of poetry in particular—as a way of giving public form to the more remote reaches of human experience. It is also to neglect one of the oldest, and in some ways the noblest, urges to create art: the urge to give voice to one's inner life precisely when one finds oneself most removed and isolated from a *common* framework of human experience—when one's subjective condition divorces one from ordinary, daily commerce with others. (We most hope to be heard when we are least likely to be understood.) What is required is a medium of expression that—like the visual image— affords others some first-personal acquaintance with the perceptions, attitudes, and emotions constitutive of the alien point of view. Visual art, I observed earlier, sometimes achieves this by effecting a reorientation of perspective at the experiential level, subjecting the viewer's perceptions (including his emotions) to the authority of the artist's point of view. It is tempting to speculate that only those art forms which compel direct sensory responses could achieve this end, and that mere words will always fail. Poetry, however, arguably occupies a psychological terrain somewhere between perception and conception; its association with imagery is not merely metaphorical. In particular, when a poem's target subject is itself an experiential point of view, poetic language can be used not so much to describe that subject as to *construct* it out of the reader's own repertoire of responses—a repertoire of non-inferential, first-personal experience. To see this, and to assess the prospects of poetry's success in this domain, I turn to an attempt to give poetic voice to ethical estrangement.

IV Celan's *Psalm*

Paul Celan is best known for poems that arise from and address his experience of Nazi oppression. Along with Primo Levi and Jean Améry, he is widely regarded as a pre-eminent literary voice of the Nazi genocide and of the moral fractures it left in European society, and in the lives of its survivors. Like several other survivor authors, Celan repeatedly returned to these concerns in his writings. Also like them, he eventually took his own life.

Celan's mature poetry is, broadly speaking, imagist in style: exceptionally spare, vivid, and elusive. That is part of its distinctiveness. But what sets certain of Celan's poems apart for many readers is not so much their formal artistry as their exceptional depth.[14] Critics and lay readers alike aver that Celan, perhaps more than any other writer, succeeded in doing justice to the unimaginable strangeness of life for European Jewry (and many other Europeans) during, and long after, the years of Nazi Germany's dominance.

Celan published a collection titled *Die Niemandsrose* in 1963. The collection does not feature a clearly discernible, connecting thread as such, and the references in the poems it gathers together range widely across Celan's personal history. John Felsteiner, Celan's biographer, says that *Die Niemandsrose* as a whole presents the reader with a problem of 'poetic intelligibility', not least because of the numerous allusions to specific places, people, and events of private biographical import to Celan. This problem is complicated by Celan's references to obscure literary and biblical sources, including plays on words in Yiddish, Latin, and German. Hence many of the poems in *Die Niemandsrose* remain bewildering and impenetrable to even the most dedicated reader. At the same time, the collection as whole, especially on rereading, yields a vivid cumulative effect through its consistent *affective* tone—a tone of wistfulness and longing, of occasional hopes restrained by regretful and sometimes resentful reminiscences of what is past. This is achieved partly through Celan's images, but also through his syntax and his many backward-looking references, creating a sombre mood of remembrance, sometimes bitter and sometimes tender, reaching back towards what once was, but now is lost.

Die Niemandsrose is also more directly drawn together by the poems' repeated invocations of absence and loss of one kind or another, with multiple references to blindness (loss of sight), madness (loss of reason), babbling (loss of the power of speech), and death (loss of life), as well as the uncountable human losses associated with the Shoah. One prominent reference to absence running through the collection occurs indirectly through the use—often an ironic use—of religious vocabulary, visual images, sacred traditions, and even verbal rhythms echoing the rhythms of familiar prayers. (This is a strategy that characterizes many

---

[14] I use the term 'depth' for want of a better one; it does not say much, in itself, besides 'psychological importance', but I mean for it to bear greater weight than that.

of Celan's post-war poems, including his renowned *Todesfugue*.) Overall, this collection is perhaps where Celan most clearly and profoundly expresses the negative transition from a safe and secure pre-war worldview underwritten by faith, tradition, and divine benevolence to a nihilistic one of moral and spiritual chaos. These are, in a phrase, poems of evaluative estrangement.

Among them, Celan's 'Psalm' is perhaps the plainest and most desolate:

> No one moulds us again out of earth and clay,
> No one conjures our dust.
> No one.
>
> Praised be your name, No one.
> For your sake
> We shall flower.
> Towards
> You.
>
> A nothing
> We were, are, shall
> Remain, flowering:
> The nothing—, the
> No one's rose.
>
> With
> Our pistil soul-bright,
> With our stamen heaven-ravaged,
> Our corolla red
> With the crimson word which we sang
> Over, O over
> the thorn.[15]

Few readers familiar with the rhythm and imagery of the biblical Psalms, whether Jewish or Christian, can fail to feel here the sting of Celan's mockery. *Psalm* voices the bitterness of the once-faithful, themselves now mocked by the indifference, even the brutality, of an absent god. The soothing pastoral imagery of the Twenty-Third Psalm ('The Lord is my

---

[15] 'Psalm' by Paul Celan, from *Poems of Paul Celan*, tr. Michael Hamburger. Translation copyright © 1972, 2002 by Michael Hamburger. Reprinted by permission of Persea Books, Inc., New York. All rights reserved.

Shepherd . . . ') hovers in the background throughout, reminding us that the speaker is not led beside still waters nor invited to lie down in green pastures; his soul is not being restored. Far from dwelling 'in the house of the lord forever', he will not be reborn at all. No future paradises await the dead, for all that exists is earth and clay and dust, and the God that will surely resurrect us and reshape us out of those lifeless materials is, precisely, No One.

As *Psalm* moves to the second and third stanzas, we hear that humanity, far from being an object of divine love, endowed with immortality, is nature's short-lived decoration, a beautiful amusement for the divine No one, flowering towards nothing, to no point or purpose, and for the 'sake of' nothing. Like the cherished rose, a human being is a bright, beautiful, and magical thing—but he is not thereby protected and loved: he is 'No one's rose'. Indeed, the rose's life-generating and reproductive characteristic—the 'pistil', 'stamen', and 'soft corolla'—are at once the sources and subjects of brutal violence ('heaven-ravaged') and coloured by blood, stained by the 'crimson word' which we once sang—the prayers and psalms of our spiritual traditions. In the absurd and demonic world of No one's rose, the only object of our prayers can be the thorn: that part of ourselves promising injury and death to those who dare to touch us.

Whatever the detail of one's reading of Celan's poem, its wider import is incontestable: it offers the form of a prayer with a message denying both the point and propriety of prayer and rhythmic song, but using the structure of both. By his interweaving of contradictory form and content, Celan succeeds in moving the reader at an immediate and pre-reflective, experiential level: the bitterness and emptiness of the abandoned believer is not only represented semantically, but conveyed viscerally. Celan achieves something rather remarkable in this respect, for 'Psalm' offers a striking *expression* (rather than a theoretical statement) of embittered nihilism: it succeeds in offering the reader an episodic experience of what it would be like, from within, to exist under the spectre of such nihilism oneself, and to find that one's only existing forms of spiritual expression—including the expression of spiritual rage—arise from and belong to the very world that one has left behind.[16] It does this in part by recollecting experiential details of the background within which our more familiar values have arisen, excavating and exploiting the symbols,

---

[16] Celan wrote throughout his life in German, which was at once his most natural poetic language and the despised language of his oppressors.

rhythms, rituals, and vocabulary that make up the fabric of our every-day, normative point of view—a fabric that is typically invisible to us until it unravels. Celan's poem thus delivers to the responsive reader the many dimensions of experience—emotional, perceptual, cognitive—with which its language is associated. In this way Celan circumvents the *semantic* limitations of the words assembled and exploits their ability to call forth experiences in the form of imaginings, memories, desires, and the emotions and moods these evoke. Moreover, by adopting the voice of a prayer, Celan moves the reader to follow the poem's course of thought from *within* the perspective of the supplicant—a perspective of private, first-personal address, making it natural for him to conceive of the words as his own. Put in psychological terms, the reader is led to introject or internalize the experiential locus from which they are delivered, that is, to experience prayer as, inter alia, a bitter accusation, and to experience himself as the estranged subject who so prays.[17]

Like Améry, Celan's narrator's evaluative framework has not merely altered in particulars, but at its foundations: the estrangement it describes is foundational. Also like Améry, the new framework it introduces is one defined by what it is not—by the transition from a traditional conception of a benevolent god to his absence. (This is not the voice of mere atheism, but the expression of an active loss of faith.) Finally, Celan's estrangement echoes Améry's in permeating his understanding of all past and future relations: not only the narrator, but all humanity is defined by the futile suffering it portends. By effecting these various dimensions of how the ethically estranged subject experiences himself and others, *Psalm* makes it possible for us to glimpse what it would be to enact this evaluative point of view. The device of speaking as one estranged from and inveighing against the very origin and arbiter of all value—a divine authority known, at least by reputation, to virtually everyone—makes it almost impossible for the reader not to experience, first-personally, at least some echoes of the absurdity, the fear, the moral confusion, and the bitter loss suffered by the survivor.

---

[17] See Kaufman and Libby, 'Changing Beliefs'. In one of the researchers' series of stud-ies on experience-taking, subjects were given similar narrative passages stated in the first-person and in the third-person voices, and then tested for levels of experiential iden-tification with the narrator. As the researchers (and common sense) predicted, narratives in the first person elicited significantly higher levels of experience-taking.

For all that, Celan's poem does not deliver a theory of value (or dis-value), as Améry's essay at times attempts to do. The epistemic merits of the poem are not those of a second-order meta-ethics. It is one thing to adduce reasons for a set of meta-ethical commitments; that is the task of a philosophical metaphysics of morals. It is another to *occupy* a given meta-ethical perspective, and to manifest in a way that affords that possibility to the reader. *Psalm* speaks first-personally, from the contradictory position of a man who finds himself compelled to continue his traditional rituals of prayer, even while his message denies his god's existence; it is the position of a survivor of faith, living on in a world that is both familiar and wholly transformed. Of course, one might attempt to construct an ideal, complete paraphrase of Celan's poem, setting out in literal terms all that can be recovered of its theoretical content, and this construction might have meta-ethical content. It might even constitute something like an ad hoc meta-ethical thesis. But however faithful it might be to the poem's semantic content, it would deliver little or none of what we value in the poem itself: it would not convey what it is to experience oneself and others *as* ethically estranged, let alone move one to take up that point of view.[18]

Outside of the context of the philosophy of language, it is just such an elaboration that we refer to as 'poetic meaning'—*not* a paraphrase of 'stand-alone' semantic content. Analyses of the settled meanings of the poem's words will not go the distance. In a successful interpretation (and even in my own amateur reading of the poem) what is elaborated typically strays very far from what can be recovered from the words alone; it is rather an exercise in recovering the experiential effects of those words—the direct, non-optional, and largely pre-reflective first-personal attitudes and motivations they elicit, compelling one to experience oneself *as* profoundly estranged. Of course, if the reader does not know the literal meaning of the words at all he will fail even to get that far; but it does not follow that this necessary condition of understanding the poem is also a sufficient one. A grasp of literal semantic content is nearer to an *occasioning* condition, setting off a psychological sequence which goes

---

[18] 'Perception' does not here mean sensory perception as in vision and hearing, but nor is it a mere figure of speech. I use it broadly to refer to any phenomenologically characterized state in which one is non-inferentially aware of some attended object or property by way of an embodied response to it; emotions are perceptions in this sense of the term.

far beyond what may be found in the words themselves, provoking in the subject an array of responses—memories, emotions, imaginings, and the rest. *Psalm*'s success as a poem consists in part in the fact that those responses so naturally and vividly mirror the character of the extraordinary perspective that is its subject. It is in this sense that the poem does its work in a psychological terrain between perception and linguistic conception. As in a visual image, its form embodies its content.

V Poetry, Perception, and Epistemic Value

Does this account of the import of *Psalm* relegate it to a play of imagination—a mere affective and perceptual provocation with no cognitive merit?[19] Are questions of truth or falsity irrelevant to the value of Celan's work? That would be so if we took no interest in whether what we grasp through the poem corresponds to the way the world is. But surely we *do* have that interest. Indeed, one motivation for the foregoing discussion of *Psalm* was to gain a better understanding of the all-too-real phenomenon of ethical estrangement, and it matters whether the poem succeeds or fails in delivering that. Celan's work, like that of many other poets, is typically regarded as an attempt on an important truth, in some sense of the word. This much is included in the attitudes we bring to bear in reading such poems: we evaluate them in part as informing or misleading us, as a process of discovery or a source of illusion.

Similarly, we often regard works of visual art as being true or false, despite the fact that a visual image, as such, makes no assertion which could be properly so assessed. Is such talk at best too casual, and at worst

---

[19] I refer to contemporary non-cognitivist accounts of figurative language, and of metaphor in particular. The most familiar defence of this view is by Donald Davidson in 'What Metaphors Mean', *Critical Inquiry*, 5/1 (autumn 1978): 31–47. Davidson holds that metaphors and other figures possess no epistemic value, because they have no semantic content other than their literal content: there is no such thing as 'figurative meaning'. Richard Rorty's conception of metaphor follows Davidson's, in spirit if not in letter, comparing the way metaphors engage us to the way we enjoy (semantically empty) birdsongs. See Richard Rorty. 'Hesse and Davidson on Metaphor', *Aristotelian Society*, suppl. vol. 61 (1987): 283–96. More recently, similarly motivated arguments are rehearsed in part II of James Grant's *The Critical Imagination* (Oxford: Oxford University Press, 2013). All of these theorists are driven, albeit from different perspectives, by their commitment to context-independent conceptions of semantic content. For a review of non-cognitivism and objections to that central commitment, see A. E. Denham, *Metaphor and Moral Experience* (Oxford: Oxford University Press, 2000).

misguided? Recall Tolstoy's fictional portrait of Anna. We have no difficulty understanding what Tolstoy means when he tells us that the
expression captured by Mihailov was 'so true that seemed to [Vronsky]
and others that they had always known it'. What is 'true' here, moreover, is not just a matter of *depictive* accuracy. Rather, it is that those who
view Anna's portrait judge that its subject—Anna—really does bear
the expression it exhibits, and that that expression really does manifest
the evaluative properties (the sweetness and spirituality) that Mihailov
shows it to have. It is not uncommon for us to evaluate artworks in this
way—to evaluate them with respect to their specifically epistemic merit,
as informing us of properties or qualities their subjects actually possess.
Indeed, among the works we typically think of as masterpieces such
valuations are very common: Michelangelo's *Pieta*, Shakespeare's *Julius
Caesar*, Rembrandt's *Self-Portrait* of 1659, and Eliot's *The Wasteland* all
lead us to notice new (or previously obscured) evaluative features of their
subjects, and the esteem in which we hold them is owed in no small part
to this effect. Works that do not do this may, of course, be esteemed for
other reasons. But it is noteworthy how few such appear in our catalogues
of artistic masterpieces.

   In the case of visual artworks, it is tempting to say that part of their
epistemic merit derives from the evaluative *perceptions* they elicit; the
phrase is recommended by fact that vision is a paradigmatically perceptual, non-inferential mode of presentation. It is also recommended
more generally by the structure of experiencing-as, where this is
non-inferential, first-personal, and phenomenologically characterized.
I noted earlier that, when we experience a work (or its represented subject) as having this or that valenced property, we typically experience
this in and through the artwork, as a property it presents—not just as
some subjective response we have *to* it. The values detected present
themselves with an immediacy and directness characteristic of perception, and as non-optional, indifferent to our preferences or whims. Once
Vronsky has experienced Anna's expression in the portrait as sweet and
spiritual, it will be difficult if not impossible for him to see it any other
way. (If ever there were a case for speaking literally of the perception of
evaluativeproperties, it is here.) Nonetheless, such a perception need not
compel a judgement that the subject actually does possess that property: Vronsky—in a variation on Tolstoy's novel—might have judged
that, whilst Mihailov's rendering of Anna captured a characteristic

expression, and that whilst *in the portrait* it manifested a sweet spiritual-ity, in Anna herself it was a manifestation of feminine cunning and prac-tised, disingenuous charm. Perceiving that a work presents its subject *as* being thus and so is one thing; assessing the work as accurate or veridical is another. A well-wrought picture or sculpture can prompt an evalua-tive perception that the viewer's judgement actively resists. This is one source of the traditional worry—and the long-standing philosophical objection—that artworks, like people, can seduce and deceive as much as enlighten us. Think of the power of a hostile newspaper caricature of someone you admire; however contrary to your beliefs its intent may be, it is impossible not to *see* in it the vices it depicts its subject as having. Experience is compelling, but cannot always be trusted. This is part of what we mean when we say that any artwork, including a poem, is true or untrue, even while it offers no truth-apt claims at all: we mean that it leads towards or away from such claims.

Likewise, in assessing the value of Celan's *Psalm* we may bring to bear different interests. One interest is in simply entertaining the experiential perspective it affords and the evaluative perceptions that it comprises. Another interest concerns whether that perspective cor-rectly represents an independently identified state of the world—in the present case, the psychological condition of ethical estrangement. If it does, this is at least one way in which it possesses epistemic value. But how is its veracity to be decided? It may seem that we have only intuitions to guide us. However, with Améry's account in view we can avail ourselves of a less arbitrary procedure, alternately comparing the theoretically identified features of ethical estrangement with the first-personal ones elicited by the poem. This will be something like a process of reflective equilibrium, in which we look for relations of fit between these two ways of elucidating the phenomenon in ques-tion. Ethical estrangement, as I characterized it in Améry's case, was distinguished by three features: it involved an evaluative change at a foundational, second-order level; those changes constituted a negat-ing transition (they consisted in an estrangement *from* Améry's for-mer evaluative convictions); and they were multi-dimensional in their psychological structure, affecting Améry's relations to others as well as to his past and future self. Of course, this characterization of ethi-cal estrangement is in part stipulative, delineating a theoretical term of art. The delineation is not an arbitrary one, however: it is directly led by Améry's account detailing the causes and consequences of his personal history. Further, it reflects the character and structure of an attuned reader's responses to Celan's *Psalm*, as these have been sketched here. To this extent, the reader who takes himself to have learned something of importance from Celan's poetic evocation of the survivor's psychology need not be merely giving voice to personal intuitions and sentiments. He may justly claim that it is true to its target, and value it for rendering more perspicuous events of which, today, most of us can only dimly conceive. These judgements are backed by good reasons, and are an apt testimony to both the complexity and of moral experience and to the power of poetic language.

10

The Inner Paradise

Tzachi Zamir

I Introduction

Recent attempts to delineate an intellectually fruitful relationship between philosophy and literature within Anglo-American aesthetics are usually proposed as compensatory epistemologies: literature, it is claimed, is able to overcome the limitations built into the traditional modes whereby philosophers construe knowledge. Targeting (usually) moral beliefs, the proponents of compensatory philosophico-literary accounts present and legitimize processes of experiential, emotional, perceptual, rhetorical and empathic belief-formation and belief-support. The knowledge-as-justified-true-belief paradigm needs to be extended, they argue; either by broadening the philosopher's default notion of knowledge, or by refusing to reduce literature's cognitive contribution to the acquisition of new knowledge.

By reconfiguring perception, by establishing a state in which philosophically significant claims can be meaningfully engaged, not via abstract reasoning alone, but through the immersion in a believable and detailed recreation of complex experience, some works of literature and poetry complement the philosopher's undertaking. By mobilizing important forms of belief-modifying attention, by establishing an embodied response to what ought to count, by clarifying the reader's own commitments, by refreshing one's grasp of what seems to be already known, by training the reader in exercising particular skills, literary works are able to foster and deepen understanding. On stronger accounts, literary works can be sometimes even *superior* to philosophical treatises in their capacity to convey genuine, full-blooded understanding—when such is contrasted to the philosopher's overestimation of argumentative defensibility. Philosophico-literary theories of this kind are not narrowly aesthetic, but are genuinely radical: they significantly broaden the critical issues that the pursuit of understanding—philosophy—should be taken to include and that philosophical methodology should, accordingly, ideally encompass.[1]

But what if a major work of literature or poetry—as is the case in Milton's *Paradise Lost*—does not merely provide experiential understanding but explicitly rejects philosophy's objective, holding that philosophy is implicated in the pursuit of an unworthy form of knowing? Harmonizing the different pursuits of philosophy and poetry would appear implausible in relation to such works, not because of the kind of cerebral analytical philosopher often imagined as the philosopher of literature's projected opponent—a mind for whom nothing but arguments should matter—but due to the resistance of poetry itself to be smoothly enlisted to philosophical pursuits. The more familiar grounds for such resistance are either the aesthetic distaste for moralistic readings or the post-humanist ideological objection to the philosophical tendency to impose trans-historical notions on complex, highly culturally determined texts.[2] The resistance posed by *Paradise Lost* is different: a direct dismissal of philosophy and its ideals.

Philosophizing—and here Milton was a child of a longstanding tradition that opposed intellectual curiosity and which, in its harshest versions, even applauded ignorance as a gift through which the unadorned word of God could be followed—is an activity which befits hell.[3] The

---

[1] The argument is often cast through moral rather than epistemological terms (see the first two chapters in Nussbaum 1990). On my reasons for subsuming such attempts under an epistemological umbrella, as well as for a detailed survey of the relevant literature, see the first two chapters in Zamir 2007. For a strong recent version of the epistemological argument, see ch. 7 in Gaut 2007. For a cognitivist argument against reducing cognitive value to knowledge, see ch. 3 in Gibson 2007. For the ways in which literary works set in motion cognitively valuable forms of attention, see Eldridge 2009, 3–17. For fictions as enabling the improving of some skills, a "knowing how" in Ryle's sense, see Landy 2012. For the power of literature to clarify concepts, see Carroll 2010, 201–34. For the distinction between stronger and weaker versions of such theories, see Nussbaum 2000.

[2] For a version of the former, see Posner 1997. For versions of the latter, see Zamir 2007, ch. 3.

[3] For a detailed exposition of the multi-faceted hostility to reason in early-modern England, its religious roots as well as its relationship to Milton, see Schultz 1955. On advocating the virtue of ignorance, see p. 187 of that work.

so-called wisdom philosophers grapple with is devoid of content, not because philosophical questions are difficult, but because the distance from God renders the preoccupation with them futile. "Beware lest any man spoil you through philosophy and vain deceit" (Colossians 2: 8) is approvingly quoted in Milton's *Christian Doctrine*, which, throughout its seven hundred pages, consistently uses the word "philosophy" disparagingly—by contrast to the guidance of the scripture.[4] Knowledge is cast as another of Satan's lures to Christ in *Paradise Regained* (IV. 285–364). Even the motivation of philosophy is insincere: the philosophical activity conducted in Milton's hell is not a genuine pursuit of understanding, but is performed by the fallen angels who hope to thereby momentarily palliate their pain (II. 561).[5]

When it comes to human beings, their aspiration for knowledge in their fallen condition is as hopeless as the state of the fallen angels—though not for the same reason. Eating of the fruit of knowledge is tantamount to eating death ("Greedily she engorged without restraint, / And knew not eating death" IX. 791–2, is how Eve's eating of the forbidden fruit is described: a form of consumption that constitutionally distorts one's capacity to adequately take in reality, XI. 412–13).[6] Succinctly put, for Milton, to fully grasp the fall entails forgoing the philosopher's optimism regarding the intelligibility of the world. Pursuing knowledge disengaged from its ties with God, with obedience, love and a full acknowledgment of one's limitations—such is nothing more than a multi-layered failure. Apostasy aside, pseudo-knowledge of this kind leads to insulation from the world—not to a deepening of the individual's bond with it. Ironically, philosophy's shortcoming is philosophical: if one genuinely seeks understanding, philosophy would send one down the wrong track. Cast through a Platonic vocabulary, Milton's point would be that, like

---

[4] For a recent defense of Milton's authorship of *Christian Doctrine*, see Campbell and Corns 2009, 424–38.

[5] Critics have debated over the extent of Milton's actual hostility to learning: some see him as changing his position throughout his life from an astute defender of the virtue of learning in his earlier works into a skeptical disparager in his later ones; others argue that he consistently held that learning is valuable, though it can be misused, leading to dangerous forms of pseudo-wisdom. For the former position, see Sensabaugh 1946. For the latter, see Samuel 1949, and ch. 5 in Samuel 1965, 101–31. Both positions are consistent with the contrast I am describing between Milton's view of knowledge as expressed in *Paradise Lost* and a philosophical concept of knowledge which is dissociated from faith.

[6] All references and citations from *Paradise Lost* are to Milton 1975.

cooking, philosophy is one of the arts of flattery; it presents a failure of understanding as if it actually were a form of knowledge. The philosopher mistakes a play of shadows on the walls of the cave for the things themselves.

It would, accordingly, be a grave simplification for a philosopher of literature to approach a poem such as *Paradise Lost* through a compensatory thesis, or through an attempt to couch its poetic insights via alternative forms of knowledge-acquisition that are palatable for philosophers. One would be reading against the implicit epistemological convictions that underpin the poem. Such readings are possible, of course: Milton's assumptions regarding understanding could simply be false, while his poem may nevertheless still contain valuable insights into issues that would interest a philosopher. Yet before coercing the poem's world in such a way—respecting its insights, but not its insights regarding the notion of insight—it might prove more interesting to tease out the poem's fuller picture of knowledge's place in a meaningful existence. The point is not merely that such a strategy is less patronizing in relation to Milton, or that it leads to a less predictable repertoire of moves in respect to those that are already familiar in contributions on philosophy of literature. The point is, rather, that to read the poem philosophically while respecting its hostility to philosophy, to sharpen rather than to bridge the philosophy–literature divide, might bring out different constitutional limitations of philosophy, limitations that a non-philosopher is better positioned to perceive. The genuine competition and irreconcilability between philosophy and poetry would be brought out, not through the standard move discussed in debates over cognitivism versus non-cognitivism within Anglo-American aesthetics—the inability of the poet to substantiate beliefs in a way that would appease a philosopher—but by showing that *it is philosophy* that falls short of establishing real understanding—"real" according to the standards of a poet.

Giving substance to this challenge necessitates a detailed engagement with the poem. For some philosophers, such engagement would take the form of transcribing poetic themes into abstract claims and arguments and then subjecting these to philosophical analysis. But such a procedure amounts to violating what was just described: the poem's precise assumptions regarding knowledge and intellectual method. A more plausible approach—which will be undertaken in what follows—is to tease out attitudes to knowledge in the poem. Milton, it will emerge, among other things relates to his poem as a theologically philosophically ethically prized *act* with language rather than merely a theoretical claim. A contemporary philosopher who wants to understand the fullness of this act as a challenge to philosophical assumptions—to philosophical method, to philosophical rigor—is invited to experience this act on its own terms. The following reading will be an attempt to explain what this kind of experience may involve. For reasons that will become obvious, I will not attempt to evaluate the emerging position regarding knowledge—*evaluation* presupposes an adherence to evaluative norms, an adherence that is itself being contested by the poem—but to clarify and identify the contours of Milton's view. By this I hope to bring out the deeper significance of Milton's particular use of poetic form in this work, but also the extent, reach, and contemporary relevance of Milton's case against a construction of knowledge that has been ingrained into philosophy.

II Forbidden Knowledge

The traditional interpretive crux posed by the Edenic Tree of Knowledge lies in its implication that God intentionally created mindless beings, hoping to keep them from knowledge and/or moral discrimination. Gnostics have even notoriously reversed the standard interpretation of the story: Jehovah is an evil entity; the serpent, an embodiment of Christ, who aims to lead human beings into the knowledge that Jehovah attempts to sequester. But even in less iconoclastic readings, forbidding knowledge seems to be a peculiar demand coming from a supposedly benevolent God. Milton endorsed the response of others to this problem: the difference caused by eating the fruit is not a categorical transition from total ignorance into illumination. Nor does it constitute a transition between an entire lack of discernment between right and wrong to its acquisition—to suppose that Adam and Eve altogether lack moral discrimination at the point in which they sin calls into question the justice of their punishment. For Milton—both in *Christian Doctrine* and in *Paradise Lost*—acquiring the knowledge of good and evil through the tree entails a transition from a state in which one knows good into a state in which one knows good *only in its relation to evil*.[7] From this

---

[7] See *Paradise Lost*, XI. 84–9, and *A Treatise on Christian Doctrine*: Milton 1825, 27–8. For precursors to this interpretation, see Williams 1948, 107.

perspective, the relationship between pre- and post-lapsarian knowledge is not merely quantitative—a shift from knowing more into knowing less—but qualitative: a shift between two altogether different experiences of the world. An all-affecting category, evil, has been injected into the human mind; from now on, it shall forever shape perception, knowledge, and value. But what does that mean? How, moreover, may the conversion from a non-corrupt into a corrupt mode of understanding be accessed by a fallen poet or be communicated to a fallen reader of his poem?

Milton's treatment of this issue can be understood by examining the three key scenes in which human beings seek knowledge in *Paradise Lost*. The first presents Adam's exchange with Raphael. The second concerns Eve's (and then Adam's) temptation by Satan. The third involves Adam's instruction by Michael, after the fall, regarding the future.

III   Edenic Knowledge

The first instance in the poem in which Adam is presented as a seeker of knowledge takes place in his encounter with Raphael, sent to warn Adam and Eve of the danger posed by Satan, when "sudden mind arose / In Adam, not to let th' occasion pass / Given him by this great conference to know / Of things above his world, and of their being / Who dwell in heav'n" (V. 452-7). Adam's desire to know is spontaneous ("sudden"), and is triggered by the presence of the angel—a potential source of knowledge to which he would otherwise have no access. We would now expect Adam to act upon this curiosity, and to bombard Raphael with questions. Yet this is *not* what follows. Instead, Adam compliments Raphael for his generosity in overlooking the humble hospitality they are able to offer in comparison to angelic standards.

Let us pause over this moment—hospitality trumping curiosity—before examining Raphael's substantive response. There is, to begin with, a spatial dimension to hospitality: inviting another to enter "one's" space (although Eden lacks property laws and possessions, Milton preserves the usual model of hospitality as predicated upon inviting another to share one's possessions). Such a transition of location is then undergirded by interpersonal gestures: breaking bread; accepting the limits of one's capacity to give; acknowledging that the host's limitations to give are noted yet not censured by the guest. Adam deepens the interpenetration

of space-sharing imagery and moral values by commending his guest
for being an "inhabitant with God": acting in the way he does in relation to his human hosts proves that Raphael regularly partakes of God's
proximity.

Hospitality's centrality to ethics has been theorized primarily as a
self-willed breach of one's borders, due to the disruption caused by a genuine internalization of the other. But the emphasis in the poem is different. What the poem does is to embed the communication of knowledge
within a broader gesture of hospitality. Pre-lapsarian pursuit of knowledge and its communication is a state in which one's curiosity is guided
and informed by an incorporation of a higher element, while simultaneously noting its distinguishing merits. Only through the humility established by such a process will knowledge be fully transmitted. Moreover,
that the hospitality is extended by *both* Adam and Eve is also significant,
particularly when readers hear overtones of Philo's allegorical interpretation of Adam and Eve as standing for parts of a single psychic unity—
an understanding implicit at several significant points in the poem. The
implication of admitting such overtones is that the hosting of the guest
and the offerings given to him are conducted on all dimensions of the
integrated soul: sensual, emotional, intellectual. Only after something
has been bestowed by man's entire being—an offering involving labor—
can this gift be genuinely received by the higher element one hopes to
momentarily take in. Only in such a state of hosting can knowledge be
pursued. The ensuing fall partly consists in a diminishing capacity to
effect such integration of giving and receiving. Finally, whereas in book
V the hosting of the higher element is actually achieved, in book XII,
upon exiting the Garden of Eden, Adam moves to a counterfactual: he
will from now on act *as if* he were in God's company and "walk / As in
his presence" (562–3). Imaginary, not literal, hosting is a fundamental
dimension of post-lapsarian faith.

The communication of knowledge which will now commence, span-
ning three books in the poem, is enveloped by this play of gestures.
Raphael opens it with a metaphysical thesis which is at once hierarchic
and egalitarian: each element in creation issues from God; it is, in that
precise sense, of equal merit. Some elements are nearer to God; they are
thus purer. Elements that are further removed from God are gradually
transformed into ones that are closer; "the grosser feeds the purer." When

it comes to reason, the latter is the very being of the soul and includes both a discursive and an intuitive dimension. The former is mostly what human beings are limited to; the latter mostly belongs to angels (486–90). The egalitarian dimension embedded in this vision of creation and knowledge warrants that, even in their limited capacity, human beings are able to receive, albeit in a diluted form, an account of their state. The hierarchic dimension implies that Raphael will have to speak in a way that accommodates itself to Adam's limitations, translating truths down to the level of human understanding. By prefacing his exposition with this thesis, Raphael's intent seems to be not only to communicate to human beings the most that they can hope to know given their limitations, but also to orient them to a mode of existence that would suit them better than a contemplative life. Each element in existence—botanical, animal, human, angelic—possesses its own appropriate sphere of activity. Each contributes singularly to creation. To pursue knowledge as such, to be a lover of wisdom, is tantamount to acting like an angel when one cannot be one.

Raphael's lines bespeak a powerful realization of the difficulty of being human. Exposed is the sham built into the repeated framing of human distinctiveness (endorsed by Renaissance humanists such as Pico della Mirandola): humans as being suspended in-between beasts on the one hand and angels on the other, becoming either through a laudable or a damning exercise of the will. Human beings cannot *be* angels or animals, as is implied when they are *likened* to them (to quote Hamlet's words, "in action how like an angel, in apprehension how like a god"). They differ in kind. Accordingly, to act *like* an angel—pretending that one can confine oneself merely to one's spiritual dimension—amounts to a denial of what and who one is. Adam is encouraged to listen to and take in Raphael's words, but to do so in full acknowledgment of his limitations—*not* by endeavoring to decode Raphael's vocabulary and attempting to access a higher mode of being. The condition of humility in and through one's aspiration for knowledge is precisely encapsulated in a tempering of the need to know by a constant awareness of one's constitutional limits. Even at one's best, one may but access a mere translation.

Such humbling is the precise effect that Raphael's lines have on Adam, indicating that a spiritually adequate grasp of divine insights is part and parcel of the pre-lapsarian state. Adam's response to Raphael is to desire to know more. This time, though, his initially generalized wish to learn yields a need to reach a better understanding of the dangers of disobedience and ingratitude to which Raphael alludes to in passing (V. 512–19). This transition from an unqualified desire to know into a quest for knowledge subordinated to obedience implies that the mediation of a spiritually higher source of instruction institutes links between the craving to know and the need to buttress one's contact with God. The pattern is repeated in book VII: instructed about the war between God and Satan, Adam asks for better understanding of his own creation (59–69). We thereby see that, rather than quench the craving that initially motivated him, the knowledge so far received merely provides a springboard to a new thirst for knowledge. Significantly, Adam *justifies* his wish to know, denying that he seeks knowledge for its own sake. Knowledge, he claims, would merely enable him and Eve to praise God more fully after comprehending what He has actually done ("not to explore the secrets ask / Of his eternal empire, but the more / To magnify his works, the more we know" VII. 95–7). Again, a generalized, undifferentiated desire to know metamorphoses into a wish to know *as an expression of a richer bond* with God.[8] Moreover, to understand one's creation is to wish to fathom one's connection to one's creator in terms that are broader than causal dependency—Adam already knows that God is the cause of his existence, here he seems to be asking for something different. Such combination of humility, hospitality, and subordination of knowledge to a greater connectedness to God characterizes the pre-lapsarian pursuit of knowledge.

IV Eve's Fall

Eve's desire for knowledge initially mirrors Adam's. Like Adam, who subordinates the pursuit of knowledge to a more profound connectedness with God, Eve—whose relationship to Adam (her co-creator in Milton) partly duplicates Adam's relation to God—explicitly avoids knowledge for its own sake. We see this when Adam requests cosmological knowledge from Raphael. Shifting attention to Eve, the narrator describes Eve

---

[8] Leonard argues that the structure of Adam's lines here (the lack of a question mark; the inability to confidently assert that Adam even asks a question) is designed to show that he is free from sheer curiosity. See Leonard 1989, 130–43 (137–8).

rising and leaving to tend the fruits and flowers. Milton's narrator is now obliged to explain what appears to be her peculiar lack of curiosity:

> Yet went she not, as not with such discourse
> Delighted, or not capable her ear
> Of what was high: such pleasure she reserved,
> Adam relating, she sole auditress;
> Her husband the relater she preferred
> Before the angel, and of him to ask
> Chose rather; he, she knew would intermix
> Grateful digressions, and solve high dispute
> With conjugal caresses, from his lip
> Not words alone pleased her. (VIII. 47–58)

Milton eroticizes Eve's desire for knowledge, thereby enabling her to copy Adam's subordination of knowledge to the desire for a tighter contact with God. Rather than merely search for wisdom, she wishes to turn its communication into a love-game: Adam, not Raphael, will do the explaining, intermingling it with amorous digressions.

The metamorphosis of this eroticized mode of knowledge (in which knowledge is interlaced with love) into a pursuit of knowledge (in which knowledge stands for more power) would take place later. Eve is then tempted by Satan, hidden in the body of his unwilling host, the serpent. How could a benevolent God prevent them from attaining wisdom? she asks, formulating a question that has been planted into her by Satan (IX. 758–60). Her physical disconnection from Adam, the higher source of instruction to which she ought to have been attached, enables the surfacing of such question. If Adam and Eve are interpreted as aspects of a psychic whole, such entails that an autonomous wish for knowledge arises only in a fragmented soul, one whose perception has been regrettably disengaged from the guidance of those elements that ought to shape and inform it. Moreover, by contrast to the model of hospitality, consisting in the integration of the higher element into one's space, by leaving Adam Eve *evicts* the higher element. The poem lingers on this separation from Adam: "Thus saying, from her husband's hand her hand / Soft she withdrew" (IX, 385). Adam pursuing her with his eye, repeatedly pleading for her quick return; the image of her situated among the flowers, unsupported by her best prop—all depict a soul in the process of losing its foundations.

Satan's successful temptation exacerbates Eve's inner insulation from Adam. Not only will she avoid taking account of Adam's opinion of her impending action, but her worldview will diminish back into the self-centred perspective which was such an immediate choice for her in her narcissism moments after her creation. Eve's recession back into an ego-centred orientation is weaved into her deliberation just prior to her eating the forbidden fruit (IX. 745–99). The plural pronouns "we," "us," and "our" are repeated eleven times, culminating in the singular "I" that terminates the deliberation and makes her reach for the fruit. Lured into a solipsistic disengagement from supportive, loving, and superior elements, thinking is demoted into a hunger for knowledge as such.

As for the process of exposure to the knowledge itself, unlike Adam's strengthening of the bonding to God via the insight he is granted, Eve's acquisition of knowledge hardens her insulation. She contemplates the pros and cons of maintaining secrecy, or even deceiving both God and Adam regarding her new enlightened state. As for the content of the acquired knowledge, eating from the fruit induces in Eve an ecstatic elation as the fruit's flavour merges with the exhilaration of attaining wisdom. But the poem systematically erodes the value of such ostensible wisdom: as she ingests the fruit of the tree of knowledge, Eve "knows not" that she eats death (Frank Kermode notes the irony[9]). Trespasses of this kind may be hid from God, she reasons. He is, after all, so far away. By juxtaposing Eve's ludicrous hope to keep her trespass unknown to God, given his foreknowledge of her act before Eve herself ever contemplated committing it, the poem casts the knowledge provided by the tree not merely as mistaken, but as sadly pathetic. Pseudo-wisdom that traps its possessor and masks from her view her own profound ignorance—such is the first manifestation of the sort of knowledge provided by the fruit. Considerations of power come next: Eve dreams of superiority (over Adam), and perceives inferiority as undesirable ("for inferior who is free?" IX. 825). Knowledge may well be related to power (as our post-humanists tirelessly claim), but only in relation to its tainted forms: indeed, it is precisely this limited outlook—relating to life as nothing more than a succession of power exchanges—that Milton builds into Satan's worldview from the very beginning of the poem. To ingest

---

[9] See "Adam Unparadised" in Kermode 1960, 98–106, here alluding to a remark from the reprinted essay in the Norton edition of the poem, p. 600.

the fruit is to integrate *this* power-driven perspective, along with its restrictions.

V Adam's Fall

In the textual span of the two hundred lines or so in which Eve has already fallen while Adam has not, two kinds of knowledge—his superior and non-corrupt one, her own fallen pseudo-knowledge— unexpectedly overlap: both decide that life without one's partner is unthinkable. In Eve's case, such attachment could be explained as an error caused by the tree, one which also infuses her act with its particular immoral strand (Adam knowingly destroys himself for love— Eve knowingly destroys *him* because of it). Yet Adam's choice cannot be excused through the same means. While the narrator informs us that in his following of Eve Adam acts "against his better knowledge" (998), it is unclear *why* he does so when his mind has not yet been corrupted by the fall. "Not deceived, but fondly overcome with female charm" is the explanation supplied by the narrator (999). But, again, *why* would Adam be prone to be undone in such a way when, unlike Eve, his own reasoning faculties have yet to be crippled by the fruit? In response to this question, Milton's theodicy must grapple with a very old crux haunting the story of the fall: either Adam is perfectly constituted, in which case he should be completely immune to temptation and should not fall (in which case God's punishment is justified but the fall becomes improbable), or Adam rather possesses a built-in weakness that leads him to fall (in which case the fall makes sense, but God becomes partly culpable of not creating a more resilient Adam). Milton sided with those who choose the latter option: Adam possesses a constitutional weakness which he, nevertheless, is also potentially able to overcome. Adam's visceral attachment to Eve *is* this weakness; it overrides his obligation to God:

> However I with thee have fixed my lot ...
> So forcible within my heart I feel
> The bond of nature draw me to my own,
> My own in thee, for what thou art is mine;
> Our state cannot be severed, we are one,
> One flesh; to lose thee were to lose myself. (IX. 952–9)

In God's anticipation of this moment and his later judgement of Adam, Milton provides his God the traditional defence: God created Adam free to fall but able to stand (III. 98–102; V. 535–40). Such liberty turns Adam's duty into a meaningful and free choice, rather than mechanical obedience. To blame God for creating a being susceptible to fall is to thus (ungratefully) also wish that God had created an inferior being. The only remaining charge against God is that He made the attachment to Eve too powerful (all other animals are created in pairs; why should Eve be formed *out of* Adam?). Such, indeed, would be Adam's complaint later in book XI. God's response is that, strong as the attachment was, Adam was still able to choose differently. God could have also mocked Adam for desiring a partner that Adam would have loved less—an advice which, had it been followed by God, would have rendered Him blameworthy in another respect. Ultimately, the only consistent option for a just god would be to bestow on Adam the best of everything: to enable him to act meaningfully—which, in turn, necessitates creating him free, which necessitates enabling him to err—and to also enable him to experience a most powerful love relation—hoping that Adam will succeed in sustaining both. The question that remains is why would a just god permit a situation in which an either/or choice between two intrinsic goods (Eve/God) has to be made. I will not discuss this question here.

For the purposes of an inquiry into competing senses of knowledge in the poem vis-à-vis philosophical knowledge, it would suffice to say that, when Adam is "fondly" (foolishly) "overcome by feminine charm," the folly consists of a withdrawal from a higher calling into a more binding one. Adam is not motivated by a wish to know at all, but rather by the desire to remain with Eve. Whereas she aspires for more, he merely wishes to retain that which he has. Unlike Eve, Adam also realizes that, by acting upon this desire, he withdraws from rather than attains knowledge. The imagery through which Adam articulates his attachment to Eve—one flesh, one self (959)—and which Eve immediately reciprocates—one heart, one soul (967)—suggests that, given a love of such depth, her corrupted understanding infects his: as she embraces him and "tenderly weeps" (990–1), she injects her new limitations into him.

Through Eve, Milton anatomizes the withdrawal from knowledge as a transition into pseudo-wisdom, self-centredness, and disconnectedness from one's partner and from God. Such are the roots of the shrewd, power-driven version of cleverness she exemplifies in her post-lapsarian cost-benefit analysis. Adam's withdrawal from knowledge stresses alto-gether different elements. His words immediately upon consuming the fruit disclose a transformation in his experience: new patterns of contact emerge between the reality he takes in and sensual pleasure (1017–26). The poem is careful to avoid suggesting that pleasure as such is height-ened. Rather, it is the *desire*—"true relish" (1023)—that becomes over-whelmingly strong. Adam tells Eve that he was never so eager to enjoy her (1028–32). Nothing is said of the augmented experience of copula-tion itself. Post-coital rest has no effect, and Adam awakens weakened "as from unrest" (the poem compares Adam to the shorn Samson rising from his sleep in Delilah's lap). Looking at Eve he puns—for the first time in the poem—on her name's proximity to evil. He feels polluted, wishing to be abandoned to a solitary existence. Book IX concludes with them quarreling to "no end."

For Adam, the effect of the knowledge provided by the tree involves constitutional emptiness and, like Eve's, a desire to be dissociated from God as well as from his earthly beloved companion. He does not wish to pursue more of the knowledge the tree can yield (neither does Eve incidentally, repeating the eating merely to join him). Unlike the love-making commended by the poem in book IV, in which intercourse has bonded them to each other and which they experienced as another of God's gifts, post-lapsarian sex, for all its intensified desire, wrenches them apart. The knowledge they obtain is directed into arguing over who is more guilty, neither taking responsibility for the trespass (IX. 1187). Most painfully, the newfound knowledge is related to a hitherto unknown experience of unbearable shame, shame not over their deeds, but over who and what they are. The broad leaves they cover themselves with embody their separation through the flora that previously served as the fabric of their labour-based unification. The broad leaves also manifest the need for concealment from the lover. The self-knowledge provided by the trespass is, accordingly, not only distorted by sensuality overpowering understanding (1127–31), but also by perceiving oneself *as* distorted. To know more than what one ought to is to learn to perceive oneself as defective.

Self-rejection of this kind colors one of the more remarkable differ-ences between Adam and Eve. The pseudo-knowledge of the tree leads Eve to foolishly fantasize that she can hide her guilt from God by avoid-ing being seen by him (she would later (X. 978–1006) repeat this move by suggesting suicide in order to prevent the transmission of God's punishment onto their future children). By contrast, Adam wishes to hide from God, not to prevent God from seeing him, but because *he* cannot face God (1080–3).[10] These different responses embody two distinct forms of disconnection from God. The first (Eve's) is predicated on the hope to avoid a God who is perceived as actively seeking one out. The second (Adam's) manifests an inability to direct one's orientation to God because of an overwhelming awareness of one's own flaws. The first orientation duplicates Satan's underestimation of God's actual power; it is thus foolish, and serves as a further ironic reminder that the fruit of the tree yields only pseudo-knowledge. The second is sadder. It suggests that, regardless of God's actual proximity, an internal barrier separating the self from divine presence has been erected by one's act. This difference, between perceiving the break from God as external or internal, will later shape the different ways whereby Adam and Eve face their guilt. Eve will advocate suicide, an *external* act through which undesirable effects in the world may be prevented. Adam proposes repentance, an *inner* act by which he hopes to mend their break from God.

VI The Paradise Within

The final form that delivery of knowledge assumes in *Paradise Lost* appears in Michael's lengthy disclosure of the future to Adam. It is this delivery—presented in the poem's final two books—that is claimed to convey the highest wisdom. In contradistinction to Eve's willing withdrawal from the earlier transmission of knowledge by Raphael, here she is unwittingly excluded by Michael's putting her to sleep (this is, once again, noteworthy: all previous separations between Adam and Eve were self-willed). Her prior wish to access knowledge through Adam's mediation in order to revive their bond can no longer be trusted.

Adam responds to Michael's instructive exposition through a mixture of dread, pain, despair—and, later, elation and happiness. By the end of this communication, Adam feels that he has attained the most that his capacity for knowledge enables, a judgment validated by Michael

---

[10] Milton relies here on a hermeneutic tradition for which "by . . . concealment [Adam] has not hidden himself from the Lord, but the Lord from himself." This citation is from Gregory's *Moralia* and is reprinted in Nohrnberg 1976, 162.

as "the sum of wisdom" (XII. 575). Here then, is what Adam says he has learnt; and what Milton, through Michael, presents as the distillation of wisdom:

> Greatly instructed I shall hence depart,
> Greatly in peace of thought, and have my fill
> Of knowledge, what this vessel can contain,
> Beyond which was my folly to aspire.
> Henceforth I learn, that to obey is best,
> And love with fear the only God, to walk
> As in his presence, ever to observe
> His providence, and on him sole depend,
> Merciful over all his works, with good
> Still overcoming evil, and by small
> Accomplishing great things, by things deemed weak
> Subverting worldly strong, and worldly wise
> By simply meek; that suffering for truth's sake
> Is fortitude to highest victory,
> And to the faithful death the gate of life;
> Taught this by his example whom I now
> Acknowledge my Redeemer ever blest. (XII. 557–73)

Michael immediately applauds this combination of obedience, love of God, belief in salvation, humility, and self-discipline. But he is then also careful to restate it in his own language, adding elements that should animate Adam's insight, emphasizing love (charity) above all ("the soul of all the rest"). Should Adam attain this state, Michael says, he will no longer lament the paradise he has just lost. Instead, he will discover a far happier paradise within (585–7).

An inner paradise—such is the counterpart to the inner hell in which Satan finds himself in book IV: "Which way I fly is hell; myself am hell" he poignantly says (IV. 75), sensing himself unable to escape his torments. Philosophers would pause over the possible overlap of internalization of space and types of knowledge. Through Satan's internalization of the image of hell from which the poem began, Milton completes his portrayal of the geography of punishment: hell as external terrain, as a physical place, giving way to hell as a state of mind. Inner hell is characterized by loneliness (Satan says that his subordinates know nothing of his suffering and self-doubt); it involves constitutional fear of something worse; it is a state of hopelessness, and of jealousy; hellish existence involves evil action, not because one desires it as such, but because one has been reduced into mere mechanical opposition to that which one has lost. Hell is also the emptiness of activity without foreseeable point or end, parasitical upon an external value scheme. Importantly for our concerns, such hell is not merely an existentially impoverished state, but a manifestation of *a form of knowing*, one limited to means–ends strategic calculations aimed at promoting ends for which the agent can find no substantive value beyond their opposition to something else.

Paradise Lost repeats the same structural movement in relation to the spatiality of Eden: an external place is gradually internalized in the moral vision closing the poem. If the inner hell described by Satan is harsher and more depressing than the dark region presented in the opening books from which he had emerged, the inner paradise painted by Michael's words is superior ("happier far") to the perfect world Adam has just lost. The initially paradoxical description of an inner paradise surpassing the original one is accounted for through the "fortunate fall": loss of Eden entails not merely an irrevocable loss, but ultimately enables the moral, spiritual, and theological elevation of human beings (XII. 473–8). To maintain the right inner bond with God—to walk as if in his company, to trust him, to enable his element (love) to infuse one's thoughts or actions—opens up a paradise within, regardless of external circumstances. The preservation of paradise by maintaining contact with God is then duplicated in Eve's relation to Adam, her co-creator: "With thee to go" she tells him, "is to stay here; without thee here to stay, is to go hence unwilling" (615–17). To maintain her bond with Adam is tantamount to remaining in paradise.

It is the *contact* with the higher element that establishes one's reality as paradisiacal, just as it is Satan's disconnection from God that constructs his hell. Heaven and hell are, ultimately, forms of connection and disconnection from the highest spiritual force; and it is this realization that is presented in the poem as the highest wisdom.

VII Poetic Form

Milton's presentation of knowledge as an objective that should be related to other ideals, foremost to the overarching wish to tighten and enrich one's bond with God, could have obviously been presented in a non-poetic, treatise-like text, as in his *Christian Doctrine*. But at least five considerations make his particular type of poetry particularly suited for his attempt "to justify the ways of God."

To begin with, we saw that, for Milton, fundamental understanding is inaccessible to the human mind even prior to the fall, and may at best be aimed for through an act of *translation* (this idea prefaces Raphael's exposition in the middle books). An epic kind of poetry, one that explicitly endorses an overly artificial anthropomorphic descriptive scheme is, accordingly, less misleading than a philosophical treatise that presupposes the descriptive adequacy of words and concepts. When angels are pictured as fighting each other on a vast battle-field with swords and lances, the reader is less likely to assume a correspondence between thought content and reality. The obliqueness of poetry thus harmonizes with epistemic humbleness: poetry is a particularly apt form through which its reader is constantly reminded of partial accessibility, of *not* reading a description, of *not* being given knowledge.

Secondly, Milton intensifies the obliqueness of poetry through an abstruse syntax of convoluted, long, bewildering sentences of which critics such as T. S. Eliot complained. Such is suitable for a rhetoric intentionally selected to arouse an awareness of the opacity of language rather than of its transparency. It thus appropriately blocks the temptation to assume that describing pre-lapsarian reality could be conducted and performed using the same descriptive methods one would employ for sticks and stones.

Thirdly, the combination of humility with the courage to approach an inaccessible subject matter is achieved through an original employment of a traditional move: the poet's summoning of the Muse. Within the context of Milton's subject matter, his invocation to the Muse in the poem's opening lines and in three later sections mobilizes a multiple operation. To invoke the Muse implies the poet's lack of autonomy and creative control over his poem—relative to the more assured stance of a philosophical treatise. It enables Milton to practice the humility which he preaches by positioning himself as merely mediating—rather than discovering—purportedly inaccessible knowledge. The aspiration is not to be a philosophical sage, a source of illumination, but to become a vehicle through which wisdom is transmitted.[11] Moreover, to summon

---

[11] Twenty-five years before the publication of *Paradise Lost*, Milton presented his vocation in life explicitly in such self-humbling terms, wishing "to be an interpreter and

the Muse is not just a rhetorical choice, but a speech act. It operates both on the level of the poet—who genuinely prays to be inspired to write well—but also provides an initiation of the reader: the reader hopefully bonds with the unworldly agency that can be the source of the sought-for understanding. If read as a prayer, the poem's opening lines—"Of man's first disobedience . . . sing Heav'nly Muse"—could, thus, also articulate *the reader's* performative speech act—a prayer to be brought into contact with an inaccessible knowledge—and not only the poet's desire to fulfill his undertaking.[12] Finally, by repeatedly summoning the Muse, the reader is constantly reminded of the process of hosting. The poet hosts another force in order to realize his intent. By implication, the reader hosts this same power through the act of reading.[13] More than a form–content agreement, such rhetoric establishes the kind of self-inhabiting by a higher force which the poem ultimately associates with the highest wisdom.

Fourthly, and in connection to this point, the poem's linguistic surface is uniquely able to perform and convey hosting through its Latinism: the implication embedded in Milton's English verse repeated hosting of another language. Critics have debated over the *aesthetic* merit of Milton's choice to make his English be haunted by Latin (as well as other languages), both by including English words that possess secondary Latin echoes, and by, sometimes, casting English formulations into Latin syntax. Such debates notwithstanding, we should not miss the *theological* dimension of this kind of poetics: that the poem's surface structure and medium would itself host a different language—one which was the original carrier of other sources of insight and wisdom—creates a complex, multi-lingual offering incorporating hospitality into its very structure. Embedding alien meanings into familiar words, or borrowing foreign

relater of the best and sagest things among [his] own citizens throughout this island in the mother dialect." See *The Reason of Church Government Urged Against Prelaty*, in Milton 1975, 357.

[12] For such a position regarding the kind of reading Milton hopes to establish, see Ainsworth 2008.

[13] Some critics would deny that the narrator should be associated with Milton himself. Even if such is the case (which I doubt), the allusion to his own blindness personalizes his speaker's use of such a tradition in a very powerful way, generating, at the very least, ambiguity in relation to a potentially genuine autobiographical use of the first person. For discussion, see Wilson 1971.

forms of sense-construction into one's native syntax, does not merely defamiliarize the presented thought; it rather invites the reader to take in the precise form of difficulty unfolded by the poet, who demands from his expressive medium, from his English, to incorporate another tongue, another way of organizing thought. Language broadens and deepens; but not through its more inventive or merely more precise creative use, as would typically be expected from a poet, but through overlaying words and sentences with the linguistic counterpart of musical counterpoint: a surface structure moving in relation to another implicit structure, establishing a harmony that transcends whatever can be reached by any single language.[14]

Fifthly, through the use of a diachronic narrative, poetry is able to establish a lived rather than a merely known relationship between its reader and the fall. Milton's religious goal of reconciling the believer to the ways of God assumes that such acceptance, even within adamant believers, is not fully engrained. Presumably, what prevents this chasm from being bridged is not some missed information, some surprising new arguments which Milton is able to supply. Believers would be perfectly aware that earthly suffering and mortality result from the initial Edenic fall. But even for steadfast believers, there exists a felt difference between a past violation taking place in some unknown place and time and the more immediate painful events which ensue as its distant ramifications. A diachronic patient poetic narrative can recreate the past as a genuine experience, turning the reader into an immediate witness and auditor of the fall—not someone who is merely aware of its consequences. Poetic recreation of this kind cannot be too smooth, and may also include evidence of its unsuitability regarding some objects of description that cannot be subsumed under a narrative.[15] However, while Milton himself opens *Christian Doctrine* with a discussion of the potential dangers of anthropopathy—anthropomorphizing God—he does not regard such

---

[14] For a convincing presentation of the debate over the extent, scope, and nature of Milton's Latinism, see Hale 1997. Hale rejects Fowler's division of Milton's Latinism into four kinds (p. 106), conceiving of Milton's incorporation of Latin as far more ambiguous and varied in form than the kinds of language-use captured by Fowler's typology. Hale importantly adds that, apart from Latin, other languages out of the ten Milton knew (he wrote in four and translated from five) underlie the poem, creating a multi-lingual structure that could have been accessed by many of his contemporary readers.

[15] Samuel Fallon (2012) has suggested that because of its timelessness, the poem's narrative mode both captures and conveys God's resistance to being narrativized.

means as fundamentally flawed. On the contrary, they were supplied by scripture precisely to facilitate some degree of understanding regarding such events.[16] By enabling the reader to repeatedly attend the transition between pre- and post-lapsarian experience—in the fallen angels as a collective, in Satan as individual, in Eve, in Adam—the reader is suspended during the reading process in an imaginative space, and is hosted by the poem in a context in which paradise is repeatedly being lost by those who have experienced it. Such reconstruction summons in the reader *the state* of living in a relationship with a momentous event. Poetry thus becomes a vehicle of imaginative relocation through language.

VIII   Poetry and Philosophy

What emerges from this discussion with regard to the "ancient quarrel" between philosophy and poetry is a fundamental difference of metaphorical clusters in relation to knowledge: knowledge as that which can be possessed (philosophy) by contrast to knowledge as that which enables the momentary hosting and channeling of something else (Milton). When such a difference is meant to orient one's mode of writing, and when writing is perceived as an act, one to which readers are meant to respond by performing a prized spiritual act of their own, an author should avoid a form of writing that describes, analyzes, or argues. Instead, a writer should set into motion an operation with words that can induce in readers a momentary hosting of a higher element: to walk as if one were with God, and to thus bring together God and reader. Through the formal dimensions surveyed here—invoking the muse, mobilizing non-immediacy by defamiliarizing syntax, construing a poly-linguistic structure, establishing and sustaining humility, constructing an experiential rather than a merely referential relationship to the fall—the poem hampers a sense of assured possession of understanding. Simultaneously, it brings the reader closer to God via a unique comingling of explanation and invitation into an imagined space. Such an opening up to God does not result from what readers would *conclude* from the poem; it would be established, rather, through the experience of reading as such, through the process the reader undergoes when pausing over the words.

[16]   See Milton 1825, 17.

Milton did not write to appease contemporary aestheticians, to demonstrate that his poetry could meet the philosophers' standards of intellectual rigor. Nor was his aim restricted to producing aesthetic pleasure. For him, broader networks and religiously valued states should infuse meaning into knowledge or underlie states like pleasure—on their own, such are worthless. *Paradise Lost*, in short, is not merely an aesthetic offering or a philosophical theodicy cast in poetic trappings, but a profound theological *act* for which Milton prepared himself during many years. To write such a poem, if one succeeds, is to achieve more than a theodicy; it is to erect a bridge between the believer and God. In a way, it is to follow in the footsteps of Christ, whose sacrifice (and not the mere delivery of sermons) is construed in the poem precisely as furnishing such a bridge.

The poet's creative act invites another act from its reader. Plato's image in *Ion*—divine meaning; poetic articulation of it; the potency of its articulation and inspired interpretation as analogous to a magnet's operation on and through iron rings; the rhapsode as a mere conveyer of insight without genuine grasp of it—is here overturned: since mastery and true possession of some kinds of understanding is not only impossible but is also vain, the highest position one may aspire to in relation to wisdom is the humbling stance of a rhapsode—opening up to wisdom's momentary visit, hosting it, and then attempting to transmit it to others. Poetry of this kind differs from philosophy in its projected effect: not merely to enable a thought to materialize, but to establish a prized state of reconciliation as part of the inspired response to the words. One should not merely *think* that one is with God (the highest ideal a religious philosopher may aspire to), but actually *be* with him through the operation of words.

I began with compensatory philosophies of literature, for which the primary question which should guide one's understanding of the separation or potential overlap between philosophy and literature depended upon one's prior answer to the question "What does it mean to know?" We arrive here at a different fundamental dimension that sets a poetic work apart from the expectations of a philosopher—the apprehension of words *as* action. If philosophy is a reasoned inquiry, Milton's kind of poetry is an offering; if philosophy is evaluated in relation to knowledge, poetry attempts to transport its reader into God's presence; if philosophy should generate articulated, well-defined conclusions, poetry facilitates a temporary hosting of wisdom; and if, finally, philosophy concerns what one believes in, poetry is an attempt to realize a higher modality of being in the world. And yet, since such becoming is also regarded by Milton as the state of being in possession of genuine wisdom—the very objective of philosophical pursuit—poetry (of Milton's kind) and philosophy (as most philosophers are likely to conceive of it) cannot be neatly integrated into some complementary pluralistic scheme, as if they participated in a similar undertaking. They are at war.

Philosophers would—perhaps should—part company from Milton's characterization of knowledge. They would say that knowledge and its pursuit should not be instrumentalized: a true lover of knowledge should follow knowledge wherever it leads, regardless of its ability to promote or hamper meaningful existence. Two immediate answers are available to Milton in response to this claim. The first is that endorsing such a stance with regard to knowledge does not adequately capture what some major philosophers believe: Plato, Aristotle, and many others have justified the pursuit of knowledge, linking the need to know with other ideals—hence instrumentalizing knowledge is not antagonistic to philosophy as such. The second answer is that, whether or not one's pursuit of knowledge is independent of other values, knowledge is embedded in networks of meaning, even if it can be pursued independently of them. Philosophical inquiry often shapes one's relationship to one's moral agency, one's assumptions regarding art, one's political stance, one's assumptions about one's happiness, and so on. The connections Milton establishes between knowledge and faith are thus not foreign to other forms of intertwining of beliefs and ends, an intertwining that philosophers on the whole welcome.

But Milton's response to such philosophers would probably be less guarded than these two responses. He would simply dismiss the assumption that knowledge can be insulated from faith. What these so-called lovers of wisdom end up with, he would say, is pseudo-knowledge. Real wisdom cannot be accessed that way, because real knowledge is essentially linked with an attempt to bond with a divine element. To know is not merely to attempt to justify or refute beliefs. It is guided and modified by a knowledge of what one cannot know, by a knowledge of one's place in existence, by a belief in what one may hope to achieve, and, ultimately, by a keen perception that moments of disunity from God are wasted moments. Philosophers would (rightly) require Milton to justify such claims. He would respond by saying that such beliefs are not themselves derived from arguments but from other sources. Such claims are meant to describe one's experience; not in the sense of picking out what there is, but of also shaping it into this form. It is within this framework, grounded in claims that are both descriptive and prescriptive—Milton would call the domain of such unique claims "scripture"—that one's pursuit of knowledge needs to take place. One would then attain wisdom, rather than place oneself within the grip of one of wisdom's numerous shadows.

We seem to arrive at a categorical impasse: since the split between Milton and philosophy is over competing notions of knowledge, over the value of argument, over underlying motivations and conflicting perceptions regarding intrinsic versus derived values, no fruitful debate can develop between such opposites. Circular definitions of knowledge would now surface, between which no mediation can be achieved. *War* seems to be the right word to use in relation to such conflicts: war as the state of deviation from argument, from what can be claimed, a transition into a clash that is conducted using a vocabulary of force: determining who can off-court who; delegitimizing the other; fighting for spiritual territory; recruiting minds; indoctrinating followers; vilifying the endorsers of the enemy; preventing the other's orientation from being articulated with fullness on one's own platforms; warning one's own camp that hosting the other's claims corrupts one's own integrity, taints the purity of one's thinking, renders flexible one's "rigor," inserts doubt into one's faith. Given this clash, the value of philosophical engagement with such a poem as Milton's is called into question. Do we, as philosophers, learn or achieve anything from reaching such categorical disjunctions between diametrically opposed conceptual worlds?

Such pessimism is unwarranted. Unlike literal wars, spiritual warfare is not wholly negative: to glimpse clearly and repeatedly the world with which one's own framework conflicts deepens one's sense of who one is, and forcefully presents the alternative to one's perspective. To sustain the ability to take in the genuine challenge of a rival perspective, a perspective that does not merely present itself as an alternative to yours, but wishes to see your world being replaced by it, demands clarifying the value of what one does, and recommitting oneself to particular objectives. Since the value of the very tools that mobilize such recommitment is being called into question—the autonomous value of arguments, of justifications, of clarifications, of refutations, of critical thinking—something of what at least some philosophers would recognize as the groundlessness of their own world is exposed. Philosophy benefits by being attacked in this way; it is both strengthened and humbled. This is why Milton's onslaught—precisely because it is launched through a vocabulary that is commensurable with philosophy's—is one of the richer and more rewarding attacks philosophy may hope for.

Philosophers of literature can neither accept Milton's poem nor enlist it into their pursuits by subsuming it into a compensatory epistemology. If they understand the poem's world, they will reject it. They must. The established pathways through which philosophers have turned to literary works are, in the case of *Paradise Lost*, unavailable. Nevertheless, if the thoughts set out here are partly right, while philosophy cannot harness *Paradise Lost* to its objectives, by engaging with the poem, philosophy accesses a valuable perception regarding its own possible limits relative to its own ends. Interestingly, philosophy attains this perception by partly adopting the poem's own modeling of the proper relationship to knowledge: by permitting itself *to host* the poem. To allow a meaningful challenge to resonate is sometimes more rewarding than merely answering it.

The poem, too, gains from being hosted in this way: only by laying itself open to philosophical questions can its fuller meaning as a superior alternative be conveyed. In attempting to *justify* the ways of God to men, the poem's immediate rival is the abstract justification that a philosopher provides. Only by distancing itself from philosophy's sense of justification can the poem block the demoting of faith into yet another abstract topic. To sustain the *war* with philosophy accordingly serves the poem's ends as well.

The war between philosophy and poetry should not necessarily be pacified. We sometimes learn more by enflaming it.[17]

---

[17] I am grateful to Sanford Budick, Stephen Fallon, John Gibson, and Talia Trianin for providing constructive comments and insightful criticisms on a previous version of this chapter.

References

Ainsworth, David. 2008. *Milton and the Spiritual Reader: Reading and Religion in Seventeenth-Century England*. New York: Routledge.

Carroll, Noël. 2010. *Art in Three Dimensions*. New York: Oxford University Press.

Corns, Thomas N. and Gordon Campbell. 2009. "*De Doctrina Christian*: An England That Might Have Been." In Nicholas McDowell and Nigel Smith (eds), *The Oxford Handbook of Milton*. Oxford: Oxford University Press, 2009, 424–38.

Eldridge, Richard T. 2009. "Introduction—Philosophy and Literature as Forms of Attention." In Eldridge (ed.), *The Oxford Handbook of Philosophy and Literature*. New York: Oxford University Press, 3–17.

Fallon, Samuel. 2012. "Milton's Strange God: Theology and Narrative Form in *Paradise Lost*." *ELH* 79/1: 33–57.

Gaut, Berys N. 2007. *Art, Emotion and Ethics*. Oxford: Oxford University Press.

Gibson, John. 2007. *Fiction and the Weave of Life*. Oxford: Oxford University Press.

Hale, John K. 1997. *Milton's Languages: The Impact of Multilingualism on Style*. Cambridge: Cambridge University Press.

Kermode, Frank, ed. 1960. *The Living Milton: Essays by Various Hands*. London: Routledge & Kegan Paul.

Landy, J. 2012. *How to Do Things with Fictions*. New York: Oxford University Press.

Leonard, John. 1989. "Language and Knowledge in *Paradise Lost*." In Dennis Richard Danielson (ed.), *The Cambridge Companion to Milton*. Cambridge: Cambridge University Press.

Milton, John. 1975. *Paradise Lost: An Authoritative Text, Backgrounds and Sources, Criticism*. New York: Norton.

Milton, John. 1825. *A Treatise on Christian Doctrine: Compiled from the Holy Scriptures Alone*, tr. Charles R. Sumner. Cambridge: Cambridge University Press.

Nohrnberg, James C. 1976. *The Analogy of the Faerie Queene*. Princeton: Princeton University Press.

Nussbaum, Martha C. 2000. "Literature and Ethical Theory: Allies or Adversaries?" *Yale Journal of Ethics*, 9: 5–16.

Nussbaum, Martha C. 1990. *Love's Knowledge: Essays on Philosophy and Literature*. New York: Oxford University Press.

Posner, Richard A. 1997. "Against Ethical Criticism." *Philosophy and Literature*, 21/1: 1–27.

Samuel, Irene. 1949. "Milton on Learning and Wisdom." *PMLA: Publications of the Modern Language Association of America*, 64/4: 708–23.

Samuel, Irene. 1965. *Plato and Milton*. Ithaca, NY: Cornell University Press.

Schultz, John Howard. 1955. *Milton and Forbidden Knowledge*. New York: Modern Language Association of America.

Sensabaugh, G. F. 1946. "Milton on Learning." *Studies in Philology*, 43/2: 258–72.

Williams, Arnold. 1948. *The Common Expositor: An Account of the Commentaries on Genesis, 1527–1633*. Chapel Hill, NC: University of North Carolina Press.

Wilson, Talbot. 1971. "The Narrator of Paradise Lost: Divine Inspiration and Human Knowledge." *Sewanee Review*, 79: 349–59.

Zamir, Tzachi. 2007. *Double Vision: Moral Philosophy and Shakespearean Drama*. Princeton: Princeton University Press.

11

"To Think Exactly and Courageously"
Poetry, Ingeborg Bachmann's Poetics, and her Bohemia Poem

Richard Eldridge

I

Poetry, when distinctly successful, involves a special use of language. This special use of language aims at the achievement of seeing, or holistic insight, or getting the sense of things. The relevant seeing, insight, or sense-getting is to be distinguished from simply understanding a message that might be communicated otherwise and from simply grasping that things are observably thus-and-so, independently of the specific invitations and guidances of imagination and attention that successful poetic language embodies. The enabling of this imaginative insight via language is a defining aim of poetic practice—epic, lyric, or dramatic—whether or not every unusual or metaphoric or distinctly formally organized string of words that is reasonably presented as poetry achieves it. Hence poetic practice undertakes to make available to its audiences not just subject-independent material quiddities, but rather things as they matter to and for human subjects, in ways that may be surprising, perplexing, terrifying, funny, and so on, as may be. Clarification of exactly how this specific subject matter *is* surprising or perplexing or terrifying or funny, and so on, is a primary aim in view for both writers and readers.

The practice of using language to invite and guide imaginative attention to what matters to and for human subjects developed historically out of song, where words are used simultaneously to convey a message and, along with rhythm and melody, to hold attention to the sound surface, hence to keep the auditors involved both in the story or information presented and in how it is presented. But poetry broke free of song by focusing on objects, events, and persons that presented difficulties to and for human feeling and by using devices of figuration such as metaphor, allusion, irony, allegory, simile, and so on more consistently and emphatically than popular strophic song does. Paraphrase can be a useful instrument for exploring the significance to a human subject that a poem is trying to convey; but when a poem is distinctly successful, the paraphrase will always fail to capture the exact way in which these words, arranged in just this way, specifically invite and guide imaginative and emotional attention.

There is wide agreement among both literary scholars and philosophers about the great bulk of this summary characterization.[1] Thus Angela Leighton remarks that "sound effects, densities of language, [and] strangeness of syntax . . . hold the key to the work. . . . [The form of the poem] makes it fit for a different kind of seeing-knowing, . . . a kind of knowing which is an imaginative attitude rather than an accumulation of known things."[2] Peter McDonald describes the successful poem as "a drama of form: the ways in which metre—the rhythms of lines, the comings and goings of sound, the demands and revelations of rhyme—perform their own transformations on the writing self,"[3] as well

---

[1] While I cite here only contemporary literary scholars and philosophers, the conception of poetry that they are urging is shared by, among others, both Wordsworth, in the Preface to *Lyrical Ballads* and Hegel, in the *Lectures on Aesthetics*, and this conception is arguably most fully and adequately worked out by them. For useful summaries of their views, see, on Wordsworth, Richard Eldridge, *Literature, Life, and Modernity* (New York: Columbia University Press, 2008), ch. 4, "Attention, Expressive Power, and Interest in Life: Wordsworth's 'Tintern Abbey,'" and, on Hegel, Eldridge, "The Work of Literary Imagination: Hegel, Rilke, and What Writers Do," *Journal of Literary Theory*, 3/1 (2009): 1–17.

[2] Angela Leighton, *On Form: Poetry, Aestheticism, and the Legacy of a Word* (Oxford: Oxford University Press, 2007), 265, 26–7, 27.

[3] Peter McDonald, "'Beside Himself': Robert Lowell's *Collected Poems*," *Poetry Review* 93 (2003–4): 64; cited in Leighton, *On Form*, 24.

as, presumably, on the attentive audience. Elisabeth Camp characterizes a poem "as encompassing more than just collections of propositions represented in a certain modality and assigned to certain functional 'boxes.' Those contents are also structured, explained, and colored in intuitive, holistic ways" by metaphors that "help us to see more clearly how things might really be and how we should act in the world."[4] Troy Jollimore describes the poem as the bearer of "a metaphorical meaning [that] must be something that cannot be precisely paraphrased, that is, expressed in a proposition or set of propositions in a way that leaves no uncaptured remainder, [and that can] give a person a special sort of *insight* into the world."[5] According to Richard Moran, an "image-making quality [that invites and guides seeing and experiencing] is what lies behind both the force and the unparaphrasabilty of poetic metaphor,"[6] while Richard Wollheim holds that "the aim of ... linguistic ... metaphor is to set what is metaphorized in a new light. Juliet, religion, the body—we see whatever it is afresh."[7]

This convergence of views about the nature of the distinctively successful poem is striking, and it gives us some reason to think that we know what poetry, as distinct from ordinary prose, is, at least in its central cases and what poetry centrally aims to achieve. Where ordinary prose communicates a fact that might be grasped independently of specific linguistic formulation, in poetry the linguistic formulation is essential to the insight. (This formulation leaves room for the fact that the extraordinary prose of the novel and short story, say, are also forms of poetic composition, along with epic, lyric, and dramatic poetry, even if they are more continuously vernacular and their distance from song is instead established by extended narrative, allegory, diction, and dialogue more than by metaphor.[8]) But what this characterization of

---

[4] Elisabeth Camp, "Two Varieties of Literary Imagination," *Midwest Studies in Philosophy*, 33 (2009): 128, 129.

[5] Troy Jollimore, "Vision, Cognition, and the Language of Poetry," *Midwest Studies in Philosophy*, 33 (2009): 138.

[6] Richard Moran, "Metaphor, Image, and Force," *Critical Inquiry*, 16 (autumn 1989): 90. Cited in Jollimore, "Vision, Cognition, and the Language of Poetry," 146.

[7] Richard Wollheim, *Painting as an Art* (Princeton: Princeton University Press, 1987), 307. Cited in Jollimore, "Vision, Cognition, and the Language of Poetry," 146–7.

[8] See Eldridge, "The Question of Truth in Literature: *Die poetische Auffassung der Welt*," in Garry L. Hagberg (ed.), *The Ethical Content of Literature: Character, Identity, Perception* (forthcoming), for an account, derived from Hegel, of poetic imagination at work in the novel.

poetry does not yet explain is *why* a practice of cultivating insight and imaginative involvement in and through attention to intensively figured linguistic forms might have developed. What interests or needs does such a practice serve? And exactly how do figuration, rhythm, and imaginative engagement in interaction with each other serve them?

It is possible that these questions have a miscellany of unrelated answers and no particular one. That is, there may just be lots of things available that it is interesting and important enough to attend to imaginatively and emotionally, via figuration, and there may be lots of particular devices of form and figuration for doing so. By taking them to respond to manifoldly diverse initiating particulars, this thought would account at least for the significant variety of poetic forms, from ode, villanelle, and blank verse to pastoral to ballad, sonnet, and sestina, among many others.

But while there is some truth in this thought—initiating particulars do matter; and poets may write for a wide miscellany of reasons, not only for the sake of clarification of perplexities—it also somewhat underplays the role of linguistic formulation in achieving imaginative insight and poetic vision by suggesting that engagement with the particular comes first, while finding the words to express that engagement comes second. While this can happen often enough, it is also false to the working habits of many poets, perhaps of most successful poets at some moments. Instead of beginning only with an object of, say, visual attention, they also *begin* with phrases or sounds, with the ear that has heard and internalized scraps of linguistic formulation and figuration that are then already at work within visual attention. (The visual attentions of painters to their subjects are similarly shaped by already existing painterly forms and achievements that they have internalized. Painters visit museums and studios in order to enter into a practice of imaginative attention that they inhabit or that inhabits them, not just to pick up devices for rendering what they already know they want to render.[9] Likewise for poets reading other poets.) As Helen Vendler puts it, "In justice to the poets we must call what they do, *in the process of conceiving and completing the finished poem*, an intricate form of thinking, even if it means expanding

---

[9] For useful development of this thought, explicating Clive Bell on significant form as not only a property of canvases, but also a means of imaginative attention that develops within a painterly tradition, see Thomas M. McLaughlin, "Clive Bell's Aesthetic: Tradition and Significant Form," *Journal of Aesthetics and Art Criticism*, 35/4 (1977), 433–43.

our idea of what thinking is,"[10] where the process often involves words entering into imaginative attention, not just coming after it.

Second, in casting the poem as an after-the-fact expression of an imaginative engagement already achieved, the thought that poems begin with particulars alone, rather than also within practices of formulation, further underdescribes the work that poetic formulation often and centrally does. To return to the passage cited from Peter McDonald, the "drama of form . . . perform[s] transformations on the writing self." There is a kind of unburdening of confused, unclarified emotion and incoherence of thought, which unburdening is achieved essentially in and through the poetic formulation.[11] Hence, as Adorno poignantly puts it, "form has its substance . . . in suffering;"[12] the search for form arises in perplexity and incoherence, and it is concluded, if it is concluded successfully, not by finding an already formed instrument, like a hammer that might be used for driving a variety of nails or for other purposes, but by finding just these words that ease the burden of perplexity. This accounts for the sense that some poets have, and that many poets have at certain moments, of being possessed by the words as they are developing, rather than clearly picking out a tool from a toolbox. Coming to find oneself in possession of, or being possessed by, the right words can be the unburdening achievement of fullness of imaginative and emotional attention, as though before finding these words one had been caught not only in perplexity, but in dullness and failure of attention. The successful poem embodies and enacts—is—a fully realized act of attention. It stands as an emblem of the possibility of fully achieved utterance and action as such, as if prior to this achievement one had not been (fully) an attentive human subject at all, but only a dull cipher of convention.[13]

[10] Helen Vendler, *Poets Thinking: Pope, Whitman, Dickinson, Yeats* (Cambridge, MA: Harvard University Press, 2006), 119; emphasis added.

[11] For an extended development of this idea, with central reference to Wordsworth, Collingwood, and Spinoza, see Eldridge, *Literature, Life, and Modernity.*

[12] T. W. Adorno, *Aesthetic Theory,* tr. Robert Hullot-Kentor (Minneapolis: University of Minnesota Press, 1998), 260.

[13] For developments of this idea see, in addition to the writers mentioned in n. 11, Charles Altieri, *The Art of Twentieth Century American Poetry: Modernism and After* (Malden, MA: Blackwell, 2006) and *The Particulars of Rapture* (Ithaca, NY: Cornell University Press, 2003); Stanley Cavell, "Music Discomposed," in Cavell, *Must We Mean What We Say?*, updated edn (Cambridge: Cambridge University Press, 2002), 180–212; and Timothy Gould, "The Names of Action," in Eldridge (ed.), *Stanley Cavell* (Cambridge: Cambridge University Press, 2003), 48–78.

II

When we accept the fact that the practice of poetry is oriented around exemplary cases, where not every object that it is reasonable to call a poem will display the features of high achievement that are present in central cases, we can move beyond summary generalities only by focusing in some detail on the imaginative work of attention done by and in particular poems. So much the better, too, if a poem on which we focus is itself the product of a major theorist of poetry with explicit training in philosophy, where the poem and the philosophical theory illuminate one another.

Among more or less contemporary poets, Ingeborg Bachmann (1926–73) developed a theoretical conception of poetry and of the interests it serves as powerfully as anyone, both as a philosopher and as a poet. Bachmann completed a Ph.D. in philosophy at the University of Vienna in 1949, with a dissertation that systematically criticized Heidegger's efforts to develop a systematic (*wissenschaftlich*) and complete account of human experience. Drawing on Wittgenstein, Bachmann argued against Heidegger that fundamental human experiences of perplexity, anxiety, unclarity, failure of orientation, and so on are part of life, but they take place in moments of intermittent, occasioned surprise, and they can be captured, if at all, only partially and in the languages of art, preeminently poetry, not in systematic theory.

> The fundamental experiences with which existential philosophy is concerned really are somehow living in human beings, and they press toward statement. But they are not rationally systematizable, and attempts at a rational system will always be condemned to fail. . . . The need for expression of this other realm of actuality, which withdraws itself from fixation by any systematizing existential philosophy, is approached, however, to an incomparably higher degree by art, with its manifold possibilities.[14]

As a text that resists doctrinal fixation and that is concerned with fugitive experiences of meaningfulness and absence of meaning rather than with material realities external to the subject, the poem is hence more the record and enactment of a developing, emotion- and attitude-infused

---

[14] Ingeborg Bachmann, *Die kritische Aufnahme der Existentialphilosophie Martin Heideggers* (The Critical Reception of Martin Heidgger's Existential Philosophy) (1948), ed. Robert Pichl (Munich: Piper, 1985), 129, 130; my translation.

encounter than it is a direct statement about things. As Peter Beicken use-fully puts it, for Bachmann "the presentation of truth in writing consists in a being underway, a direction-giving, a permanent designing, and as a result also a self-actualizing,"[15] not in either the statement or the expression of something already known or felt distinctly prior to the process of writing.

In Bachmann's particular case, the need to get underway, find a direction, and move toward a more sustainable subjectivity is overwhelmingly marked by a sense of pain or loss, omnipresent, but not yet registered. In her 1959 poetological speech upon receiving the radio play prize of the Austrian Blind War Veterans for her *The Good God of Manhattan*, she ascribes a need for coming to terms with not-yet-registered pain to human beings in general, at least under current conditions of life.

For we all want to come to see. And that clandestine pain makes us for the first time open to experience and especially to the truth. We say very simply and correctly, when we enter into this clear, aching condition, in which the pain becomes fruitful: my eyes have been opened. We say this not because we have perceived a thing or an incident externally, but rather because we have grasped what we otherwise could not see. And this is what art should accomplish: that for us, in this sense, our eyes are opened.[16]

Crucially, however, this opening of the eyes that art should accomplish is accomplished *only* by means of art, which is hence more than an instrument for transmitting something already grasped. The language of poetry must itself make something happen. Poetry is neither a matter centrally of pleasing formal intricacies nor of transmission of a message, but rather of an understanding that is itself both achieved and transmitted essentially through the form of the particular poem. Insight and form come together, or not at all. As Bachmann puts it in her 1959–60 *Frankfurt Lectures* on poetics,

Actuality will always be encountered just there, where, with a new language, an ethically recognizing jolt takes place, and not where one tries simply to make the language new in itself, as if the language itself could drive home the knowledge

---

[15]   Peter Beicken, *Ingeborg Bachmann* (Munich: C. H. Beck, 1988), 155–6; my translation.
[16]   Bachmann, "Die Wahrheit ist dem Menschen zumutbar," in Bachmann, *Werke*, iv, ed. Christine Koschel, Inge von Weidenbaum, and Clemens Münster (Munich: Piper, 1993), 275; my translation. The title of this speech is all but untranslatable, with "zumut-bar" embracing all of "reasonable for," "accessible to," and "entitled to."

and could proclaim the experience that one had never had. On one who merely busies himself with language just in order that it feel novel, language itself soon takes revenge and unmasks every intention. A new language must have a new gait, and it has this new gait only when a new spirit retains and preserves it.[17]

The result of Bachmann's pursuit in poetic practice of a new way of seeing, motivated by pain and a felt sense of lack of orientation in the face of historical, social, and personal circumstances, and bound up with an attempt to generate a new language in and through which something is to happen, is a powerful balance of and competition between a wounded subjectivity and a subjectivity coming to vision and voice. Each poem is an experiment in both seeing and voicing, as the speaking subject attempts to work its way out of pain and perplexity and into fuller clarity, self-possession, and attention to the poem's topic. As Beicken puts it, the development of a Bachmann poem is typically marked by

two chief tendencies. The first brings forward the poetic evidence, the exemplary showing of the injurious effects of history on the human subject and on the sphere of life that is essential to him. The other tendency refuses to remain with the evidence of vulnerability, but instead unfolds an inexhaustibly self-expressing vision of a breakthrough of the negatively existent, a breakthrough that corresponds to the wish to outrun the limits of what can actually be experienced.

The poem is then the enactment and the record of a movement—a something happening—that arises out of holding these two tendencies in tension with one another: an engaging with perplexing, injurious actuality, and an envisioning of a more meaningful, emotionally and intellectually coherent life otherwise. When this movement is especially well developed, then neither tendency is sacrificed to the other. Both escapist utopianism and simple documentation of the horrific must be avoided. Instead what takes place is a modulation between these two tendencies each coming into expression, until a controlled balance of attention to painful actuality and continuing longing for life otherwise is achieved.

The speaking poetic subject is itself shaped by and within this modulating movement between these two tendencies, rather than controlling it from outside. Hence it acts as what Irmela von der Lühe aptly characterizes as a "participant in [a] process of the loss of self-certainty

---

[17] Bachmann, *Frankfurter Vorlesungen: Probleme zeitgenössicher Dichtung—I: Fragen und Scheinfragen*, in Bachmann, *Werke*, iv. 192; my translation.

(*Ich-Gewißheit*)"[18] that takes place both historically and in the poetic
work that both responds to and is situated within that history. As
Bachmann characterizes it in her *Frankfurt Lectures*, the poetic I is
now an "I without guarantee (*Ich ohne Gewähr*)" in any immediate
self-certainties of thought or feeling, an I that must be "read off" its own
formulations (*ein abgelesenes Ich*) rather than something that controls
them out of clear thought and feeling in advance of utterance or inscription.[19] In the face of the horrors and perplexities of the modern world—
immediately those of Austria during and after World War II, but more
broadly those of modernity as such, understood (as in Hofmannsthal's
"Lord Chandos Letter" and Musil's *The Man Without Qualities*: two significant influences on Bachmann) as a scene of the loss of possibilities
of coherent and stable identity, the poetic I is unmoored from any clear
self-presence. As von der Lühe puts it, for Bachmann "what was once
pronounced with a claim to the greatest possible authenticity, what was
once when pronounced an indicator of an unchallengeable identity, of an
unbroken self-consciousness—this guarantee that was once articulated
by means of the personal pronoun 'I' is gone."[20] Surrounded by social
opacity and flux, without anchors for thought and feeling, the I is itself
destabilized. In a 1953 radio play, Bachmann has the character called The
Critic praise the Wittgenstein of the *Tractatus* for his "intellectual hon-
esty and awe in the face of an actuality that has withdrawn from human
understanding."[21] In her own voice, she remarks that "A walk around the
corner is enough to make one insane. The world has become a sickness."[22]
As a result, nothing can be taken for granted—not how conditions will
develop, not one's own thoughts and feelings, and not any way of life that
might afford satisfactions and embody meaningfulness. Without givens
in external conditions, thoughts and feelings, or modes of life, we must,

[18] Irmela von der Lühe, "'Ich ohne Gewähr': Ingeborg Bachmanns Frankfurter
Vorlesungen zur Poetik," in Christine Koschel and Inge von Weidenbaum (eds),
Kein objektives Urteil—nur ein lebendiges: Texte Zum Werk von Ingeborg Bachmann
(Munich: Piper, 1989), 577; my translation.
[19] Bachmann, *Frankfurter Vorlesungen—III Das schreibende Ich*, in *Werke*, iv. 217–18;
my translation.
[20] Von der Lühe, "'Ich ohne Gewähr,'" p. 577; my translation.
[21] Bachmann, "Sagbares und Undsagbares—Die Philosophie Ludwig Wittgensteins,"
in *Werke*, iv. 125; my translation.
[22] Bachmann, "Jede Jugend ist die dümmste [Entwurf]," in *Werke*, iv. 334; my
translation.

as Bachmann puts it, "incessantly justify ourselves and everything that we do, desire, and think; life as we have lived it for millennia is nothing that can be taken for granted (*nichts Selbstverständliches*)."[23]

And yet, despite her sense of pains and opacity, both contemporary Austrian and more generally modern, Bachmann holds fast to the convictions "that our power (*Kraft*) reaches further than our unhappiness, that one, though robbed of much, still knows how to raise oneself up (*sich zu erheben weiß*)."[24] The key to this movement aimed at re-establishing and stabilizing the speaking subject and its modes of attention and involvement is "to think exactly and courageously,"[25] that is, not to give in to cliché, journalistic representation, or wallowing in muddles of feeling, but instead to embrace attentiveness and openness, so that one both lets something happen to oneself amidst chaos, perplexity, pain, and dullness and finds oneself coming to words that fitly achieve and enact the dawning of stabler attention. The poetic "I" is, as von der Lühe puts it, initially rhetorized, medialized, and formalized: emptied out, as it were, into a loss of clarity and self-presence as a result of modern practices of technologization and fragmentarily particularized communication. But this emptied out I also bears within it a dream of greater and stabler self-unity and a power of beginning to actualize this dream in the achievement of fuller attentiveness, against the sways of medialization, by means of poetic language.[26] "At the end of the lectures," we then find, in von der Lühe's formulation, "not resignation or a fashionable confession of an in principle loss of meaning, but rather a hope that repeatedly shines through all skepticism, an expression of the inability to give up, of a holding fast, along with all the doubts about language with which it is bound up, to the possibility of the I *through* language and *through* poetry."[27]

The result is that the "I without guarantee," as it develops itself in poetry by means of language, functions "as a placeholder for the human

---

[23] Bachmann, "Auf das Opfer darf keiner sich berufen' [Entwurf]," in *Werke*, iv. 335; my translation.

[24] Bachmann, "Die Wahrheit ist dem Menschen zumutbar," in *Werke*, iv. 277; my translation.

[25] Bachmann, "Ins tausendjährige Reich," in *Werke*, iv. 28; my translation.

[26] Von der Lühe, "'Ich ohne Gewähr,'" 578; my translation.

[27] Von der Lühe, "'Ich ohne Gewähr,'" 586–7; my translation; emphases added.

voice,"[28] itself here understood as a metonym for more fully achieved and stabilized subjectivity.[29] Though it involves within daily actuality "a peculiar, strange way of existing, asocial, solitary, and cursed,"[30] the life of a poetizing human subject moving into such fuller subjectivity, by means of poetic language, in relation to existing conditions stands in turn as a metonym of human attentiveness and human life as such, above the levels of cliché and animal reactivity. "I speak; therefore I am."[31] In order to raise oneself up to fuller subjectivity by means of poetic development, what is required is a "thinking-with (*Mitdenken*) of despair and of hope."[32] Insofar as this poetic development can take place, we are not condemned to be ciphers of the conditions that surround us. We can, by means of poetic composition, make a move in relation to the actual. "In the interplay of the impossible and the possible, we expand our possibilities."[33]

---

[28] Bachmann, *Frankfurter Vorlesungen III: Das schreibende Ich*, in *Werke*, iv. 237; my translation.

[29] In a useful survey of the development of various forms of speaking personae in Bachmann's œuvre, Amy Kepple Strawser charts a development from (i) a voice speaking as a member of a collective "we" in relation to immediate historical conditions, to (ii) a "cosmic I" concerned with questions of death, existence, and nature, to (iii) a male persona, to (iv) an unspecified "you," to (v) the marked subjective I of the author. Strawser argues further that "the discovery of her subjective voice contributed to Bachmann's desertion of the lyric form" in favor of the novel. Her "growing awareness of herself as a woman writer" blocked her ability to speak lyrically, with, as it were, ontological exemplarity in relation to existing conditions. ("The Development and Ultimate Cessation of Ingeborg Bachmann's Lyric Voice," in Gudrun Brokoph-Mauch (ed.), *Thunder Rumbling at my Heels: Tracing Ingeborg Bachmann* (Riverside, CA: Ariadne Press, 1998), 186). (Bachmann gave up writing poetry altogether in 1967.) This seems right, but it may be wondered which of these authorial voices—the cosmic-ontological-lyrical or the markedly personal, social, particularized, female, novelistic—enables Bachmann to develop her greatest artistic powers. Perhaps courting an ontological voice is a requirement for successful lyric.

[30] Bachmann, "Rede zur Verleihung des Anton-Wildgans-Preises," in *Werke*, iv. 294; my translation.

[31] Bachmann, *Das schreibende Ich*, in *Werke*, iv. 225; my translation.

[32] Bachmann, *Frankfurter Vorlesungen I: Fragen und Scheinfragen*, in *Werke*, iv. 183; my translation. Von der Lühe usefully notes that the preposition in this passage is "von" (of), not "an" (about) (Von der *Lühe*, "'Ich ohne Gewähr,'" 583). The task is to think in, through, and by means of these moods, in relation to the objects that prompt them and the possibilities of language that develop in relation to them, not to describe these moods from outside them.

[33] Bachmann, "Die Wahrheit ist dem Menschen zumutbar," in *Werke*, iv. 276; my translation.

III

"Böhmen liegt am Meer" / "Bohemia Lies By the Sea" is one of Bachmann's last poems. Written in 1964, it was first published in November 1968, after the Prague Spring uprising in 1968, ended by the arrival in Prague of Soviet tanks on August 15. It addresses social conditions abstractly, whether those of the Soviet invasion, of the post-war Austrian economic recovery and silences about the war, of fascism during and after the war, or of all these all at once as symptoms of modernity; and, like most of Bachmann's best lyrics—and arguably like the strongest lyrics in general—it addresses the nature, function, and value of lyric vision and accomplishment in relation to social conditions, paradigmatically in its rehearsals of what its poetic speaking will do or is unable to do, has suffered and will continue to suffer, in virtue of the possession but difficult exercise of poetic powers. Here is the poem in its entirety.

Böhmen liegt am Meer

Sind hierorts Häuser grün, tret ich noch in ein Haus.
Sind hier die Brücken heil, geh ich auf gutem Grund.
Ist Liebesmüh in alle Zeit verloren, verlier ich sie hier gern.

Bin ich's nicht, ist es einer, der ist so gut wie ich.

Grenzt hier ein Wort an mich, so laß ich's grenzen.
Liegt Böhmen noch am Meer, glaub ich den Meeren wieder.
Und glaub ich noch ans Meer, so hoffe ich auf Land.
Bin ich's, so ist's ein jeder, der soviel ist wie ich.
Ich will nichts mehr für mich. Ich will zugrunde gehen.

Zugrund—das heißt zum Meer, dort find ich Böhmen wieder.
Zugrund gerichtet, wach ich ruhig auf.
Von Grund auf weiß ich jetzt, und ich bin unverloren.

Kommt her, ihr Böhmen alle, Seefahrer, Hafenhuren und Schiffe
unverankert. Wollt ihr nicht böhmisch sein, Illyrer, Veroneser
und Venezianer alle. Spielt die Komödien, die lachen machen

Und die zum Weinen sind. Und irrt euch hundertmal,
wie ich mich irrte und Proben nie bestand,
doch hab ich sie bestanden, ein um das andre Mal.

Wie Böhmen sie bestand und eines schönen Tags
ans Meer begnadigt wurde und jetzt am Wasser liegt.

Ich grenz noch an ein Wort und an ein andres Land,
Ich grenz, wie wenig auch, an alles immer mehr,
ein Böhme, ein Vagrant, der nichts hat, den nichts hält,
begabt nur noch, vom Meer, das strittig ist, Land meiner
Wahl zu sehen.

Bohemia Lies By the Sea

If houses here are green, I'll step inside a house.
If bridges here are sound, I'll walk on solid ground.
If love's labour's lost in every age, I'd gladly lose it here.

If it's not me, it's one who is as good as me.

If a word here borders on me, I'll let it border.
If Bohemia still lies by the sea, I'll believe in the sea again.
And believing in the sea, thus I can hope for land.

If it's me, then it's anyone, for he's as worthy as me.
I want nothing more for myself. I want to go under.

Under—that means the sea, there I'll find Bohemia again.
From my grave, I wake in peace.
From deep down I know now, and I'm not lost.

Come here all you Bohemians, seafarers, dock whores, and ships
unanchored. Don't you want to be Bohemians, all you Illyrians,
Veronese and Venetians. Play the comedies that make us laugh

until we cry. And err a hundred times,
as I erred and never withstood the trials,
though I did withstand them time after time.

As Bohemia withstood them and one fine day
was released to the sea and now lies by water.

I still border on a word and on another land,
I border, like little else, on everything more and more,

a Bohemian, a wandering minstrel, who has nothing, who
is held by nothing, gifted only at seeing, by a doubtful sea,
the land of my choice.[34]

Bohemia, of course, does not lie by the sea, since it is entirely surrounded by Germany, Austria, and Moravia-Silesia. The title refers to the stage directions to Act 3, Scene 3, of Shakespeare's *The Winter's Tale*: "Bohemia: a desert country near the sea." Hence it invokes a counterfactual, imagined place of magical rescue, since Bohemia in *The Winter's Tale* is the place where Perdita, the daughter of King Leontes of Sicily, is refound. (Leontes, falsely suspecting his wife Hermione of adultery, had ordered the infant to be put to death; the shepherd Antigonus, charged with this task, after being visited on ship by a vision of the now dead Hermione, has followed her instructions and left Perdita to death by exposure on the coast of Bohemia, where she is then found and raised by an itinerant, elderly shepherd.) Bohemia by the sea is then, one might say, the imagined place where things are set right, where violence is undone, misunderstandings are overcome, and meaningful life is achieved. And the question of this poem is then what this place might mean, and how if it at all it might be entered, by one who is a Bohemian, a vagrant, and who wishes to find Bohemia again—a place where things make sense. The poem is hence thematically structured by what Peter Horst Neumann aptly calls "a yearning for salvation" (*eine Erlösungs-Sehnsucht*)[35] in the face of a troubled and fallen actuality.

Metrically, the poem is carefully organized to balance and hold in tension a regular, highly formal meter—the alexandrine or iambic hexameter—with both slight deviations from this and a smaller number of lines that are more prose-like. (The English translation captures some but not all of this metrical ordering.) As Horst Neumann puts it, "the alexandrine is written into the poem as a principle of order, but through the breaking of this norm the language swings into the open."[36] The effect of this breaking free of the alexandrine is, however, less liberation than a loss of intensity and control of voice. It as though the poem were continually establishing a gait and then stumbling away from it, as though poetic vision were being successfully all but naturally housed in achieved unity of form, only repeatedly then to founder almost instantaneously

Filkins. Reprinted with the permission of The Permissions Company, Inc. on behalf of Zephyr Press, <www.zephyrpress.org>.

[35] Peter Horst Neumann, "Ingeborg Bachmann's Böhmisches Manifest," in Koschel and von Weidenbaum, *Kein objektives Urteil*, 387.

[36] Neumann, "Ingeborg Bachmann's Böhmisches Manifest," 384; my translation.

back into the prosaic. Hence the poem mirrors metrically the thematics of salvation or magical recovery into fuller meaningfulness (a gait established), glimpsed and achieved for a moment, but always again lost.

More specifically, lines 1, 2, 7, 9, 16, 19, 21, and 22 (a third of the 24 complete lines of the poem) are perfect alexandrines, each with a caesura in the exact middle of the line. Lines 5, 6, 8, 10, 12, 17, 18, 20, another third of the poem) are almost alexandrines, with a syllable either missing or added either at the end of the line or just before the caesura. Here the effect is one of slight stumbling or unsettling, while the overall sense of the meter is maintained. Line 11 is an iambic pentameter—a compression of metric intensity from the alexandrine hexameters. Lines 3, 4, lines 13, 14, 15, and lines 23, 24, 25 are then distinctively prosaic and colloquial, not metrically organized. They enact a stepping back of the speaking subject from immersion in the songlike development of the meter (already itself fraying in the imperfect alexandrines), as though the subject were both not able to go on with them and were thrown into distantiated reflectiveness on what just has, or hasn't, been accomplished metrically and visionarily. The four sets of strongly marked non-alexandrines—the prosaic 3–4, 13–15, and 23–5, plus the iambic pentameter 11—invite special attention as metacommentaries on the achievements and limits of poetic vision and poetic form.

Lines 3 and 4 initiate this metacommentary. "If it's not me" who has entered into a house, walked on solid ground, and gladly lost love, then "it's one who is as good as me." Perdita, or Shakespeare, or the speaking subject living in the poem imaginatively and outside daily actuality, has made meaning somehow, and that can matter for an empirical I within daily actuality. The other "I"s may suffice, at least for a few lines or moments, to establish movement, entry into a house, and love. As a result, after this first interrupting reflection in lines 3 and 4, the rhythm reasserts itself, with some stumbling, in lines 5–10. But the desire of the subject that is caught up in this metrical development is a desire for a life otherwise and sustained within this movement, not a desire for ordinary life, ego-identity, and violent social differentiation within the fallen actual. Hence it is, for an actually living, socially situated subject, a desire for release or death, a *Sehnsucht nach dem Tod*: to find Bohemia again, at the sea, would be, like Hölderlin's Empedocles, to go under, to be directed to collapse or ruin ("*Zugrund gerichtet*").

In the compressed, iambic pentameter line 11, the speaking subject awakes or reawakens abruptly and in a way that fractures the rhythm, and yet also calmly or in peace ("ruhig") from this desire and its partial or fleeting fulfillment in the rhythms of the poem and into actual empirical identity. From deep down, from the bottom or fundament of things ("Von Grund auf") the nature of the desire that motivates poetry is recognized, accepted, survived, and remembered or held in consciousness. "I know now and I'm not lost."

The second prosaic interjection in lines 13–15 is then an oratorical call, from the standpoint of the surviving, existing, empirical subject who remembers, to others to join in coping with the pains of actuality by playing, by living unanchored, as Bohemians, in at least temporary withdrawal or escape from socially compelled seriousness and socially anchored identity. Such refuges—now marked as intermittent—will not be wholly redemptive. Crying will come, and error, and, with luck and persistence, survival: tests or challenges ("Proben") may be withstood, and imagination and the counterfactual ("Böhmen/Bohemia") may survive, stand, even if one is not quite sure how, by moving, as the speaker of this poem moves, into and then again out of poetic organization and metrical movement.

What remains is then a speaker or subject who, like Bohemia, borders or touches on another word or land—another, more meaningful, less troubled, way of living and feeling—without being able actually quite to enter it, like Moses who died on Mount Pisgah, on the east bank of the Jordan, overlooking the promised land of Canaan, but without being able to enter it,[37] Bordering on a word, the poetic subject is able to form and sustain itself in the perfect alexandrines of lines 21 and 22, but only as a wanderer, seer, and borderer on another land of choice, and the last three lines 23–25 stumble back into prose and into the distantiated recognition of this fact of actual, empirical identity and of the impossibility of living within imagination unfreighted by actuality's difficulties.

The "noch"—"yet," "still," "nevertheless"—that occurs five times in the poem, toward the beginning in lines 1, 6, and 7, then again at the end, lines 21 and 24, is a marker of having been able to make enough of a

---

[37] Erich Fried, "'Ich grenz noch an ein Wort und an ein andres Land': Zu Ingeborg Bachmanns Böhmen-Gedicht," in Koschel and von Weidenbaum, *Kein objektives Urteil*, 392, notes the parallel to Moses. See Deuteronomy 32: 48–34: 5, especially 33: 52, where the Lord says to Moses, "Yet thou shalt see the land before *thee*; but thou shalt not go thither unto the land which I give the children of Israel" (Authorized King James Version, ed. Robert Carroll and Stephen Pickett (Oxford: Oxford University Press, 2008), 260).

movement, but only fleetingly, and only just enough: a marker of having arrived fleetingly at achieved vision and poetic formation, but also of having been unable to enter and live wholly within poetically formed life.[38] This "noch" qualifies the verb forms—"enter" or "step inside;" "lies" (for Bohemia); "believe;" "border;" and "gifted" or "talented" ("begabt")— that describe relations to the meaningful, the imaginative, the poetically formed, and to counterfactual life otherwise. The speaker almost, or still, or yet, or nonetheless has such relations, but they are too weak in the face of the ways of actuality to yield any standing redemption. Prose and distantiated reflection return to undo poetic formation, as the poem drifts off toward its end, leaving the speaker with only a sense of having been able to see life otherwise and been able to formulate it poetically for a moment, for a few lines, but without having been able to enter it or live within it.

IV

What, then, has been achieved in "Böhmen liegt am Meer, its achievement exemplary of the possibilities of achievement in lyric poetry more generally? Crucially, the poem is both the expression and the enactment of a multiply overdetermined and repeated experience of suffering, in particular of a failure to live in the world with others in reciprocity and mutual intersubjective fluency. It registers an experience of being blocked in fulfilling a desire for reciprocity and intersubjective fluency, together with an imagining of life otherwise, an imagining that expresses that fundamental desire half-fulfilled. And equally crucially, it registers a sense that this desire persists as unfulfilled, or as at best partly fulfilled in and through the work itself, as a placeholder for life otherwise. Thus it offers us not an opportunity to know ourselves in the way we might know the dispositions of measurable empirical objects in space, but rather an opportunity to acknowledge a shared condition as enacted and expressed.[39] Stendhal's conception of art as a *promesse de*

---

[38] Fried notes the occurrence of these five "nochs" and argues that they indicate the co-presence and intermixing of a resistance ("ein Sich-Sträuben") and surrender to death and a movement within which one has no place as a subject ("ein Zugrundegehen"). "Ich grenz noch," 393.

[39] For an important discussion of acknowledgment as a central cognitive aim of literary practice, see John Gibson, *Fiction and the Weave of Life* (Oxford: Oxford University Press, 2007), 102–20.

bonheur and Adorno's conception of art as a plenipotentiary of a future praxis come to mind (art and beauty as placeholders for and anticipations of more meaningful life)—marked elegiacally by a sense of always only bordering on the realization of any such anticipation, promise, or practice. Or as Kant describes the workings of poetic imagination in §49 of the *Critique of the Power of Judgment*, "On the faculties of mind which constitute genius,"

The imagination (as a productive cognitive faculty) is, namely, very powerful in creating, as it were, another nature, out of the material which the actual one gives it. We entertain ourselves with it [this other nature] when experience seems too mundane to us; we transform the latter [actual nature], no doubt always in accordance with analogous laws, but also in accordance with principles that lie higher in reason (and which are every bit as natural to us as those in accordance with which the understanding apprehends empirical nature); in this we feel our freedom from the law of association (which applies to the empirical use of that faculty), in accordance with which material can certainly be lent to us by nature, but can yet be reworked by us into something entirely different, namely into that which steps beyond nature.[40]

That the pains of the material and social actual—in all its varieties—are enough to prompt imaginings of life otherwise, that human subjects have powers to form materials, whether of words or of life, poetically, so as to sustain more meaningful life, even if only momentarily, and that human subjects can recognize and accept this fate of always only bordering on another land of choice—all this is more than enough to give lyric poetry, in all its textual densities, in all its devices of figuration and attention and rhythmically controlled movement, an enduring place in the imaginative economy of human life, if we but enter into its modes of development. What would it be to live as a human subject without a desire for life otherwise, without the exercise and development of poetic practices that articulate this desire, and without recognition of their limits and hence of the standing force of desire and imagination? Poetry is a face of the human.[41]

---

[40] Immanuel Kant, *The Critique of the Power of Judgment*, tr. Paul Guyer and Eric Matthews (Cambridge: Cambridge University Press, 2000), 5: 314, p. 192; translation slightly modified; Kant, *Kritik der Urteilskraft* (Frankfurt am Main: Suhrkamp, 1974), A190–1, B194–5, p. 250.

[41] I am grateful to Sarah Eldridge, Hannah Eldridge, and Joan Vandegrift for helpful comments on an earlier draft of this chapter.

Index

Adorno, Theodor W. 195, 236, 249
Ainsworth, David 223
Altieri, Charles 6, 173, 236
Améry, Jean 190–5, 199–204
Ammons, A. R. 90
analytic aesthetics 5–8, 63
analytic philosophy 38, 42–3, 47, 54, 57, 111–26, 136, 188, 206
Apollinaire, Guillaume 6, 73, 75
Aristotle 172, 227
Ashbery, John 4, 10, 46, 52–3
Autin, J. L. 136
avant-garde (poetic) 5, 100, 106, 146

Bachelard, Gaston 174–5
Bachmann, Ingeborg 15, 232–47
Barthes, Roland 175
Baudelaire, Charles 6, 49, 152
Beardsley, Monroe C. 29, 179
Beicken, Peter 238–9
Bell, Clive 234
Bennett, Louise 107
Bernstein, Charles 6, 100, 102
Bishop, Elizabeth 172–4
Blackburn, Simon 13
Bradley, A. C. 21–3, 27–8, 31, 33, 117
Brooks, Cleanth 24–5, 28–30, 156
Brooks, Gwendolyn 104–5
Budd, Malcolm 22–3

Cavalcanti, Guido 158
Cavell, Stanley 171, 175–6, 236
Camp, Elisabeth 2, 234
Campbell, Gordon 207
Carroll, Noël 206
Celan, Paul 5, 9, 15, 189, 195–204
Chomsky, Noam 33–4, 46
cognitive value of poetry, see knowledge
Coleridge, Samuel 25
Cohen, Leonard 57
Collingwood, R. G. 29, 133, 236
compensatory thesis 205, 208, 226, 229

compression, of poetic meaning 7, 18–9, 28–9
Corns, Thomas N. 206
Critchley, Simon 45, 178
criticism 102, 116, 156, 158, 167; see also interpretation
cummings, e. e. 72–3

de la Mare, Walter 169
de Sousa, Ronald 12, 56
Davidson, Donald 16, 25–7, 47, 201
Davies, David 133
Dean, Jeffrey 64
declamation-based practices 131, 138–47; see also inscription-based practices
defining art 22, 63–5, 83, 175
Denham, Alison 14–15, 201
Dickinson, Emily 9–10, 125
Donne, John 30, 36, 48
Dué, Casey 135

Eldridge, Richard 1–2, 15, 206, 233, 236
Eliot, T. S. 6, 10, 55, 70, 107, 154, 156–65, 202, 222
Elliott, R. K. 155
Emerson, Ralph Waldo 66, 81
epistemic value of poetry 188–90, 201–22; see also knowledge
estrangement
  ethical 189–203
  poetic 103
experience-taking 183, 186–90
experiencing-as 183–9, 202
experiential-thesis 20–4, 28, 36
expression 19, 24, 26–32, 42, 49, 99–102, 113, 125, 157–9, 174, 177, 183–5, 195, 198, 236–9, 248

Fallon, Samuel 224
fiction 3–5, 11, 71, 112, 151–2, 183, 206
Filkins, Peter 244–5
Fodor, Jerry 39, 64, 70

form, poetic 10, 21, 27–8, 35, 42–4, 48–9,
    58, 68, 73–7, 83–5, 141, 150, 209,
    221–5, 232–3, 236–8, 242, 245–6
form/content relation 21–2, 27–36, 77,
    84, 95, 106, 198, 201
Frege, Gottlob 8, 47, 70, 119–25, 152
Freytag-Loringhoven, Elsa von 74
Fried, Erich 247–8
Friedrich, Casper David 185
Frijda, Nico 41, 55
Frost, Robert 67, 142–3, 169, 179

Gaut, Berys 64, 206
Gaynesford, Maximilian de 2
Gioia, Dana 147
Gibson, John 56, 178, 206, 248
Goldie, Peter 8
Golding, Alan 6
Goodland, Giles 18–9, 28–32
Goodman, Nelson 69, 130, 133, 136
Graham, W. S. 169
Grant, James 201
Greenlaw, Lavinia 93–4

Hale, John K. 224
Hardy, Thomas 114, 152
Hegel, George Wilhelm Friedrich 118,
    164, 233
Heidegger, Martin 116, 149–50, 153–4,
    160–1, 175, 237
Hollander, John 34
Homer 134–7, 140, 144, 148, 153
Houlihan, Joan 88–103
Howell, Robert 136–7
hyperintensionality 25–8, 31

Irvin, Sherri 13, 104, 105
imagination 11, 32, 108, 116, 122, 173–4,
    232–4, 247, 249
inscription-based practices 131, 140–1;
    see also declamation-based
    practices
interpretation 11, 24, 30, 34, 66, 84, 96,
    101, 104–6, 131, 142–4, 149, 168, 200
    relevance of authorial intentions
    to 104–6, 140
Izenberg, Oren 6, 10, 103

James, Henry 7, 171–2
Jarrell, Randall 164
John, Eileen 2

Jollimore, Troy 2, 105–6, 234
Joyce, James 5, 152

Kant, Immanuel 115, 118, 154, 164, 249
Kaufman, Geoff F. 186, 199
Keats, John 111, 116, 154
Kermode, Frank 215
Kivy, Peter 2, 23–4, 29, 132, 177
Koethe, John 2, 55–6, 156–7
knowledge 112, 150, 205, 207
    in Paradise Lost, 205–29
    relation to poetic form. 221–5;
    see also form/content relation
    in/through poetry. 19, 112, 150–2, 155,
        159, 162–82, 190, 205
    see also truth
Kripke, Saul 70

Lamarque, Peter 2, 12, 24, 28, 35, 50, 55,
    90, 95, 106, 156, 178
Landy, Joshua 206
Larkin, Philip 53, 55–6
Leighton, Angela 10, 4, 233
Leonard, John 213
Lepore, Ernie 2, 25–6
Libby, Lisa K. 186, 199
Levinson, Jerrold 134, 136
Lombardo, Gian 98–108.
Lowell, Amy 73, 146
Lühe, Irmela von der 240–2

Macaulay, Thomas Babington 111–12
Mandelbaum, Eric 12–13
Martindale, Colin 53–4
McDonald, Peter 233, 236
McLaughlin, Thomas M. 235
McGregor, Rafe 2
Mengert, Christina 88–9, 91–6, 99,
    104, 108
Mill, John Stuart 113
Milton, John 5, 42, 134–5, 205–29
modernism 5–10, 18, 74
Moran, Richard 106, 234

naive reading 6–10
Neumann, Peter Horst 245
Nicholls, Peter 94
Nietzsche, Friedrich 40, 150,
    163–4, 166–9
nonsense 74, 125, 163
Nozick, Robert 38, 59

Oatley, Keith 41
Olsen, Stein Haugom 90, 106
Ong, Walter J. 134
ontology of poetry 22, 127–48
opacity of poetry 7–8, 30, 36, 63–85, 222,
    240–1; *see also* semantics/semantic
    meaning, semantic opacity

paraphrase 26, 68, 115, 156, 168, 188,
    200, 235
  heresy of paraphrase 21–9, 35–7, 156
Peacock, Thomas Love 112
Peacocke, Christopher 184
Peake, Mervyn 162
Pessoa, Fernando 50–2, 59
Plath, Sylvia 5
Plato 37–8, 40, 42, 111, 118, 121, 164, 26–7
Ponge, Francis 49
Pope, Alexander 116–17, 155, 30, 36
Porter, Peter 164–5, 174
Pound, Ezra 6, 78–9
Prinz, Jesse 12–13

Ribeiro, Anna Christina Soy 2, 13–14,
    43–4, 48–50, 60, 128
Rich, Adrienne 108
Rilke, Rainer Maria 6, 150, 160
Rossetti, Christina 72
Rowe, Mark 2
Ruskin, John 113

Samuel, Irene 207
Sappho 14, 148
Saussure, Ferdinand de 46
Scruton, Roger 14, 174–5
semantics/semantic meaning 33, 46, 53,
    56, 66–7, 95, 106, 108, 118, 120, 149,
    154–5, 188, 198–201
  semantic density 21, 23, 29–30, 33–5
  semantic finegrainedness 18–36
  semantic innocence 25
  semantic opacity 68–70
Sensabaugh, George F. 207
Shakespeare, William 48, 59, 75, 114,
    116, 129, 151, 157, 159, 202, 245–6
Shelley, Percy Bysshe 111–12, 156
Simmias of Rhodes 138–9, 143

Smith, Barbara Herrnstein 136, 139
Stecker, Robert 2
Stern, Joseph 2
Stevens, Wallace 5, 9–10, 45, 55, 65–7, 71,
    136, 155, 163–6, 173–4, 178–80
Stewart, Susan 6
Strawser, Amy Kepple 242
Sundararajan, Louise 41, 54
Suppes, Patrick 2, 95
Swinburne, Algernon Charles 19

Thomas, Dylan 75
Thomasson, Amie 132–3, 140
Tolstoy, Leo 183–7, 202
truth 33, 38–9, 47–8, 56–60, 67, 113,
    115–16, 120–1, 149–52, 188, 203,
    235, 238
  in poetry 58–60, 114, 149–61, 238
  see also knowledge
Tzara, Tristan 73
twofoldness, poetic 75–80, 84–5

Valéry, Paul 165, 177
value, poetic 4, 19–26, 29–36, 96, 98,
    100, 114, 117, 154–6, 161
Vendler, Helen 6, 235–6
Verlaine, Paul 40, 155
Voegelin, Salomé 175
voice 66, 142, 147, 195–9, 239, 241–2, 245;
    see also expression

Wagner, Richard 150
Walton, Kendall 2
Williams, Bernard 118
Williams, William Carlos 79–80 118
Winnie the Pooh 170
Wittgenstein, Ludwig 34, 40, 63–4, 111,
    115, 124, 163, 166–70, 237, 240
Wollheim, Richard 75, 77–8, 131, 234
Wordsworth, William 5, 7, 35–6, 44, 112,
    123, 233, 236

Yeats, W. B. 5, 30, 40, 151, 236

Zamir, Tzachi 15, 206
Ziff, Paul 46, 53, 63
Zwicky, Jan 58–9